WHEN THE SHOPPING WAS GOOD

Woolworths and the Irish Main Street

Barbara Walsh

IRISH ACADEMIC PRESS
DUBLIN • PORTLAND, OR

First published in 2011 by Irish Academic Press

2 Brookside, Dundrum Road, Dublin 14, Ireland	920 NE 58th Avenue, Suite 300 Portland, Oregon, 97213-3786 USA

www.iap.ie

British Library Cataloguing in Publication Data
An entry can be found on request

ISBN 978 0 7165 3053 4 (cloth)

Library of Congress Cataloging-in-Publication Data
An entry can be found on request

Typeset by FiSH Books, Enfield, Middx.
Printed by MPG Books Group Ltd, Bodmin & King's Lynn

Contents

Illustrations

Every effort has been made to obtain permission for the images, but we will rectify any omissions if we receive new information on the copyright holder.

Acknowledgements

The research for this book has been drawn from a number of sources which include some of the archive records of the formerly named F.W. Woolworth & Co. Ltd. The privilege of being allowed to examine some of their earliest documents when I began my preliminary research in 2007 was very much appreciated, and I would like to acknowledge the excellent support received from Paul Seaton and Woolworths plc at that time. As the book progressed, privately held material from a number of other sources was made available to me, and I am deeply grateful for all the kind assistance I have received from so many people.

Several published historical discourses on social, economic and political aspects have contributed useful commentary to aid this study, and I would like to acknowledge the work of these authors. I am grateful also to the many librarians and newspaper editors who have offered help during the research: for a complete list of libraries, see the bibliography. My thanks, too, to all those who have assisted in providing photographic images.

My sincere appreciation and thanks goes to Lisa Hyde and her team at Irish Academic Press; their support and enthusiasm for the book has been an inspiration. It has been also a special privilege that Senator Feargal Quinn has graciously agreed to write the foreword for the book and I am truly grateful to him for this gesture.

Words of deep gratitude are due to all the former Woolworth employees and their families, who gave generously of their time in order to be interviewed or to assist in other ways. Their opinions, advice, information and practical help have been immensely valuable, and their shared memories have given life to this book. I would like to thank them for their patience. Moreover, in addition to all these good people, there are many others who have also assisted me in different ways and I would like to included them in my thanks:

Robert Anderson, Mike Barry, Margaret Butler née Nestor, Peter and Pat Carr, Alice Carroll, Chris Caulfield, Sean Curtin, Paddy Dundon, Padraig Doyle, Joan Fenton née McKegney, Nicholas Furlong, John Haycock, Philip Haycock, Kitty Hayes, Irene Irish, Pat Kelly, Joe Lynch, Helen McKeown, Seamus MacRedmond, Gerry McTernan, Aileen McVey née Doran, Joan Mulholland, Gerry O'Hea, the late Daphne Perrett née McCarthy, Jonathan Perrett, Josie Murph Ruane née Ruane, Jim and Barbara Rafter, the late Pat Quinn, Gordon Revington, Brian Small, John C. Walsh, Sean Walsh, Stephen Walsh, Tony Walsh, Bernie Whitmore née Duffy, Betty Wyse née Hallihan and Kieron Wyse.

Foreword

At the age of 17 my father ran away from home and boarded a ship in Liverpool en route to New York. He made friends on board and agreed to meet up in Manhattan. But where? Well, the best known building in New York, probably the only one they had heard of in 1919, was the Woolworth Building. They never met again because the Woolworth building was so big that there was a main entrance on four different streets. Thus I grew up with the Woolworth story as part of the family folklore.

No visit to town for any youngster was complete without a visit to Woolworths for ice cream or sweets. So a book about Woolworths in Ireland should be of great interest to those of us whose youth included weekly treats at Woolworths.

However, history is all about dates, wars and revolutions so I assumed this book was going to be of value only to those who are studying retailing. How wrong I was! Of course the story will fascinate any aspiring retailer with its description of the changes in serving customers over the past century. Nonetheless it is not limited to shopkeepers because it will also engross the mind of any reader who wants to learn about the changes in the way we lived our lives since the first Woolworth store opened in Dublin's Grafton Street in 1914, three months before the start of the First World War and two years ahead of the Easter Rising.

For the younger reader (and I mean anyone under 60!) an understanding of what life was like in Ireland in those early decades emerges from the description of the challenges that faced the company at that time. The goods that were sold then differ from the needs of today – long woollen socks to wear, coal scuttles for the fireplace and stationery for the pre-email days. The Grafton Street store was sited next door to the Singer Sewing Machine shop and cornered a large share of the market for haberdashery items.

During those years there was a strong protectionist economic policy in the world's markets. Woolworths had to handle 'Buy Irish' campaigns south of the border, 'Buy Ulster' campaigns in the North, 'Buy British' or 'Empire goods' in England and 'Buy German' in Germany.

The management handled the challenge of 'Buy Irish' by encouraging their best suppliers to set up subsidiaries in the twenty-six counties. As a result, Nugget Shoe Polish and Aspro had labels attached 'Packed in the Free State'. Irish-owned companies such as Jacob's Biscuits and Urney Chocolate were favoured. One long association was with Hughes Brothers Ice Cream in Rathfarnham that continued from 1926 right through to 1984.

Children were a prime target for the Woolworth Sales Team and as they opened more shops, ice cream, Pick 'n' Mix sweets and biscuits became a major attraction. The stories of giving great value for broken biscuits bring a smile to the lips, even of competitors! As a rival retailer I remember the battle for the Dundalk customers' money when our supermarkets' pre-packed biscuits were being undercut by the loose biscuits of Woolworths across the street.

What went wrong? Why did F. W. Woolworth close down in the Republic in 1984 but remain open in Northern Ireland until 2009?

The answer to that question probably lies in the strict manner in which the company was directed from the top. The stores in the Republic were managed, on a very tight rein, from the District Office in Liverpool. Very little freedom was allowed to cater for any town's particular tastes or customer needs and the District Office in Liverpool would appear to have forgotten that the founder of the company F. W. Woolworth himself was an innovator par excellence.

The assumption that there was no need to change, that what worked last year will work next year, is emphasised by the Woolworths Henry Street manager looking at H. William's first supermarket and saying 'It won't work – it's just a gimmick!' It is not unlike the Chairman of Liptons in the 1960s who told his shareholders at their AGM that self service would never catch on in Britain.

By 1984 the decision to close the shops in the Republic came from London. There were different levels of VAT and different laws but the new break with sterling may have been the crucial factor.

One of the greatest compliments to any enterprise is to breed look-alike competitors. In 1936 two Moore brothers opened a store called Wellworths in Enniskillen. They expanded that company to a number of branches throughout Northern Ireland – and even across the border – and competed with Woolworths for many years.

One enterprising neighbour in Tipperary town, on learning of the closure of Woolworths on the Main Street, opened a new store called Wellworths which I visited recently and appears to be able to survive 30 years later.

Barbara Walsh has produced a work which is a joy to read for those of us who participated in the revolution of Irish retailing over the past century. But even more so, she entertains and whets the appetite for more from those who never experienced a time when a visit to Woolworths was the event of the week!

Senator Feargal Quinn,
July 2010

Introduction

For the best part of the twentieth century and beyond, one firm, F.W. Woolworth & Co. Ltd, held a dominant position in many of Ireland's main streets. For several generations of Irish shoppers, a visit to a Woolworth store was an essential part of a day's outing, and the aim of this book is to examine how communities in Ireland's towns and cities reacted to this distinctive style of retailing.

Every province in Ireland had its share of Woolworth outlets. As the story unfolds, decade by decade, the spotlight will fall on how they were received and perceived. The people who worked in these branches and the goods they sold from their counters are examined. The role played by store managers was central to how chain-store retailing developed in Ireland, and these men, in turn, made valuable contributions to Irish business and commercial life. Their recollections of the firm's early days, together with many other personal reminiscences from former Woolworth employees, their families and their customers, bring a lighter touch to the narrative.

The difficulties experienced in the 1920s and 1930s, the 'Emergency' and the immediate post-war era are among the topics focused on. Questions arise, such as why Woolworth stocked different merchandise in their branches in Northern Ireland in contrast to outlets in the Republic? How important was the Irish tourist industry to these stores?

The opening of a new Woolworth branch in an Irish town was as much welcomed for the local employment it provided, as for the variety of goods it sold. When rival chain stores finally appeared on the scene, how did Woolworth managers handle the competition? How did they fare during the Northern Troubles? And, why were all the branches in the Republic shut down in the 1980s?

Throughout the narrative a brief background portrait of the corporate growth and development of the Woolworth Company from 1914 to 2008 will be given. The final years of the twentieth century saw the company undergo several radical changes, and the first years of the new millennium brought promise of a bright future. Shoppers in Northern Ireland liked the Woolworth concept of the 'everyday store for everyone', and the company's Irish branches have continued to thrive in the Province up until the end of this story.

The elements contained in this book are varied and it has been necessary at times to use a broad brush to cover areas that carry the potential for further research. I hope the book provides some entertainment for readers and that it will also trigger inspiration for more specialist studies. There are additional avenues to explore and alternative views and perspectives to be opened up.

My sources have included many first-hand accounts of events that interface with some of the background history provided in my bibliography. Readers who are interested to learn more about the early life of the multimillionaire American founder, Frank Winfield Woolworth, (1852–1919), and of the firm's corporate and brand-building history, will find Paul Seaton's recently published *A Sixpenny Romance: Celebrating a Century of Value at Woolworths* (2009) a useful source of informative detail on the development of the Woolworth chain in the United Kingdom from 1909 to 2008.[1] Otherwise, for those who wish to gain more insight into the founder's private life, there is a solidly conscientious biography, written almost seventy years ago, by John K. Winkler entitled *Five and Ten: The Fabulous Life of F. W. Woolworth*.[2] This work quotes extensively from collected private papers and other company and family memorabilia.

It is now over one hundred and thirty years since the American company founded by Frank Winfield Woolworth made an appearance in the world of retail commerce. He opened his first store in New York State in 1879, and a chain of similar outlets grew to be a runaway success in the United States of America. In his later years, Woolworth fulfilled a long-cherish ambition to establish a foothold in the British Isles when he personally travelled to Liverpool in 1909 to establish a British Registered Company bearing his name. He appointed his cousin, Fred Moore Woolworth, as the managing director of the new company, and the first of what was to become well over one thousand Woolworth stores in the United Kingdom and Ireland opened in Liverpool within a few months. Five years later, in 1914, F. W. Woolworth & Co. Ltd established their first branch in Ireland.

For generations of shoppers everywhere, all Woolworth stores have become identified colloquially in speech and in print as *Woolworth's*, *Woolworths* or

Woolies. However, since the firm's incorporation as a British Registered Company in 1909, F.W. Woolworth & Co. Ltd preferred the use of *Woolworth* without an *s,* or, for that matter, an apostrophe *s* in their own documentation. The subsequent use of *Woolworths* to replace *Woolworth,* which came about as a result of corporate changes of title in more recent times, now causes some confusion as to the correct terminology to use. Therefore, for clarity and consistency the older, more formal *Woolworth* appellation has been retained throughout the narrative of this book, until the year 2001 is reached, at which time it became *Woolworths plc.* Otherwise, in those instances when quotations, interviews, advertisements or extracts from other work added the colloquial *s* or apostrophe *s,* this form has been kept.

Chapter 1

The First Years

1914–1918

On Thursday, 23 April 1914, Messrs F.W. Woolworth & Co. Ltd opened the doors of their first store in Ireland. It was the forerunner of over forty similar retail outlets this firm was to establish in Ireland within the next eight-four years. The subsequent expansion of their presence in other Irish towns and cities went on to create not only a piece of living heritage that changed shopping habits and, in some instances, the visual streetscape of a main street in a rural town, but it also created a folk memory that remained held in great affection for future generations.

In 1914, by contrast to the exaggerated excitement their appearance was to later generate in provincial centres, the arrival in Dublin of what was perceived to be yet another British retail firm passed off without creating any noticeable concern. The existing department stores in the city considered themselves sophisticated, and this newcomer in Grafton Street was loftily ignored as presenting no direct competition. Many other multiples had made quiet inroads into Ireland since the latter part of the nineteenth century. Lipton's grocery stores and their associated London and Newcastle Tea Company could be found in many locations outside of the capital; likewise branches of the Home and Colonial and Maypole chains. Various branded shoe shops, men's outfitters such as Burton's the Tailor, and the ubiquitous Singer Sewing Machine shops were also well distributed. However, these incoming retailers had all merged into existing streetscapes with only minimal visual or commercial impact. Their exterior and interior appearance differed little from neighbouring Irish shops. They stocked a similar range of goods and served their customers in a traditional, old-style way, from behind long counters with goods for sale stacked up on shelves behind the assistant or hidden in storage drawers or back stockrooms.

Figure 1. The counter and interior of a Maypole shop.
Courtesy Robert Anderson, *Memories in Focus,* Vol. 1 (1981).

Dublin's largest emporiums nurtured an air of hushed formality. Male shop-walkers in morning suits ushered customers to the relevant departments where a few samples of stock were ensconced in glassed cabinets or special counters for this purpose. A chair would be brought for the intending shopper, and an attentive assistant behind one of the counters would then produce whatever selection of goods the customer requested. Only the sales person had access to the merchandise. Sometimes goods were held in glass-fronted boxes to reveal their contents, but more usually items were stored in wooden drawers and, for the most part, kept tidied away out of sight. Unlike today, there were no open racks of ready-to-wear clothing laid out in serried rows. Dressmakers and tailors still held sway, and the fabric departments of the best shops stocked huge bolts of cloth from which their customers could make selections.

Ordinary people did not enter the portals of such exclusive houses of fashion. Instead, they patronized the less formidable drapery stores of substance that stocked clothing, hosiery, white goods and fabrics. For household wares, shoppers sought out a hardware shop. For toys, they went to a toyshop. For sweets, there were confectioners or sweet shops. Fancy goods and small wares could be purchased in shops known as hucksters, and toiletries were stocked by the chemist. Stationers, bookshops and newsagents restricted themselves to their own specialist lines.

By contrast, the carefully designed shop-floor format of a Woolworth store sold a variety of goods that could be found in a dozen shops or more. Their stock was laid out along aisles of open-counter displays to encourage all who came into a store to move around and examine everything before selecting their choice of purchase. There was no pressure from floor-walkers or sales assistants. People felt free to browse as long as they liked and could leave without buying anything at all. This brought a touch of wonder for shoppers, who were more used to finding a similar style of open display trading only available from makeshift streetside stalls during fair days in market towns, or in designated market areas in the cities.

Figure 2. Open counter display in a Woolworth store.
Courtesy 3ᴰ and 6ᴰ Pictures Ltd.

There was nothing temporary or makeshift about the Woolworth stores; the elegance of the shop fittings and window displays, their well-regimented uniformed staff and the excellent quality of their wares never failed to impress commentators. The image they aimed to present was one of serving an upwardly mobile clientele; shoppers who desired 'nice' things at reasonable prices, who were keen to better themselves, their homes and their lifestyles but who had little or no surplus income to spend on 'luxuries'. Company strategy had always been reliant on bulk buying goods for an enormous spread of retail outlets. This gave them the power to flourish on lower price margins than their rivals without any lack in the quality of the products being offered.

How this impacted on shopping patterns in Irish towns became more apparent when, in due course, F. W. Woolworth & Co. Ltd began to open many identical outlets outside of the three major urban centres of Dublin, Belfast and Cork. Their arrival in market towns not only made a considerable visual impact on streetscapes, but often introduced an unwelcome challenge into an established and conservative retail climate. Yet, for the most part, as shall be demonstrated, the opening of a new branch would be recognized later as having been a boost to the commercial viability of many of the smaller rural communities.

The American founder of the famous store chain, Frank Winfield Woolworth, (1852–1919), would have felt very much at home in Ireland. As one of two sons born into a family small-holding that struggled to make a living from mixed farming in New York State in the mid-nineteenth century, he had inherited something of the determination and commercial acumen of his mother's people, the McBriers, who had emigrated to the United States from County Down in 1825 to become modestly successful in farm and associated rural business ventures.[1] When Frank Woolworth created the concept of 'an everyday store for everyone' in a small New York State town called Lancaster in 1879, he had aimed to draw in the custom of its surrounding rural community. The patrons of his stores were mostly farming families, thrifty and wary but ready to respond to offers of reliable bargains and novelties. Thirty-five years later, when his style of doing business came to Irish market towns, the reaction his stores received was very similar to those early days in America. Lifestyles that mirrored his parents' hard work and frugal living standards were still very much in evidence in early twentieth-century rural Ireland.

What was the magic every Woolworth store managed to create? It was partly a visual familiarity, or 'branding', long before this term came into common use. Taking the cue from the American experience, the directors of the British subsidiary company knew it was essential that every store had an identical presence. Their familiar red and gold fascia-board was instantly recognizable in every location. Legends such as 'Nothing in these stores over 6^D' matched imaginative window displays that lured shoppers in to browse and buy. Once inside, whether in a busy large city or a sleepy small town, customers were then assailed by that distinctive 'Woolworth' smell. Even today it is still remembered by older generations as a strange mixture of oiled pitch-pine floors, marshmallow sweets, paper bags, bath salts, biscuits and the faint odour of leather goods and greased metal hardware.[2]

Every Woolworth store not only smelt the same, it looked identical. The lighting, fittings and the style of shop floor layouts were invariably uniform. Solid mahogany counters displayed wares that were laid out with military precision within easy reach of customers. There were few packaged goods, and merchandise was mostly sold loose. Use of this display format was still relatively novel, but since its foundation, the Woolworth Company had made good use of a traditional marketplace axiom, 'When a customer picks up an item to examine it, the sale is already three-quarters completed'.

Store aisles were wide. There was plenty of room for browsers. At weekends, whole families would descend *en masse* while, on quieter days, housewives, pensioners, schoolchildren and lunchtime shoppers ebbed and flowed in predictable patterns. In towns and resorts that catered for holidaymakers or visiting tourists, an afternoon saunter around the local Woolworth store could offer entertainment and distraction, especially when rain spoiled other plans.

The morning routine for a store's manager ran like an army exercise, and it never varied. His first task before opening the doors was to look over the front window displays to make sure everything on view from the street was still in perfect order. If he spotted any dirt or litter around the entrance or pavement, a staff member had to go outside to clean it up immediately. Inside, floors and counters were checked. Everything had to be gleaming clean and all lights in perfect working order. Uniformed counter assistants – who were always referred to as 'Miss', including the rare married ones – were then allowed to file on to the shop floor. Their entrances and exits were regimented by a series of buzzers, or sometimes a whistle, which signalled a coordinated opening of all cash registers to 'till up', followed by another buzzer to allow the front doors to open for the public. Such strict regimentation was the norm in that era.

In those days, store layouts were designed to have several assistants behind each counter to answer questions or help make a choice. They also took payments and wrapped purchases, but their principal task was to watch very closely how their stock was moving during the day. A form to be written-up later then detailed items that were selling well, the favourite colours and styles being chosen and any changed trends in popularity. This process was of particular importance when new lines were put out on temporary sale as 'try-outs' in a few selected outlets.

Demarcation lines were firmly drawn and counter assistants were never allowed into the stockroom. No supervisor could 'stock-up' without putting in an order form, and each and every item was coded by number, colour and department. Long before computerized systems of control were invented, Frank Woolworth's well-tried methods carried an efficient trail of crucial information that linked each store counter to the office desk of a senior buyer. Herein lay one of the secrets of successful trading.

When Woolworth came to Grafton Street

One may ask what prompted Woolworth to extend their business into Ireland in 1914? Might it have been the consequence of some special desire expressed by its founder? Frank Woolworth would have been aware of his mother's family connection to Ireland, and there is anecdotal evidence that on at least one of his frequent transatlantic ocean trips to Europe he had taken time to come ashore at Cobh in order to make investigative enquiries about the emigration of his Irish grandfather, Henry McBrier.[3] It is not known if he was successful. Subsequently, the Woolworth decision to open branches in Ireland had a relatively slow gestation in comparison to the speed by which the new British company expanded across the rest of the United Kingdom. The first store had opened in Liverpool in November 1909, and by the end of 1912 the British company was trading out of twenty stores, nineteen of which were in England and one in Wales. Profit for that year had totalled over £29,000. Expansion continued at the same rapid pace. Eight more English stores and another store in Wales had been opened by the end of 1913. Results were excellent. Sales totalled £431,000 and the profit generated from this figure came to £58,000. The commission paid out to their managers had been £8,000, and the average profit per store was £1,312.[4]

Plans for the first store in Ireland were put in motion on 14 November 1913, when the board of directors of the British Woolworth Company gathered in their Liverpool office to finalize the legalities for the first of three adjoining properties in Dublin's Grafton Street.[5] A thirty-year lease for the ground floor and basement of a children's outfitters at number 66 Grafton Street was ready for the directors' approval and signature. Negotiations were almost complete for the already vacant premises at number 67, together with the shop next door, number 68, which ran a brisk trade in fancy goods and jewellery. Just under two years later the company would acquire the lease of number 65.[6] These four fine properties together comprised a prime position close to the St Stephen's Green end of Dublin's premier shopping street.

Figure 3. Ireland's first Woolworth store in Grafton Street, Dublin.
Courtesy 3[D] and 6[D] Pictures Ltd.

The Woolworth Company's strategic move into the Irish capital city had been conducted according to their tried and tested formula. The firm's practice was to first target the most up-market shopping street in a selected town or city. Led by a bright young American called Louis Denempont, who had been sent from their New York office in 1910 to act as a property scout for the fledgling new company, a team of experts would then seek out a commercial outlet that had neighbouring premises noted to be already well patronized by a passing trade. Their flair for picking prime sites with potential often produced several options for selection. Negotiations with the owners for a long lease or, as later became more favoured, the outright purchase of a freehold, would then begin.

The location of Dublin's first store was an excellent example of this strategy. The Grafton Street premises they had targeted was clearly flanked on either side by desirable commercial neighbours – one of the Singer Sewing Machine's busy and popular shops occupied the street level of number 69, with the Misses Clarke and Power, described as Court Dressmakers, accommodated on the second floor; the Alliance and Dublin Consumers Gas Company was conducting its business from the adjoining number 65. (When the Gas Company moved to D'Olier Street the following year, Woolworth also took over these premises to provide a café for customers. Further expansion took place, much later, in 1927.)

In the decades to come, the speed by which the British Woolworth Company continued to accelerate its presence in every major shopping area was remarkable. Each new store opened was identified within company records not only by the street address in each town but also with an individual Woolworth store number (see below, Appendix I). Therefore, as preparations for the opening of the Grafton Street store went ahead, this Woolworth outlet was given it own special number, 31, which indicates that it was the thirty-first store of the chain and known henceforth by all company employees as '31 Dublin'. The second Irish store to be opened was located in Belfast's High Street the following year. This was the firm's fifty-ninth store, '59 Belfast', which opened on 6 November 1915.

On 17 August 1918 trading began from another outlet across the River Liffey in Henry Street, to be known for the next sixty-six years by Woolworth people as '76 Dublin'. Almost four decades later, the city's third but comparatively short-lived store, '839 Dublin', began trading in Thomas Street in 1954.

The selection of premises in Grafton Street to introduce the Woolworth style of shopping to Irish customers in 1914 was an excellent decision. Its location was in the middle of the most prestigious shopping area of the capital, known informally as the 'Golden Square Mile', which stretched from the Shelbourne and Russell Hotels, bordering St Stephen's Green, to include Kildare Street and Dawson Street, which ran parallel to Grafton Street. These thoroughfares were graced by important buildings, such as the Royal Dublin Society's Leinster House (later to become the home of Dáil Éireann), the Royal Academy and the City's Mansion House, the official residence of Dublin's lord mayors since 1715, built twenty years before London came to bestow a similar honour on its first citizen.[7]

Not far away around the corner, past where Nassau Street skirted the railings of Trinity College, two of the most well-known rival shopping emporiums, Brown Thomas and Switzers (Dublin's equivalent of Harrods and Harvey Nichols) had already faced each other across the northern end of Grafton Street for well over fifty years. Moreover, this part of the city was bordered by a fashionable residential area which encompassed two university colleges, art galleries, museums, libraries and gentlemen's clubs within its Georgian squares. For Woolworth, the procurement of a retail outlet with an address anywhere within the immediate environs of such a swathe of privileged living was a real coup. Their Grafton Street neighbours were all well-established high-class retailers of repute, and to have settled in their midst bestowed an unmistakably dignified cachet of excellence and style. On opening their doors for their first day of trading, Woolworth had truly 'arrived'.

The street's role as a genteel shopping location also made it a popular gathering place, well serviced by a number of cafés where people of leisure could meet and mingle. Bewley's renowned Oriental Tea Rooms was not to arrive for another few years, but the rather more elite Mitchell's Tea Rooms had been favoured by the ladies who shopped in Brown Thomas for decades, while patrons of the Robert Roberts café were regularly regaled by the music of a string quartet. Woolworth soon opened its own restaurant and added a touch of transatlantic pizzazz by calling it a caféteria. Its facilities soon became a popular venue, to be hired out by social organizations for sedate evening events, such as, for example, lectures on heritage and the arts run by the Dublin Literary Society.[8] Likewise, the rather more spacious caféteria on the upper floors of the second Dublin store, in Henry Street, found favour with a number of groups running charity whist drives and dances.[9]

It should be remembered that, in those days, Dublin was looked upon as the second city in what was then the United Kingdom of England, Wales, Scotland and Ireland, and their having a strong presence here fitted in perfectly with the Woolworth Company's forward planning. After five years in existence, the company was aiming to gain a new level of authority and prestige within the retail trade. Since 1910 their executive office headquarters had been based in London WC2. From here they had carefully selected all the top-class shopping districts of each provincial region for a major store. Branches in Swansea (1912) and Cardiff (1913) had introduced them to Wales. In 1914, shortly after arriving in Dublin's Grafton Street, the first store in Scotland had opened, in Glasgow. It may be assumed that, while intuition and a well-honed instinct for the 'right' new location may have been the starting point, a careful assessment of all the pros and cons would have been conducted before final decisions were made.

Experience had taught the team of property scouts that one of the best places to site a new Woolworth premises in any town was often beside a Singer Sewing Machine shop. It was a bonus enjoyed by the Grafton Street store. This situation was favoured, not merely because Woolworth counters stocked a huge range of sewing threads, trimmings and other notions sought by customers at a time when home-dressmaking was all the rage, but because the Singer shops attracted the 'right' kind of shopper Woolworth wished to woo. Ladies who patronized the Singer shops were probably still using old hand or foot treadle machines in preference to the expensive new electric models being displayed – but this did not mean they did not want the most up-to-date and stylish range of laces, ribbons, bias bindings, nets and stylish hat trimmings and dressmaking patterns that Woolworth offered at bargain prices. Ladies with aspirations to improve their lifestyles and homes would also seek out merchandise such as toiletries, house-wares, fine china and 'modern' gadgets. The promise of 'Nothing over sixpence' was the lure.

As business in their new store in Grafton Street got off to a satisfyingly good start, the directors of the new British company could have had no inkling of the momentous historic events that lay ahead. Within months of their arrival in Ireland, the Great War (1914–18) would be upon them and – not long after – domestic political difficulties, commencing with the 1916 Easter Rising were to bring problems lasting up to and beyond the foundation of the new Irish Free State in 1922.

The Effect of the Great War

Although there had been rumours rumbling for some time over the possibility of an armed conflict with Germany, most people were taken by surprise when the German kaiser ordered his troops to mobilize for war, on 1 August 1914. Many official administrations all over Europe were away *en vacances* to enjoy the summer when the German Army swept swiftly through Belgium and on into northern France, to come within 30 miles of Paris. In France, the Woolworth Company's office at 52 rue du General Chanzy in Calais was caught unprepared, like everybody else. For decades, Woolworth buyers had purchased heavily from European manufacturers, and the whole distribution system from suppliers was now confronted by huge difficulties. At least 25 per cent of everything sold from the firm's American store counters originated from Europe. New York had to face the problem that shipments of goods from Europe were likely to be stopped immediately.

Figure 4. Nothing over Sixpence.
Courtesy G. McTernan.

Figure 5. A range of products for all family members.
Courtesy 3^D and 6^D Pictures Ltd.

As hostilities escalated, German U-boats increasingly threatened all shipping lines across the Atlantic, but manufacturers in the United States soon started upgrading production techniques so that they could respond to demands for more home-produced products. For firms like the Woolworth Company in America, their decades-long reliance on goods supplied by European and British factories and workshops would undergo substantial changes as a result of the war, and, in England, the company's subsidiary branch was to be directly affected, also. Regular supplies of stock for their counters was seriously disrupted, and London buyers went scouting for British and Irish firms which could make products to replace European or American-made imports. This experience would later prove to have been a particularly useful exercise. Not before too long, the buyers would have to be ready to facilitate sales of Irish-made merchandise in preference to 'British' goods in many of the company's Irish stores.

Meanwhile in Ireland, as in the rest of the world, it was commonly assumed in August of 1914 that this little dispute with Germany would be all over by Christmas. Nonetheless, all Irish reservists were immediately mustered in 1914 and there were calls for volunteers to enlist in the British Army's expeditionary force. A large number of young Irish men were swept up by the excitement of the moment. Thousands rallied to the cause.

One interesting outcome of the Great War years, which can illustrate how the Woolworth store chain in Ireland developed a slightly different style to the British company's outlets elsewhere, relates to the appointment of women manageresses. With so many men gone off to the war, the number of experienced male store managers and trainees available for promotion within the firm was soon badly depleted. Yet, Woolworth had continued to open up new stores, and it was necessary to upgrade girls who were former staff supervisors or cashiers in order to fill the gaps at store management level. Ten posts for women as manageresses were created between 1916 and 1924. All were placements in English stores. Excluding one or two, most of these postings were located in the south of the country or in London. Several of the ladies were married and most retained their position for a number of ensuing years. By contrast, the first official appointment of a Woolworth manageress to an Irish store was not to take place for another forty years, although many senior female staff members acted *pro tem* for absent male managers from time to time. Eventually, just over halfway through the century, Irish stores would go through a period of having a high proportion of manageresses for a short while.[10]

Although calculations for female employment in Ireland are recognized as unexact, even in census returns, evidence of 'gainful' or paid work for women for the greater part of the twentieth century always showed a marked difference between the more industrialized north of the country and what became the Free State, mainly because women's employment was traditionally associated with farming or home-based work, and not with industry or the distribution services.[11] In this regard, the Woolworth Company's Irish stores were to become unique institutions within rural areas, providing high levels of employment opportunities for young women.

Woolworth Expands its Presence in Ireland

Throughout the Great War, despite running into the difficulty of finding enough senior staff during the war, the Woolworth directors had continued to press ahead with a planned schedule of expansion.

In 1915, on 6 November, the 59 Belfast High Street outlet was opened. The date marked the sixth anniversary of the company's first British store, in Liverpool.

Belfast was Ireland's most highly industrialized city, dominated by the shipyards and linen industry, and it was not long before the volume of business being done in this busy high street store justified expansion into the next-door premises. In due course, having been rebuilt and extended several more times, it would become the oldest surviving Woolworth branch in Ireland. By the time Belfast celebrated the millennium, it was still one of the most well-known and imposing retail buildings in the city centre.

Rebellion in the Streets of Dublin: 1916

By 1916 the Woolworth directors who planned for further expansion in Ireland would have been aware that the long-drawn-out negotiations over

Figure 6. Celebrating the first opening: the new Belfast store takes
everyone on a jaunt to Bangor in 1915.
Courtesy G. McTernan.

Irish Home Rule legislation had been put in abeyance for the duration of
the First World War. It was not a matter for their immediate concern, in any
case, as no adjustment to trading conditions in Ireland was anticipated. The
possibility of a sudden onset of civil disorder in Dublin would not have
entered their minds. Consequently, like everyone else, when the Easter Rising
began, in April 1916, the manager of the Woolworth store in Grafton Street
was no better prepared than any of his commercial neighbours. Fortunately,
only minor incidents of looting were experienced. As one press report put it:
'Amongst the Grafton Street houses which have suffered by the marauders are
Mansfield's boot warehouse, Knowles's fruit store, Woolworth's bazaar, Knapp
and Peterson's pipe and tobacco shop, the Maison Phillippe chocolate shop
and Noblett's toffee house.'[12]

It would seem that the looters may have considered the Woolworth sweet
counter a special attraction. James Stephens, in his famous eye-witness account

of the 1916 Rebellion, has recorded how 'the shops attacked were mainly haberdashers, shoe shops and sweet shops', adding: 'There is something comical about this looting of sweet shops – almost innocent and child-like. Possibly most of the looters are children who are having the sole gorge of their lives. They have tasted sweetstuffs [*sic*] they have never toothed before, and will never taste again in this life, and until they die the insurrection of 1916 will have a sweet savour for them.'[13]

Use of the term 'bazaar' by the press to describe the Woolworth store in this incident reflects common parlance employed at that time. Many of the early outlets were listed in local trade directories in this way, or else called 'Variety Store' – another description that has since dropped out of favour. They were also categorized under the heading 'Fancy Goods'. Occasionally, and rather more grandiosely, the compiler of a trade directory might allocate them the title 'Department Store'.

When Dublin's second Woolworth branch at numbers 18 and 19 Henry Street (later to be expanded to include number 20) was opened for business, on 17 August 1918, the building might, indeed, have qualified for this description. This section of the street had been destroyed by fire during the Easter Rising, and the Woolworth store thus occupied a fine new premises rebuilt on the site of the Bewley Tea Company's former shop. The Woolworth real estate scouts must have been quick to spot the opportunity to snap up this prime location. Their negotiations for a fifty-year lease with Bewley Sons & Company Limited was completed and ready for the directors' approval almost exactly twelve months later.[14]

The new building had utilized all the most modern construction techniques and the work was nearing completion when it was visited by a group of architects from the Architectural Association of Ireland. The building materials and techniques received acclaim, and 'the care taken in the choice of essential details' had impressed.[15] Furnishings such as locks, bolts, hinges, mats, shutters and grates were thought to be excellent. In time to come, there were to be many more similar appreciative assessments, and occasional amazed comments, in regard to the professionalism and high standards used in the building and the interior fitting-out of other Woolworth stores in Irish towns and cities.

Shopping in a Woolworth Store, 1914–19

In the early days, many items on Woolworth counters were sold for as little as 1d. The cheaper items were not prepacked, but mostly sold loose. This was nothing unusual. Display packaging was almost unheard of. Goods purchased were served to customers in paper bags or parcelled up with wrapping paper and string after the sale was completed. Up to this time, when typically out shopping, an Irish customer's daily list might require several separate forays into different establishments. There would be visits to the grocer or butcher; then the stationer, chemist or hardware store could be next; perhaps something from the draper was needed? And a look into the sweetshop before going home was a must. The arrival of a new Woolworth store in a town's main shopping street meant that almost all that was needed could be found under one roof.

What did Woolworth sell? Just about everything. Today's pensioners will remember their parents speaking about many of the lines that are never seen today. Although there are far too many to mention here, there are some which merit recollection, if only to recall a style of life that had begun to disappear almost a hundred years or so ago.

During the first decades of the century the bicycle remained by far the favourite mode of privately owned wheeled transport for a lot of people. Hardware counters in Woolworth, therefore, carried puncture repair kits and pumps in addition to a range of useful tools, spanners, oil and spare bicycle chains. They also sold a wide selection of carpentry tools and fretwork kits, hammers, screwdrivers and saws, together with loose nails, tacks, screws, brackets, nuts and bolts. They displayed boot and shoe products, including laces and innersoles, and also shoe trees, spare repair heels and soles, both in leather and rubber, and metal segs (small studs) in a variety of sizes, which helped save wear and tear. People were in the habit of walking greater distances at this time; many carried out their own maintenance of boots and shoes at home, and shoes were never thrown away until the uppers were worn beyond repair.

Haberdashery counters have all but disappeared from shops today, but in past decades this was a department of great importance to shoppers. While ribbons and lace were sold by the yard, packets of needles, pins and bodkins, thimbles, thread, buttons and bias binding each had their separate sections on counter displays. Small skeins of different coloured wools for darning woollen socks were popular, until the concept of thrift went out of fashion with the invention of hard-wearing synthetic yarns.

Domestic washing machines were unheard-of. Home laundry was done by hand, and the weekly wash meant housewives struggling with soap, washboards and tubs. While a few branded soapflakes were marketed in packets, it was still a common practice to have loose soapflakes and washing

GOOD THINGS TO KNOW
THE SOLE OF ECONOMY

'MARVEL'
RUBBER SOLES

—give shoes
TREBLED
WEAR!

THE gigantic demand for MARVEL soles is ample proof of their amazing durability and sterling value. Fit them to all the family shoes and halve your footwear costs. Obtainable from Woolworths Stores everywhere.

IN ALL SIZES
BLACK or TAN

BROAD or NARROW
TOE FITTINGS

6d
PER PAIR

INVISIBLE WHEN   FITTED

Figure 7. Shoe care was an
important chore.
Courtesy 3ᴰ and 6ᴰ Pictures Ltd.

soda sold by weight. These could be bought in hardware stores, grocers – and in branches of Woolworth.

Another series of products that have long disappeared from modern-day shopping lists are the household items made from tin and enamelware. Bowls, plates, mugs, dishes and picnic sets were also made from Bakelite, a hard but brittle synthetic material that would be replaced by plastic products after the Second World War. All kitchen appliances were manually operated. A simple wire whisk used for whipping up cream or mixing the ingredients for baking a cake was only occasionally replaced by a more sophisticated mechanical gadget, worked by hand. There were also hand-operated rotary mincing machines, which had to be clamped on to a table top before being put to use. In the days before refrigerators, pierced metal larder safes kept food cool, while heavy pottery crocks, pudding bowls and jugs were used to provide as much insulation as possible before and after dishes were cooked.

It could be said that every aspect of people's day-to-day life was mirrored by the products to be found on a Woolworth counter. What may be noted especially is how children were dressed during the decades, and one striking example is the large amount of boy's woollen knee socks sold by the firm's knitted goods department right up until the 1970s. The sons of 'respectable' families at every class level habitually wore short trousers until the age of 12 or 13, at which time the donning of a pair of long trousers often became the mark of starting work, or, for the more privileged, entry into the senior school classes. Other lines in knitted goods for men, women and children included lock-knit vests, ladies knickers and men's underpants. Short ankle socks, most popularly white in colour, were worn by children of all ages and even by girls well into their late teens.

Homes were chilly places in the days before central heating. As a rule, houses relied on gas or open turf or coal fires, which were only lit to heat

The Well-Equipped Work-Basket

EVERY woman, whether she is fond of needlework or not, should possess a really well-filled work-basket. In fact, if she is really a good worker, it is especially important for her to have suitable mending appliances and materials. For instance, if she does not do very fine darning, she must be especially particular to choose silks that blend really well with her hose. Very dainty darning work is inconspicuous, and bad darning shows less if the mending is exact to tone. Many women find that their work of darning for the family is much lessened when they use Visylka mendings, because they wear so well. They save many hours of work, because once a hole has been darned it does not break through again in spite of hard wear. It is very wise to keep also in the work-basket a good choice of sewing cottons and silks in many shades. If you have your frocks made for you, ask the dressmaker to send you a little of the material for emergency mending, and part of a reel of silk or cotton to match. She is sure to have some left over, and they are certain to be useful on many occasions

Figure 8. Woolworth had everything for the lady's work basket.
Courtesy *Coleraine Chronicle*.

kitchens and living rooms, and there were many icy corners in remaining areas of a home for at least six months of the year. To keep people warm in winter, women and children wore cotton liberty bodices or long-sleeved woollen vests – and in the severest cold weather – men, women and children alike donned woollen combinations. Naturally, Woolworth stocked coal scuttles, shovels and fire irons and the blackening paste that was used to clean the metal grates of fireplaces and ranges.

Figure 9. Thrifty tips were always welcomed.
Courtesy 3ᴰ and 6ᴰ Pictures Ltd.

A huge volume of sales was generated by stationery and toy departments, especially at Christmas, and while window displays were lavish, the foremost message was always 'Nothing in these stores over 6d'. Keeping all prices down to this low level was achieved by the policy of bulk buying direct from manufacturers. When Woolworth bought merchandise from a supplier, these orders were rarely given for goods to be packed and delivered in dozen lots, but rather for hundreds, even thousands, of gross. Most of the deliveries were made to a central warehouse for subsequent distribution via rail and boat, to reach the counters of stores right across England, Scotland, Wales and Ireland.

Selling to Woolworth

The procedure a manufacturer had to undergo in order to have a new line or range of merchandise vetted, tested and finally accepted by a Woolworth buyer was tough. The first hurdle was to get one of these executives to consider a new product. The company's founder, Frank Woolworth, had always eschewed the use of agents and middle men, although this was a policy which time eventually and inevitably eroded away, as shall be shown. Factory owners were encouraged to make submissions to the Buying Office in London, where, if after an initial inspection, the item they made looked interesting, then they would be given permission to apply for some painstaking 'try-outs' on the counters of a few selected stores. Each 'try-out' included the new piece of merchandise being subjected to counter-staff assessments at point-of-sale to time how quickly and in what quantities these new items moved. If customers were offered a choice of colours or styles, the written reports also included this data and the outcome of several 'try-outs' would be then submitted before a final decision was put forward for the final approval of the buyer and his colleagues at board-room level. This procedure guaranteed that by the time a manufacturer was given the go-ahead to start production and planning delivery dates, every aspect of the manufacturing process and delivery schedules had been worked out.

A Clash with the Law

It was probably inevitable that the simplification of buying in bulk, while cheap and uncomplicated, might sometimes run the company into trouble. Such incidents did arise from time to time, especially when the original source for items of merchandise became unaccountably blurred.

Within a short time after opening in Dublin, the first of several legal clashes triggered by the Woolworth policy of keeping prices at rock bottom appeared in one of the city's leading newspapers. The company's bulk buying strategy had swiftly come to the attention of the Irish Industrial Development Association, a body founded in Cork in 1903, whose officials were assiduous in their efforts to ensure that not only trade descriptions for wares were accurate, but that the sale of home-produced goods was favoured over imported items. More specifically targeted campaigns to promote locally made goods were shortly to become a very familiar recurring sight. It will be shown in later chapters how similar patriotic concerns to support 'protectionist' legislation aimed to assist local manufacturing industries were to emerge almost everywhere during the inter-war period.

The Ulster Quality Mark

FOLLOW THE STAR

AT BALMORAL
KING'S HALL.
INDUSTRIES' EXHIBITION

AT MARKET

Buy from the retail merchants who stock and recommend Ulster products. Those traders who foster home industries, create work for potential customers, for your relations, friends and neighbours, and for the youth of the province who seek work and opportunity here in their own country. Retail merchants may become Associate Members of the Ulster Industries Development Association by permanent display of the "Star" Window Sign, and signing the membership pledge.

Visitors to the Royal Ulster Show are particularly directed to those Stands displaying the "Star" hanging sign, which indicates a display of Ulster products. Examine the exhibits and note their excellence in quality and value, then remember that their manufacture represents work and wages for your own countrymen. On the Balcony, full particulars of the "Six Pointed Star" may be obtained at Stand 126. You may enrol as an Associate Member of the Ulster Industries Development Association, thus signifying your willingness to help yourself and the people of Ulster as a whole.

STAND 126
FRONT BALCONY

AT HOME

Every member of the family should wear the Ulster "Star" and practise the principle of commonsense patriotism. Buying home products means increased employment.

"UNEMPLOYMENT" is your problem, and not only a governmental worry. Fathers, mothers, sisters, brothers, friends and neighbours, can do much to supply an effective answer by a concerted effort to create more work. Become an Associate Member now, and an active worker in the advance of Ulster to greater comfort, security and prosperity.

THE PRINCIPLE REPRESENTED BY THE SIX-POINTED STAR IS

BUY ULSTER GOODS
AND INCREASE EMPLOYMENT
Always Buy Within the Empire

Figure 10. The Ulster Star Quality Mark.
Courtesy *Armagh Guardian.*

A six pointed star symbol for 'Buy Ulster Goods' was promoted in Northern Ireland in the 1930s, and, across the water, retailers and suppliers increasingly urged shoppers to 'Buy British or Empire Goods' in all their newspaper advertising.[16] By 1933 totalitarian Germany was also to experience rather more sinister moves against 'foreign' merchandise. American-owned Woolworth stores in Essen and other towns in the Rhur were picketed with placards that read 'Germans, Buy German Goods'. Several of these stores were forced to close their doors when the managers were threatened with arrest.[17]

The Woolworth Company's first clash with the law in Ireland, in September 1916, was nowhere near as drastic as this. Keen to display his alertness over an infringement of the law, the secretary of the Dublin branch of the Irish Industrial Development Association, which had its offices at 102 and 103 Grafton Street, brought the nearby Woolworth store to court to answer a complaint over the sale of men's silk ties. These had been displayed during August as 'special value for 6d' and had been described as 'made in Dublin'.[18]

In presenting his case, counsel for the I.I.D.A. informed the court that the association's secretary 'wanted to stop this illegal traffic'. Several samples of the ties had been rigorously examined and were found to be 'only 25 per cent silk'. Moreover, they were 'certainly not made in Dublin' and they could claim that the Woolworth Company's shop in Grafton Street was guilty of selling goods to which 'a false trade description had been applied'.

In their defence, the counsel for Woolworth pleaded that the company's representative had tendered an apology to the court and offered to pay all costs. But the distinctly waspish presiding magistrate was not to be mollified by any notion of obsequious apologies. 'Am I to understand that [the defendant] pleads guilty to the offence?' he asked. When told that this was so, he imposed a fine of £10.

The Woolworth counsel rose to his feet. He was quite prepared to enliven a dull day in court with a bit of light swordplay with an old adversary on the bench. '£10 is a very severe fine,' he argued. The magistrate, however, was in no mood to engage in the fun. 'I don't think so. I think this is a gross fraud.' Counsel was not yet ready to give up too readily, nonetheless. He reiterated the point that the company bought the ties in Dublin in the honest belief they had been made here. 'Would his worship not make this fine £5?' he pleaded. The response was withering, 'I will not. £10 and £10 costs.'[19]

It was a lesson learned. The Woolworth Company soon discovered the need to tread warily in Ireland. The commercial climate here was finely tuned to many sensitivities within retailing, especially in relation to Irish-made goods.

They were to find that official and non-official vigilance over standards and protectionist laws in Ireland easily created conflict and often required a high level of compromise to placate local shoppers. The case of the sixpenny silk ties was not to be the last such confrontation.

A decade later, the store in Dublin's Henry Street settled another claim. This time it cost them 20 guineas. This challenge had been brought by a firm of local photographers over the copyright ownership of some photographs for sale on the store's fancy goods counter.[20] The photographs were reproductions of three executed leaders of the 1916 Rising: Clarke, O'Hanrahan and Colbert. Apart from the breach of copyright, it has to be wondered if the London buyer for this department was aware of the more subtle nuances that might be attached this type of merchandise? While the summons was not brought about over a political issue per se, this incident nonetheless points up how easily an underlying political message could become attached to something sold from a Woolworth counter in Ireland.

Trade organizations and worker's guilds in England were just as keen to rap the company over the knuckles whenever standards slipped, and there were instances when a buyer was either hoodwinked or was not as alert as he should have been. A store manager in Oxford faced a summons in his local police court 'for selling six table knives bearing the words "Best English Cutlery, Sheffield"'. The knives were described as not being made of Sheffield steel as implied, but from 'a kind of zinc' with 'shafts of low quality celluloid'. A plea of having been 'ordered from a reputable manufacturer' cut no ice whatsoever. Woolworth was fined £5 with £75 costs.[21]

By contrast to the Irish scenario, having to face such charges in the United Kingdom was relatively simple to handle. Any supplier found to be untrustworthy was dealt with ruthlessly. But it was to become an increasing struggle for Woolworth buyers to ensure that the counters of their Irish stores were stocked with acceptable merchandise. While adhering to the company's rigid trading strategies and quality rulings, these men had to retain a carefully neutral stance when confronting the mercurial political, economic and social conditions in Ireland. Each ensuing decade was to introduce a spate of legislative refinements that required constant delicate negotiation with government departments, trade boards and other official bodies. And that was the easy part. Throughout the war of Independence of 1919–1921 and the following strife of the civil war, the problems to be met with in dealing with official and unofficial protests became all the more difficult because they originated from both sides of the conflict.

Historians now recognize that the Great War 'had beneficial effects on the Irish economy north and south'. This was because during this period 'those goods traditionally produced in and exported from Ireland were heavily in demand'.[22] Many Irish manufacturing firms were awarded British government contracts and a wide range of military supplies was shipped off to the war.

Between 1914–18, linen was much in demand for military purposes, tents haversacks, hospital equipment and aeroplane fabric … Shipbuilding also saw a great expansion … and the industrial prosperity was not confined to the North. Many of the southern food-processing industries, dairy products, biscuits and flour milling also experienced a period of buoyant demand. Irish producers North and South were operating very much in a sellers' market.[23]

Stealing from Woolworth

Trading in the Dublin and Belfast stores in those early years soon settled into a satisfactory pattern, but inevitably, the Woolworth practice of allowing customers to browse and handle goods before making a purchase created an increase of opportunities for light-fingered shoppers intent on shoplifting. Staff members were trained to be vigilant, and within months of the opening of the first Dublin store a regular stream of culprits were being hauled up in front of the police courts. The bench was, at first, prone to be lenient, perhaps realizing the temptations being offered by the novelty of the open counter displays would take some time to wear off, as, for example, when 'two respectably-dressed young women … were charged with having in December [1914] stolen two bottles of brilliantine and two combs, the property of Messrs, Woolworth's Ltd., Grafton Street, also with stealing on another date a hat pin and a brooch'. On this occasion, the bench merely cautioned the girls in front of him 'to be more careful in future', although adding the rider that, 'He wanted to give notice that that was the last time he would look on any similar charges from Woolworth's with clemency.'[24]

It was not too long before the attitudes of magistrates hardened considerably. Later reports tell of miscreants accused of stealing even as little as a sixpenny handkerchief, a shoemaker's knife or a similarly priced imitation gold ring being sent down for a full fourteen days. And no signs of leniency appear to have been shown to unfortunate cases who may have fallen on hard times, such as the young grocer's assistant in Dublin, described as 'of no fixed abode', who was charged with 'the larceny of shirt fronts, ties and soap to the total of 3s 6d from Woolworth's store in Henry street'. One could imagine such items being stolen in a moment of desperation by the homeless young man in order to keep up a clean and tidy appearance – and his job behind the grocer's counter. But no concession was made. He went to jail.[25]

Things were no less easy in the Belfast Custody Court. No hint of grace was forthcoming under this jurisdiction, either. The advanced years of an 80-year-old man caught stealing a number of 3d and 6d articles from the Woolworth branch in North Street generated little sympathy. The store manager gave evidence of 'a considerable amount of pilfering' – and the accused received fourteen days.[26]

At the other end of the social spectrum, one can still find light-hearted evidence in literary memoirs that display how stealing from a Woolworth counter became an acceptable rite of passage for generations of middle-class schoolchildren. Not prompted by genuine poverty or desperate situations, filching small items from the open counters was apparently thought of as a mere harmless childish folly: 'we mitched in the afternoons, we spent hours in Woolworth's, stealing rings and brooches, racing down Grafton Street, pissing ourselves with laughter'.[27]

The Management System

In those early days, having to attend court hearings at regular intervals was just another of the many duties that fell within a Woolworth store manager's remit. All the company's managers underwent training through several grades of position. The system ran with military precision. Indeed, a great number of the earliest employees were ex-army personnel who were accustomed to the regimentation and respect for higher authority the Woolworth hierarchy insisted upon.

By the standards of the day, everyone who worked for Woolworth benefited from excellent conditions of employment and pay. This system was, however, based on the premise that pay packets that were boosted by personal or teamwork incentives produced the best results. In return, the workforce was expected to be totally loyal, not only to the company but also to each other, and there was the understanding that those who ruled from the top accepted considerable responsibility for their employees' health and well-being. Unshakable belief in the company's ethos bound them together.

Until the final part of the twentieth century, the business of running the company lay in the hands of directors and board members who took pride in the fact that each one had risen through the ranks on the same career ladder.

Without exception, all had started off as raw recruits in one of the stores' stockrooms. Their favourite claim, to have 'learned the business by sweeping a stockroom floor', was an often repeated axiom by management for decades to come. It also ensured that even the most lofty executive knew from personal experience how an ordinary working person's life could sometimes take a bad turn. Many behind-the-scenes acts of kindness, grants of long-term sick leave or early retirement were quietly approved by the board. By contrast, no quarter was given to anyone whose disloyalty let them down.

Within the ranks of middle management and higher, a collegiate system ran on the assumption of mutual support. It was matey, and it was entirely male. No woman rose to an executive level of management until the latter end of the century. These men knew the importance of good staff and customer relationships, nonetheless. They learned how to display the ranges to best advantage; how to monitor sales and prevent shrinkage. Several developed a particular flair for identifying good merchandise – an important attribute for those who became buyers – but, most importantly, all knew how to sell. There was no corner of the retail business that each director would not have had some experience of at some stage of his career. At the same time, like a family, each man knew the others' strengths and weaknesses.

When Frank Woolworth set up the British F.W. Woolworth & Co. Ltd in 1909, he advised the new board to train up store managers who had plenty of local knowledge of their areas. He had set the example by immediately recruiting a young Yorkshire-born Englishman and former wholesale shipping agent, William L. Stephenson, to be the first managing director's right-hand man. Stephenson had been well placed to guide the new company in the right direction. He already knew a great deal about the Woolworth operation, having handled British-made merchandise for them for years for a firm in Birmingham. He knew the market and he knew the suppliers. He had also acquired a wide circle of useful business contacts.

In 1909 the fledgling Woolworth Company's ambition was to expand across the United Kingdom very quickly, and by the time their first four stores had opened, a big recruiting drive for potential managers was already underway. This strategy eventually led to the foundation of a number of district offices. A northern office in Liverpool and a southern office in London were the first to be set up. Ten years later, the firm's day-to-day business was organized into the Liverpool, Birmingham and Metropolitan (London) Districts, and the company's Executive Office was based in London. In 1954 the Kensington (south-east England) District Office was added. This structure was retained until the 1980s. Responsibility for Ireland, which was initially administered by the Northern Office in 1914, came under the direction of the Liverpool District Office in 1929, together with the greater part of northern England, Scotland and the Isle of Man.

Irish Manpower were soon to the Fore

By 1911, with eleven stores now opened, several young men, either from Ireland or with a claim to Irish roots, like the company's founder, had been recruited and trained up into management. One of these men, Charles McCarthy (1883–1979), was to be closely associated with the company for the next three decades. The son of a Wexford farming family, he had left Ireland at an early age and was doing well as a self-made entrepreneur in Lancashire when he was headhunted into the firm, possibly by Stephenson, in 1910.[28] The firm needed men with experience of the retail trade, and, following his introductory stint in the first Liverpool store, McCarthy (known by all as 'Mac'), was subsequently involved in the setting-up of several new stores. However, in January 1914, when the chairman called Mac in to tell him he was sending him back to Ireland to take over the management of the soon to be opened new store in Dublin's Grafton Street, Mac drove a hard bargain. This 30-year-old businessman's sights had been set on gaining a post in Executive Office in London, and Woolworth would have to make this move to Ireland attractive if he wanted to keep him. A greatly enhanced salary and commission were negotiated, and, in a move which was typical of the way the American Woolworth Company had always persuaded top people to become business partners rather than mere employees, a batch of preference shares was put in his name.[29] He and Stephenson were thus the first British shareholders in the private company. In due course, both men added to their shareholding at every possible opportunity.

Mac's stint in Grafton Street was interrupted by war service as a pilot in the First World War, but he later returned to Ireland to manage the outlet in Henry Street for a short time.[30] Men at the top like Mac became extremely wealthy very quickly. In later years, he liked to tell the story of how, during his time in Dublin, he had had been approached by one of the city's best-known department stores. The directors of this large emporium in O'Connell Street were looking for a new general manager. Their offer of an annual salary of £1,000 was an almost unheard-of sum at that time. But the offer was swiftly rebuffed. 'That would only be enough to pay for my cigars', Mac told them.[31]

Within a year or two of this incident, Mac's appointment to the post of buyer in Executive Office in London realized his ambition to rise to the very top. Many of his compatriots would follow in his wake, to make their mark as powerful men within the Woolworth Company.

There is no mystery attached to why Ireland could supply such a rich source of suitable management talent. Not unlike Scotland, a century earlier, whose brightest and best engineers, chemists and entrepreneurs had fuelled their neighbour's Industrial Revolution, early twentieth-century Ireland had produced a core of forward-looking and innovative business brains. There were few openings at home to be exploited, however. Lucrative advancement in the commercial world usually required candidates to seek opportunities abroad.

Commercial enterprise in Irish market towns was drawn, in the main, from the rural middle-class merchant or strong farming classes who had survived the famine years of 1845–50. These were astute and canny traders. For at least a couple of generations such families had flourished on the proceeds of the licensed trade and its traditional association with general grocery and funeral undertaking, or branched into ironmongery, hardware and animal feeds. Shopkeeping was in their blood. As was the practice among the farming community, it was normally only the eldest boy who inherited or, at least, received the lion's share of the family's commercial concern. The other male siblings, therefore, had to seek employment as befitted their education. Their hard-working parents were ambitious. Money spent on higher levels of education of children was never stinted in the hope that improved learning skills would allow the option of a career in one of the professions, in the public service, banking or insurance. Following the revision of the education curriculum in 1924, it became customary for sons to receive an academic and sporting education up to, and sometimes beyond, Leaving Certificate level, as a pupil of one of the prestigious religious-run colleges, which often supported a seminary, and in the first half of the twentieth century it was not unknown for almost half a senior class to be soaked up by a missionary order or local diocesan college.[32] But for boys with flair who were hungry for success in the commercial world, the range of subsequent career options was usually still very limited. Exciting opportunities beckoned when the F.W. Woolworth & Co. Ltd began visibly expanding its retail chain more vigorously across Ireland.

What may be taken into account also, in this respect, is that young men from these backgrounds quite often enjoyed the benefit of a family with local links within the Irish dynastic political system. When it came to networking in order to advance the prospects for a son, many parents of young hopefuls had 'pull' within certain closed circles, or a way of getting access to it.[33] It was not unheard-of for favours to be called up from leading politicians when an extra push was needed to persuade a local Woolworth store manager to take on a likely lad as a 'learner'. 'Getting him into Woolworths' was often the answer to the anxious prayers of not a few Irish families.[34]

All Woolworth Company employees enjoyed good conditions and rates of pay by the standards of the day, but they were subject to strict disciplinary regimes which would now be regarded as intrusively paternalistic. A manager was paid on a scale graded by the size of his store's retail floor area, and, each year, a bonus was added to his salary that was based on a percentage of the twelve months net profits he had generated. Employees at every level benefited from the firm's pension scheme and retirement at the age of 60 was compulsory for all. For Woolworth men who made it to the top, there were additional benefits within their pension funds, and many who had served at executive level since the company's early days became extremely wealthy. By the next decade, it was thought appropriate that the store managers should be given increased incentives by allotments of a small amount of shares in addition to their year-end bonus.[35]

While the Woolworth Company in its early decades might be viewed as being an organization that was run on strict militaristic lines, it was not constrained by the class-consciousness that was characteristic of the military at the time of the Great War in 1914. One scholar, commenting on the recruitment of volunteers from Ireland, has noted how 'the Lieutenant-General in command of the 16th Irish Division wrote contemptuously of applicants for commissions who "write their applications in red or green ink on a blank bill-head of a village shop"'.[36] Any similar letters of application for management training would have received an entirely different reaction from the top brass in the business world of the Woolworth Liverpool District Office. Far from sneering at these ambitious youngsters from families of middle-class market town merchants, they had been quick to recognize the potential leadership qualities and innate business acumen within the strong farmer class. This reputation became so patently evident that, three-quarters of the way through the century, there was the belief, doubtlessly an apocryphal exaggeration, that the only way to get continuous promotion from some of the more influential executives in this district office was to be not only Irish, but a Catholic and born in Limerick. Whether true or not, nevertheless, what is now apparent – in some minds at least – is that without the loyalty and communication skills of so many good Irish managers who were willing to be continually moved around, the success of the company's trading during this expansionary era would not have been so successful.[37]

By the time the Great War ended with an armistice signed in November 1918, F.W. Woolworth & Co. Ltd had almost doubled in size. Eighty stores were up and running and the firm had branches throughout the whole of England, Ireland, Scotland and Wales. This high level of infiltration had been achieved in less than ten years, and the pace of growth continued to accelerate. Plans were now in hand to concentrate more fully on increasing the number of outlets in the south of England, particularly in the London area, but, nonetheless, there were to be several more new outlets in Ireland within the next eighteen months. At board level everything was very satisfactory. There was no hint of fear that the excellent reception the firm had received in Ireland some four years earlier could not be smoothly and successfully built upon in the coming decades. How wrong they were.

Chapter 2
Difficult Times
1919–1926

The New Year of 1919 saw Woolworth executives in London making ready for several new store openings. These would include one in the city of Aberdeen in Scotland, followed by two in the rural south of England and one in London. Further expansion in Ireland was envisaged, too. They aimed to have a store in Cork and another in Londonderry (Derry). They also wanted to build on the success of the two Dublin stores by locating another new outlet for the capital in the wealthy urban borough of Kingstown (Dun Laoghaire). As spring approached, the board looked forward to a period of steady and positive progress in Ireland for the next eighteen months or so.

A cable from New York on 8 April 1919 stalled plans briefly, with the announcement that the company's president and founder, Frank Winfield Woolworth, had passed away, suddenly and unexpectedly, just short of his 67th birthday. It was the end of an era, but not the end of the retail empire he had founded. Woolworth's vast private fortune was left to his family and his death did not affect the Woolworth retail chains on both sides of the Atlantic. These firms had been organized into corporate structures more than a decade earlier and would continue to run smoothly and efficiently until the end of what came to be called 'the roaring twenties', ten years later.

In 1919, with only three outlets in Ireland, it may be assumed that the British firm's directors were not anticipating that Ireland's scattered cities and towns would hold the promise of being able to carry anything like the saturation patterns achieved throughout core areas of England. For the most part, the typical Irish town had a low and static, occasionally even shrinking, urban population. Yet, as has been already indicated, the hinterland of the cities and large market towns presented a scenario quite similar to the founder's

experience some thirty years earlier, in New York State. For rural communities, the holding of a set market day or days each week in their local
town was the focus of the surrounding population's main commercial activity.
People came into town from the wider catchment area in order to shop or
maybe to conduct some business – and also to enjoy themselves. The inclusion
of a visit to a local Woolworth store soon became established as providing
pleasure to a day's outing. In this respect, an Irish market town was no different
than its counterparts in rural America or England. The shopkeepers in these
areas relied on the spending power of frequent and predictable waves of
visiting shoppers.

In Ireland, only the cities of Dublin and Belfast had any sizable resident
population. Provincial cities were many times smaller. Cork could only muster
a population of about 78,000 and other provincial centres carried from around
40,000 to just under 12,000. Clearly, the potential of any retail outlet was
reliant on being able to draw customers in from outlying areas which often
straddled more than one adjacent county. The creation of a good reputation
for reliability, variety and value was going to be a crucial tactic. Spreading this
reputation by word of mouth was important.

Nonetheless, by 1919 F. W. Woolworth & Co. Ltd was well settled in Dublin
and Belfast and the board was ready to target the next most important city in
Ireland, Cork. They had found an excellent site located in the middle of this
city's premier shopping area and planned to open the doors of their third
outlet in Ireland, at 39–41 St Patrick's Street, in early 1920.

A Woolworth store opening in those early decades was almost always
organized according to a set formula. A large advertisement was placed in the
local newspaper to announce a half-day 'inspection' of the store, during which
no goods would be sold. Instead, patrons were invited to come and to look
around at their leisure. Some form of musical entertainment was often laid on
and tea might be served if the outlet was a large one with cafeteria facilities.
Newsprint shortages and other disruptions during the war years of 1914 to
1918 would appear to have curtailed this practice, but by 1920 normality was
thought to have returned, and on the afternoon of 6 February 1920 the *Cork
Examiner* carried a three-column six-inch high notice inviting 'inspection' of
the range of goods they would be carrying when the doors opened for
business on the following morning at 9 o'clock.[1] Clearly, some thought had
gone into the preparation of the advertisement, and care had been taken to
include the statement, 'with a complete local staff', to defuse any misunder-
standing over employment issues. A store of even modest dimensions would

carry up to thirty or forty female counter assistants as well as two or three male trainees to assist the manager. A large city store also might have what was called a 'permanent' man in the stockroom for odd jobs, but in the same way that female staff were never moved from one store branch to another, his position was a fixed one.

The final line of the Woolworth advertisement that added the information that the Woolworth Company had '82 branches in the United Kingdom', does raise a question, nonetheless. The London and Dublin newspaper columns at that time were clearly reflecting an increasingly volatile and unstable situation in Ireland over the Partition and Home Rule negotiations, and it would seem that the Woolworth executives who planned the Cork opening were not as highly tuned-in to the sensitivity of political issues in Ireland as they should have been. They were soon to be enlightened. It is very noticeable that this statement to highlight Woolworth outlets as part of a 'United Kingdom chain' was swiftly dropped from all the subsequent notices.

The launch of their branch in St Patrick's Street, Cork, went ahead apparently without incident, despite seriously escalating disturbances centred in the Munster area that week. The atmosphere was tense. Seventy political prisoners were being held in Cork jail and the national newspapers were full of dramatic reports. Arms and ammunition had been seized in a 'Raid near Cork'; the post office in Spike Island was cleared out by robbers 'who were not yet apprehended'.[2] On the very day that the *Cork Examiner* carried the Woolworth announcement for the 'Opening Inspection', the news stories on other pages wrote of 'armed and masked men raiding a house in Clare' and of anticipated arrests in Blarney, where 'quantities of ammunition, explosives and revolvers had been found'.[3] One month later, a hastily convened British auxiliary armed police force, the notorious 'Black and Tans', arrived in the area. A very difficult time lay ahead.

In the meantime, the opening of the next Woolworth branch, on Londonderry's Ferryquay Street, had proceeded as planned on 27 and 28 February. The company's preliminary 'afternoon for viewing only' notices were impressive. Advertisements emblazoned the front pages of both local newspapers, the *Londonderry Sentinel* and the *Derry Journal*, to inform the city's townspeople that 'Musical selections by a local orchestra' would provide entertainment that afternoon. A carefully worded caveat stated that this branch would have 'a complete local staff' in attendance.[4] This time Ulster town's traders watched and took note. Several were ready to pose an immediate challenge to the Woolworth 'nothing over 6d' competition. A large

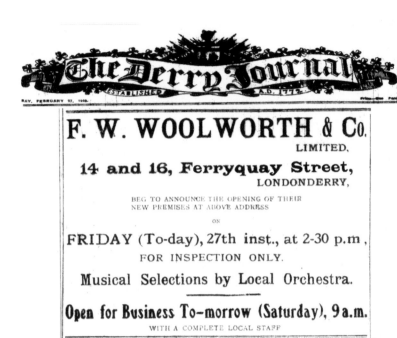

Figure 11. Musical selections from a local orchestra
entertained on Preview Day, 27 February 1920.

Courtesy *Derry Journal.*

advertisement in the following week's *Derry Journal*, inserted by another
recently opened firm, R.J. Matthews, reminded readers to 'Note the address:
6, Sackville Street' and announced a 'Great Realization Sale of Drapery, Wool
& Haberdashery stock to be cleared at 50 per cent less than today's prices'.[5]
It was clear that local competition was not going to allow Woolworth to have
everything its own way.

But beyond all the optimism surrounding the business activity, what cannot
be overlooked is the fact that the current political situation was escalating in
its intensity. The proposals for partition had enraged both communities in this
city and there was soon to be chaos in the streets. Incidents of violence
erupted more regularly. By the summer, the situation had deteriorated to
unthinkable levels of savagery.

Yet, apparently non-plussed by all the political upheaval, the Woolworth
expansion programme for Ireland continued as planned. By August, Liverpool
District Office had installed the first manager of a new branch in readiness for

its opening in the salubrious suburb of Kingstown, County Dublin. (This township's name was officially reverted to Dun Laoghaire around the same time by the District Urban Council.[6]) Headlines in the local Dublin papers were worrying.[7] They reported: 'Irish towns in a state of siege'; 'Main roads barricaded'; 'Extraordinary military activity around Dublin'; 'Curfew imposed'. It is not altogether surprising, then, that the Dun Laoghaire branch of F.W. Woolworth & Co. Ltd would seem to have opened quietly and without any fanfare at the end of August or early September.[8] By that time, what the press was calling 'Munster's reign of terror' was in full force. The *Irish Independent* reported reprisal raids, as 'Crown Forces run amok', and within days curfews were being imposed in three counties and the holding of markets was prohibited in Limerick, Tipperary and Cork.[9] By the end of the month, the newspaper headlines carried nothing but tragedies: 'Shootings'; 'Terrible unrest'; 'Cork very bad'.[10] The Anglo-Irish war had gathered momentum. And worse was to come.

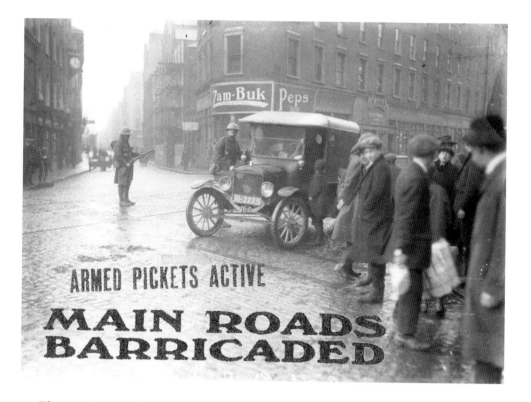

Figure 12. British soldiers in Dublin: Press reports of increased military activity.

Main image: © National Library of Ireland.

On 11 December 1920, in reprisal for repeated attacks on Munster police barracks and Crown forces, a large section of Cork, including the greater part of the southern side of St Patrick's Street, was set on fire. Some of Cork's finest department stores were among the buildings that were completely gutted. Whole blocks of retail shops on many of the streets succumbed to the flames. How interesting it is to note that one city block in the section of St Patrick's Street bordered by Montague Street, which included numbers 39–41, was left untouched by the perpetrators. This section of the street contained the newly opened Woolworth store.

Next morning, the citizens of Cork were described in press reports as 'being in a state of terror'. 'Lorries jammed in the street to remove the surviving merchants' most valuable goods', it was reported, and an announcement went out that 'looters would be shot on sight'.[11] Nonetheless, in the aftermath of this setback, what would seem apparent is that despite all the civil disorder and obvious dangers, the Woolworth board was undeterred from ploughing ahead. Their determination to carry on with their expansion in Ireland must have reflected the directors' confidence that the business to be done in their Irish branches was a viable commercial undertaking. Six months later, work to prepare an outlet in Portadown was complete and the store was ready to begin trading. 'Inspection day' was advertised as 18 February 1921.[12]

A branch in Limerick was to be next. The opening here, on 7 May, may have been a quietly organized affair. Raids, arrests and shootings were dominating the news. There were skirmishes between the police, Crown forces and 'the rebels', and violence in the area continued to escalate. By 18 June, however, the attention of the top management in the Woolworth company had switched back to the progress being made by their construction teams in the Province of Ulster. Trading from a second store in Belfast was about to commence. These new premises were located in North Street, where the offer of 'Special Bargains' for the opening day provoked some unruliness in the overexcited crowd that had gathered. One of the store windows was broken in the fracas and a 12-year-old child was hurt and brought to the Mater hospital. A contemporary report noted that, 'a force of police had to be requisitioned to form a queue'.[13] It would be five years before another outlet was opened in Ireland (see below, Appendix I, Table 2).

Ballymena Welcomes Woolworth

On 19 February 1926 the town of Ballymena, County Down welcomed the arrival of their new Woolworth branch in some style. Once more the advertisements in both local newspapers, the *Ballymena Observer* and the *Weekly Telegraph*, announced an inspection afternoon was to be held. The townspeople were invited to come to the store to look around. No goods were to be on sale, but, as was usual for these openings, a touch of culture was provided. In this instance, the entertainment was provided by musical selections performed by Boyle's orchestra. The store opened for normal business the following morning at 9 o'clock.

F. W. WOOLWORTH & CO.,

LIMITED,

BRIDGE STREET, BALLYMENA.

SHOP OPENS for inspection by the public at 2·30 p.m., FRIDAY, FEBRUARY 19; all are invited. No Goods Sold this day. Orchestra.

SATURDAY, FEBRUARY 20, at 9 a.m. the Shop will OPEN FOR BUSINESS with a full line of Special and Regular Merchandise.

Sweets	Chocolates	Jewellery
Ribbon	Handkerchiefs	Millinery
Hosiery	Drapery	Toilet
Stationery	Fancies	Haberdashery
Boot Goods	Paint	Polish
Gas Goods	Cutlery	Ironmongery
Toys	Woodenware	Crockery
Tinware	Enamelware	Hardware

F. W. Woolworth & Co.,

Limited.

Figure 13. Woolworth opens in Ballymena.

Courtesy *Ballymena Observer*.

The report that accompanied this publicity in the *Ballymena Observer* presents an excellent example of how the local press in market towns all over Ireland tended to react to these carefully organized opening ceremonies. Newspaper coverage was almost always based on a standard piece of copy supplied by the Woolworth company to newspaper editors in the area. Consequently, many of the published write-ups contained much the same plaudits and a great deal of repetition can be recognized. Nonetheless, on each occasion a journalist would have woven the salient facts into a piece that had appeal for readers at the time. Much can be learned about people's attitudes and lifestyles from these commentaries.

The reporter for the *Ballymena Observer* took a measured approach, writing: 'Great interest was manifested by the general public of Ballymena and District in the opening of a local branch of F.W. Woolworth, Ltd, in premises formerly occupied by Mr J. Stevenson, Bridge Street, last week'; the piece goes on to note that the building in Bridge Street, which had been 'remodelled and palatially [*sic*] equipped in a remarkably short space of time', had made use of local labour 'to the fullest extent.'[14] The latter comment was an important point to make.

The final appearance of Ballymena's new branch had made a big impression. The scribe goes on to note:

> Outside and inside the store is very attractive … along each side wall are panel plate glass mirrors which greatly enhance the appearance of the building, and the system of gas lighting gives the store and exceedingly bright and cheery appearance … upstairs has every modern convenience for the staff, including a dining room, cloakroom and kitchen for the female staff.[15]

The remark that all the counter staff had been recruited locally was also an important point to observe and one which the Woolworth publicity never failed to emphasize when a new branch was opened in Ireland.

The Ballymena launch was entirely successful. It was said that 'from the moment of opening until closing time, a never ending stream of people surged through the building. Inside the first fifty minutes 1,000 had passed through the doorway … on the following day the shop was packed. Very brisk trade was done.'[16]

Coexistence with Trade Unions

In the aftermath of the First World War trade in Ireland went into decline, financial markets remained shaky, and the ensuing air of uncertainty prompted greater militancy within the labour movement. As may be expected, despite the Woolworth Company ethos, which aimed to offer old-fashioned, if paternalistic care of their employees in return for unquestioned loyalty, the Woolworth store outlets in Ireland did not escape this general unrest over wages and conditions. The Woolworth Company's relationship with the Trade Union Movement in the United Kingdom and in Ireland is a topic worthy of treatment as a separate study, however, and observations can only remain generalized. The pattern appears inconsistent.

In the first decades of the twentieth century the IWWU (Irish Women Workers Union) was the female wing of the Irish Transport and General Workers Union, but, as Mary Daly has pointed out, this organization 'was ambivalent about women's rights' and it was their view that 'women working outside the home was a social evil which should be rectified by paying men sufficient wages to maintain a wife and family'.[17] At that time there was some disarray in the organization of union representation for shop assistants. The Draper's Assistants' Association saw themselves more as a trade association than a union, and Woolworth counter staff may have been members of the IWWU prior to joining the IUDWC (Irish Union of Distributive Workers and Clerks), a forerunner of IDATU (Irish Distributive and Administrative Trade Union). It may be noted, in addition, that Woolworth cafeteria staff in Ireland (in those branches that provided this facility for customers) would seem to have been members of the Irish Hotel and Café Workers' Trade Union in the early years.

For example, in 1918, within a week or so of the opening of Dublin's new Henry Street store, its cafeteria workers were taking part in a short-lived but widespread strike that was affecting many of the city hotels and restaurants.[18] A similar strike by Woolworth girls in January 1919 was settled by a conference held under the presidency of the lord mayor; but it was not too long before several more strikes came to once more interrupt the normal business of the Dublin and Cork outlets.[19] Dublin citizens seem not to have taken some of the disputes too seriously, if a piece in one of the city's broadsheets is anything to go by. 'Lusty-lunged strikers' was the heading over a piece in the *Irish Times*, which went on to comment how

in Henry street, two deep [the strikers], moved to and fro outside
the establishment, chanting grievances and repeating injunctions,
and, incidentally, amusing onlookers, who seemed to enjoy the
crescendo of discord reached when there was a suspicion of
anyone entering the premises. The girls were all young, many with
their hair down, and it was surprising what lung power they could
command in declaring a strike. They demanded better conditions
and declared that their union had been ignored.[20]

Later, a situation that arose in Cork was rather more grim. In January 1922
a serious dispute by all the staff in the Cork store had culminated in the
complete closure of the outlet. No mutual agreement was reached and trading
in the St Patrick Street store, 83 Cork, was not resumed for eighteen months.
When this branch reopened, in mid July 1923, no union staff were
employed.[21] This state of affairs may not have lasted for long. Unions were
reinstated here eventually, and the Cork branch soon gained a reputation for
being one of the most strongly unionized Woolworth outlets in Ireland.[22]

Protectionism: Boycotts and Pickets

The Irish War of Independence came to an official end with the truce that
commenced at noon on 11 July 1921. The eruption of the civil war that
followed was to bring even greater problems for the smooth running of
British-owned stores in Ireland, not the least of which were the bitter
confrontations over the source of goods sold from their shop counters. The call
for greater levels of protectionism in the years following the First World War
was not, of course, a trend confined to Ireland. There is plenty of evidence of
equally wide post-war concern voiced by various pressure groups elsewhere,
because of the growing unemployment and economic downturn. These
campaigns aimed to pressurize retail traders everywhere to support their own
local industries.

One of the first instances of disruptive protest against the sale of non-Irish
goods was instigated by a number of Sinn Féin activists in the United States
of America. In October 1920 a campaign was waged in New York for several
months, aimed to encourage shoppers to boycott firms that sold British goods
and services.[23]

In their American-published journal the *Sinn Féiner*, strident rhetoric was
used to rally support in 1921, declaring: 'While American workers starve don't

buy a cent's worth of British goods of any kind. Be loyal to America and to the American worker. Strike the British Hun through his pocketbook and save America for Americans … the efficacy of the boycott is bringing John Bull to his knees'.[24] There is evidence that leading New York retail stores such as Macy & Co., Gimbel Bros. and Saks & Co. were being targeted during the campaign, but what is striking to find is that the name of the American Woolworth Company was not included in the published list of offending stores carrying British-made products.[25] As already noted in Chapter 1, the Woolworth Company in America had pragmatically switched from buying merchandise from European suppliers during the 1914–18 war years, when supplies were cut off from crossing the Atlantic. They had, instead, offered support and instruction to assist producers of home-manufactured goods, thereby creating a huge boost to the fortunes of hundreds of small industrial firms as well as jobs for workers in the United States. After the war the American Woolworth buyers continued to place their orders with the same suppliers and in this way helped keep a selection of industries alive throughout the depression years.

In Ireland in May 1921 a newspaper appeal was launched that exhorted the 'Women of Ireland' to bring a list of 'approved' suppliers and manufacturers with them on shopping trips, asking: 'What are you doing for your country? In your hands lies the power to effect [*sic*] the economic liberation of Ireland.' The message goes on to claim that 'four-fifths of all the money that was spent in Ireland was spent by women', adding that 'Last year £64,000,000 was spent on imported goods while Irish men and women emigrated for lack of work'.[26] A long list of Irish-made commodities in alphabetical order then followed. The call was clear: readers were exhorted, 'Do your share to remedy this … Bring this list when Shopping'.[27]

Although clearly backed by a number of solidly respectable and patriotic business concerns whose products were dutifully acknowledged in the suggested 'shopping list', the unsophisticated copy supplied by the organizers displayed a rather touching ignorance of advertising techniques. The inclusion of 'Agricultural Drain Pipes, Bricks and Tiles, Fire Extinguishers and Revolving Shutters' among items listed for attention could hardly have galvanized much response from the ladies going out with shopping baskets over their arms.

It was not long before more militant support for a strict protectionist policy came to regard the British Woolworth Company and other similar retailers as obvious targets. However, it would seem that the scale of the trouble to come

Women of Ireland

WHAT are you doing for your country? In your hands lies the power to effect the economic liberation of Ireland.

Four-fifths of the money spent in Ireland is spent by the women of Ireland. Last year they spent £64,000,000 on imported goods, while Irish men and women emigrated for lack of work.

Do your share to remedy this. Let every purchase you make in the future be of Irish make. Begin with these brands—their quality is unrivalled.

Bring this List when Shopping.

Account Books	Hely's, Ltd., Dublin.
Advertising..	Kenny's Advertising Agency, Dublin.
Agricultural Drain Pipes	Courtown Brick & Tile Works, Courtown Harbour, Gorey.
Bacon and Hams	Donnelly's, Ltd., Dublin.
Biscuits	W. & R. Jacob and Co., Ltd., Dublin.
Boots , ...	Michael Goretney, Carlow.
Boxes (Wood)	Bottle Cases, Butter Boxes— Legg Bros. (Dublin), Ltd.
Bricks and Tiles	Courtown Brick & Tile Works, Courtown Harbour, Gorey.
Brushes	J. S. Varian & Co., Dublin.
Chocolates	Dublin Chocolate Works, Sweet- lunds, Kilmainham. "Savoy."—Savoy Cocoa Co., Ltd., Dublin. "Urney." — Urney , Chocolates, Ltd., Urney. Williams & Woods, Ltd., Dublin.
Church Candles	Lalor, Ltd., Dublin.
Cleaners and Dyers	Eustace Bros., Dublin.
Clothing ...	Irish Co-operative Clothing Manufacturing Co., Dublin.
Coach and Motor	

Figure 14. Appeal to the Women of Ireland.

Courtesy *Irish Times.*

was underestimated by the Woolworth management. Had early warnings been ignored? In the summer of 1921 a report in the *Anglo-Celt* had announced that 'English-made soaps were seized by armed men in Woolworth's in Dun Laoghaire',[28] and by October the campaign was escalating. The other Woolworth stores in Dublin were now being accused of selling Belfast manufactured candles, soap and tinware. One morning, a Dublin broadsheet ran the headline 'Interrupted Sale: Scenes at Dublin shop'.[29] Readers were told of picketing and trouble in the capital: 'The operation of the decree of Dáil Eireann prohibiting the sale of certain classes of goods in Dublin led to exciting scenes yesterday afternoon at Messrs. Woolworth's establishment in Grafton Street and Henry Street'. The piece explained how bill posters had been pasted on to the shopfront doors overnight and that additional notices were affixed on to windows later in the afternoon with the legend: 'Warning. This shop is selling boycotted goods'.[30]

The previous evening, news of the boycott had been rushed out on the front page of a late edition of the city's *Evening Herald*: 'Those responsible for putting up the bills refused to allow them to be taken down and some trouble ensued between the parties. An immense crowd collected in the thoroughfare [Grafton Street] and traffic was blocked for some time. The police moved on the crowd which showed some hostility to the firm.'[31] By the following day, the agitation had spread. Once more, an *Evening Herald* journalist provided graphic reportage, writing:

> The activity over the Belfast Boycott was extended to Dun Laoghaire today. The branch shop in Upper George's Street of the city firm which is affected was found this morning to be placarded [*sic*] with large printed notices. The result was that the shop has been deserted. Two girl pickets walked up and down in front of the premises but no disturbance has taken place. The firm has placed a notice in the window as follows: No boycotted goods are being sold in this store as we can prove to an enquirer.[32]

It was not the sort of publicity any shopkeeper would welcome. Woolworth sought political assistance, and the Dáil's trade minister (Prohibition Department) began immediate negotiations with the central committee of the Belfast Trade Boycott, 'with the result that the matter at issue is now satisfactorily settled'.[33] Announcing the 'End of the Boycott', the *Dublin Evening Mail* reported: 'a settlement has been reached in the dispute which led to the temporary interruption of business in the Dublin and Kingstown establishments of Messrs Woolworth, and arrangements are made for immediate carrying on of the sale which is attracting such widespread attention'.[34]

This incidence of a seemingly trivial spat between the Woolworth Company and Sinn Féin activists might seem lightweight in its retelling. Yet, there was sufficient importance in the event to bring about press coverage of a question put to a cabinet member in the Westminster parliament shortly afterwards. Under the headline 'Boycott of British Goods', a Dublin newspaper reported an exchange on the floor of the House between Sir Hamar Greenwood and Sir John Butcher, the Unionist member for the City of Cork. As Lloyd George's Chief Secretary for Ireland, Greenwood was notorious for his close association with the activities of the Black and Tans, and Butcher had been putting pressure on him over the large number of boycotting circulars that had been causing serious loss to many small traders in the South of Ireland.[35] His stonewalling had now prompted Butcher to enquire if the Honourable Member had 'read the report of the meeting of Sinn Féin delegates a few days ago stating that 225,000 notices boycotting British Goods had been distributed' and asking 'has he taken any steps?'[36]

Lieutenant Colonel Archer-Shee, a Conservative MP, then entered the fray by asking if Sir Hamar Greenwood 'was aware that Woolworth's stores in Dublin were closed by so-called Irish Republican Army police while eight Dublin Metropolitan Police were looking on and that no steps were taken to prevent those stores being closed because they were selling British goods?' But Greenwood was not going to be further drawn or provoked on this issue. The press report ends with the unsatisfactory observation: 'no answer was returned'.[37]

The extent to which these boycott campaigns were successful is difficult to assess. One cannot overlook the clues that surface later – such as this small but ominous press notice in the columns of the *Irish Times* on Saturday, 6 May 1922, just over twelve months following one incident. Under the headline '£200 Fine', it reads: 'The manager of Messrs Woolworths and Co., Henry Street having been ordered by officers of the Army Executive to pay a fine of £200 for a breach of the 'Boycott Regulations', visited the Four Courts in connection with the matter. He was informed that if the fine were not 'paid by noon tomorrow, action would be taken by the irregular forces'.[38] Could it be assumed the fine was promptly paid?

After the foundation of the new Irish Free State, efforts to encourage consumers to 'Buy Irish Goods' were taken on board by retail firms and manufacturers. Their tactics did not employ boycotts or threats, but instead relied on slogans in their regular advertisements to remind shoppers to support locally made goods and services. As shall be discussed in the next chapter, many of these retailers tiptoed carefully between a demonstration of patriotic nationalism and a desire to woo customers with cosmopolitan fashions from Paris or London.[39]

Following the death of the Sinn Féin founder, Arthur Griffith, in August 1922, whom one historian has described as 'an out-and-out protectionist', the fledgling Irish Free State at first adopted a more relaxed attitude, having been persuaded by the influential Fiscal Enquiry Committee of 1923 that too great an imposition of tariffs would simply raise the cost of living, increase agricultural wages, push up costs and prices and thereby diminish exports.[40] It has been also suggested by historian Roy Foster that despite the 'Sinn Féin pedigree of the government's theorists, [the State] did not develop a coherent policy of protectionism. Some tariffs were imposed on imported goods to encourage home production'.[41] For example, the budget of 1924 imposed duties on boots and shoes, sugar confectionery, soap and candles, cocoa preparations, table waters and glass bottles.[42] However, 'no overall fiscal readjustments were made with a view to develop new industries'.[43] A far more positive thrust to encourage Irish manufacturing would be developed in the decades to come. Methods were devised to ensure that the Woolworth Company could continue to offer their standardized range of goods on their Irish counters by using agents for products or by encouraging some of their best suppliers to set up subsidiaries in the south of Ireland.

The eagerness of regional communities in England and elsewhere in Europe to adopt support for protectionism during the 1920s undoubtedly created problems for Woolworth's London-based buyers. These senior men carried the responsibility for the company's strictly controlled format for the buying and distribution of many lines. The stock they bought in from foreign suppliers had been sold in branches without question on both sides of the Atlantic for years. It was of little concern to a buyer whether the merchandise for sale on his department's counters was manufactured in Belfast, Birmingham, Bremen, Bangkok or Bantry. The Woolworth bottom line was to ensure that their suppliers' cost price and quality never varied and that the company's merchandise men could rely on orders that were efficiently filled and delivered on time. If shoppers refused to buy specific items because of their origin or, indeed, for any other reason, it can be certain that these ranges were swiftly discontinued. There was no hidden agenda at work – political or otherwise – merely a desire to provide a satisfactory margin of profit on their fixed low prices for the best-quality goods that could be found.

For the next three decades it was Woolworth policy to stock counters in the South by relying on several alternative systems: Irish-made merchandise was one; goods manufactured in Ireland under licence for English brand names was another; and items distributed under licence via an Irish agent yet another. It should be noted though, that this policy was not employed in regard to goods sold across the counters in the company's stores in Northern Ireland. Stock for the Ulster branches was delivered and processed through the same operational system used in the United Kingdom and was, for the most part, British-made.

Raiders Armed and Unarmed

Vocal disruption caused by strikers, pickets and boycotts were not the worse of the problems young managers of newly opened stores in Ireland had to face during the early 1920s. On Tuesday, 15 November 1921 an *Irish Times* journalist reports: 'Three armed and masked men "held up" the staff at Messrs. Woolworth & Co.'s shop in Limerick on Saturday night after the closing hour and seized the day's takings.' By the standards of the day it was an entirely minor incident, and the report merely notes that, 'a policeman in plain clothes seized one of the men, who fired a shot. Nobody was injured and the man got away. In their flight they dropped £11 in silver.'[44] No further intelligence seemed to have surfaced about the raid. The fact that nobody was shot had lessened its value as a news story.

The managers of Irish stores soon got used to being exposed to exciting and dangerous situations. Very often violent incidents were provoked by labour disputes. One such incident around this time targeted the Woolworth premises in Grafton Street during a strike. On 5 June 1922 a large body of about forty men, led by a band and armed with hatchets and revolvers, marched up Grafton Street and entered the Woolworth store. Once inside, they set about the destruction of everything that lay to hand. A press report records how 'The smashing up operations were carried out methodically, and the wreckers did not leave before destroying the mirrors and plate glass windows. No estimate of the damage is yet available, but it is stated a very considerable sum is involved.'[45] The same report noted: 'For some weeks past, a strike has been in progress at Messrs. Woolworth's. The firm's Henry Street house was closed down for a time in consequence, but the Grafton Street branch remained open despite the continued activity of the pickets'.[46] It would seem that it was the management's disregard of the picketing that had provoked this attack.

Similar incidents may have taken place elsewhere at different times, but details are sparse. The Woolworth Company would not have courted adverse publicity, and it is only possible to speculate on the details. Clues are rare, but, for example, a claim for damages to their Woolworth premises in Limerick costing £2,000 was lodged by the company against the Offices of Government in August 1922.[47] The amount of compensation being sought was large. The incident must have been one of some significance, but no available records have been found.

Just under two years later, a well-documented piece of drama took place in Dublin's Grafton Street store. However, on this occasion, the use of guns was rather more menacing. The store's 22-year-old manager at the time, Gilbert Powers, had only recently arrival in Dublin, having been promoted from his former post as the manager of the Woolworth outlet in Preston, Lancashire. More accustomed to dealing with customers caught engaged in petty shoplifting, nothing in his training had prepared him for robbery conducted by armed revolutionaries. It was a traumatic moment when, just before lunchtime one bright May morning, a gunman thrust a loaded revolver close against his chest.

Figure 15. Gunmen in Grafton Street, 1922.

Photograph: © Hutton/Getty Images.

The next day's newspaper headlines, for 20 May 1924, gave their sub-editor an excuse to be dramatic: 'Daylight Robbery in Dublin. Armed Exploit in Messrs. Woolworth's. £355 carried away'. The paper's correspondent had caught the moment exactly:

> In broad daylight and in full view of forty or fifty persons, some of them Free State Soldiers, three 'gunmen' yesterday seized and carried away two money bags containing £355 from the premises of Messrs. Woolworth, Grafton St, Dublin. The robbery caused a panic. Women screamed and men swore, and one or two aged persons were knocked down in a wild rush to get out of the shop … policemen barred the entrance; but the robbers had left by a back door. They are said to have driven away in a Ford car.[48]

The report went on to note that the three gunmen obviously knew the daily routine of the store and had arrived just before the time a lodgement of money was normally taken to the nearby bank. Two of the robbers had posed as customers. The gripping excitement of the scene was captured later by a reporter from the *Irish Times*, who described how these intruders had been

> lounging in the shop, examining the goods on the stalls, when there was a commotion at the door which leads into Chatham place and the manager of the firm and his assistant entered with their hands up. Behind them came a man who wore motor goggles and held a large revolver. The supposed customers then sprang to action. Pulling out revolvers they ran towards the cashier's desk and by threats compelled the officials to put up their hands. The man who wore goggles was dressed in a fawn overcoat. One of his companions was tall and clean-shaven, with a fresh complexion and the other, a stoutly-built man was about 5 feet 8 inches in height and wore a navy blue suit. One of the stolen money bags contained £220 in notes and the other £133 in silver.[49]

Four days later it was reported that the raiders had been caught. Two men were later charged and each was subsequently sentenced to 'ten years penal servitude and to receive fifteen lashes before entering on their imprisonment'.[50]

There is a postscript to this story. The young store manager's not-to-be-envied experience in Dublin did not deter him from continuing what was to be a spectacular career within the Woolworth Company. Identified by the board in London as an eager high-flyer who clearly did not show panic in desperate situations, the young man steadily rose through the ranks. By the age of 46 he had made it to the top. As will be shown, he was to become a formidable presence in Executive Office.

Incidents of robbery and violence involving Woolworth employees were not only confined to Ireland, of course, and reports of 'raids' occasionally struck a lighter note. One Sunday afternoon in 1927, when the manager of the Tooting branch of Woolworth in London, stopped by to make a routine check of his store, he was surprised to find 'two men busily engaged in drilling operations at the safe'. The would-be robbers tried to make their escape through a skylight, but he and a friend who had accompanied him on the store visit held on to the miscreant's legs and having armed themselves with a couple of spades from the hardware department, held the intruders at bay until the police could be called.[51]

In Clonmel, several years later, another account of a Sunday incident raised a few smiles for readers of the company's staff journal, the *New Bond*. The piece was written by Lena Mackay, who would later manage the Tipperary outlet for more than twenty years until her retirement. Today she is still remembered as one of the first ladies to be a manageress in Ireland. Headlined by the journal's editor as 'Troubled Times in Ireland and the Result', she relates how the Clonmel manager had been woken up at home at 3 o'clock in the morning by the local Garda sergeant. A night watchman had heard two explosions coming from inside the premises. It was thought that 'a person or persons were raiding the Store'. The story continues to explain how

> The Sergeant collected his men and instructed them to surround the building as best they could by hiding in doorways and laneways, waiting to catch the intruders [as it was] believed that the explosion was the bursting of the safe ... but when the manager quietly opened the door they were not left long in doubt as to what had happened. There on the Toilet Counter were about one dozen burst bottles of Peroxide! The manager gave one gasp and spluttered 'Well! I'll eat my hat and coat!' The Sergeant and his men were speechless. The night-watchman quickly disappeared.[52]

One can safely assume that either her own or editorial propriety may have seen fit to water down some of the rather more colourful language aired on that occasion.

What the chain's late founder, Frank Woolworth, might have made of developments in these early days of the start-up in Ireland, involving armed hold-ups, picketing and the boycott of goods for sale, must remain in the realms of speculation, although, doubtlessly, his views would have been typically forthright. Woolworth's strict Methodist-inspired precepts put strong emphasis on honesty, fairness and the value of hard work and meticulous thrift. These came to form the base of his business formula and remained so for the greater part of the company's trading life. His biographer, Winkler, credited him with a number of 'nuggets of wisdom', which he liked to impart when interviewed. They were straightforward, if folksey exhortations: 'No man can make a success of a business which he does not like'; 'small profits on an article will become big profits if you sell enough of it'.[53] The multimillionaire's habit of quietly walking into a store, unannounced and unrecognized, to run a finger along counters to see if he could pick up any traces of dust on the displays, with which to later confront the manager, became the stuff of legend. Indeed, the routine was copied by senior management for decades to come. Woolworth's obsession with tidiness, cleanliness and merchandise that staff could be proud of selling became a legacy that was passed down to succeeding generations. And moreover, adherence to these traditions was sustained as much by the continued loyalty of customers as by the commitment of Woolworth employees.

A Change at the Top

For the British board of directors in London, it can be said that the 1920s had brought many new and unexpected challenges. The unexpected death in 1923 of their company's managing director, Fred Moore Woolworth, a cousin of the late founder, might have come as a serious blow if high street trading had not been so buoyant and its executives so well geared-up as a team. His passing caused no ripples, however, and the steady march forward of the company did not miss a beat. The former MD's right-hand man, Yorkshire-born William L. Stephenson, moved smoothly into the position vacated by his boss. Eight years after the end of the Great War, the company controlled a chain of 242 retail outlets. Only ten of these stores were located in Ireland by 1926, but the next few years were to see the number of Irish towns with a Woolworth store in its main shopping street double in number from ten to twenty (see below, Appendix I, Tables 1, 2 and 3).

The Woolworth Management Trainee: Setting off on the Career Ladder

One of the strongest elements of the company's ethos was the belief that management should be completely *au fait* with every aspect of the business. Until major changes were introduced towards the end of the century, all the top men had drawn immense benefit from having spent their early working life within the firm. The mantra 'I started by sweeping the stockroom floor' was never allowed to be forgotten by those who later made decisions at boardroom level. They knew the ranges; they knew the systems; they knew the problems, set procedures and protocols. Up to well past the half-century mark, company recruiting literature was still extolling the virtues of Frank Woolworth's original belief that this was the only sure way to train up and assess the potential of all new employees.

Nothing changed for decades in this respect. The declaration 'Woolworth trains you for success' was the title of an introductory pamphlet for would-be managers produced in the late 1960s. Within its pages lies the proof that how things were done in the 1920s remained basically unchanged for four more decades. By 1967 a young 'learner' starting off in the stockroom was still being told:

> Over a limited period you would be employed in the store stockroom with responsibility for receiving, checking, storing and issuing of merchandise to the sales floors. This training will enable you to learn the vast number of suppliers and something of the organization behind the variety of goods sold, and of the qualities demanded. It will help you to understand the importance of knowing the merchandise, the items which sell quickly and others that need careful handling, and of essential importance, seasonal merchandise which has to be made available at the right quantities and at the right time. This knowledge is an essential part of a successful manager's make-up.[54]

Recruits were warned that their progress would be strictly monitored and, as will be shown, life was made deliberately tough for these young men. The process was not unlike the army-style regime used by other formalized institutions of the era: the hospitals, the religious orders, the civil service or the Post Office. The aim of a training-in period was to knock off corners, break down resistance to taking orders and then to reshape the minds of raw squaddies into efficient, meticulous machines that responded to set systems with a computer-like precision. Regular reports would be sent by each trainee's store manager to his superiors in his District (later called Regional) Office. Store visits by an inspecting superintendent from District or Area Office would include a vetting of the progress being made. What the pamphlet did not spell out so clearly, however, was the level of regular transfers from location to location, often at short notice and often many miles apart, which the system imposed on young 'learners'. The explanatory paragraph was bland and held no hint of the traumas that lay in wait: 'As experience is gained and ability recognized you will pass on from one category to the next until such time as you are considered ready for Store Management. Each step forward will of course carry with it appropriate salary increase. All the time assessment will be made of your potential.'[55] And therein lay the clue to the success of this strategy. As in the armed forces, there were leaders and followers. This was made obvious: 'Progress will depend upon you and rapid advancement will always be open for the right type of man.'[56]

And the incentive? Again, the practical touch; the message Woolworth gave to a truly ambitious candidate was clarity itself: 'The more competent you become the greater salary you command', adding how 'there are many wonderful opportunities available to men of vision and determination and remember, all promotions are made from within the organization'.[57]

There were, of course, both strengths and weaknesses within a rigid method of training, which had remained unchanged since 1909. In later years, former executives often recalled the horrors and tribulations they endured as young trainee managers under the 'old guard'. Learning the ropes under the tutorage of senior men in those days – and indeed right up to the mid 1950s – meant having to suffer strictly old-fashioned discipline and Victorian values that had long since been abandoned by most of their contemporaries.

A manager's aim was to make life as tough as possible for his learners. The fledglings under his care were taught by using a sharp tongue. Praise was rare. Expected to be visibly 'on duty' and alert at all times when on the shop floor, trainees were subjected to an endless stream of scathing sarcasm. If a 'learner' was spotted taking a break by leaning his back against one of the high mahogany counters while engaging a colleague in conversation, the manager would send down a word of congratulation for his attention to an overlooked safety issue. His message would ask, was the counter in danger of falling over without the support of the young man's back? Should the store's odd-jobs man be sent for to fix some defect?

Likewise, when a manager felt a trainee was spending too long standing at the end counter of one of his departments, pencil in hand and stock folder in front of him, diligently checking and filling in sheets of analysis data on merchandise forms, there was often a message sent to enquire if young Mr X would like to have the shop's front doors closed to keep customers out on the street until he had completed his paperwork undisturbed?[58]

There was also rigid management dress code for male employees which had never changed since 1909. A dark suit, grey or navy, but never brown, with a white shirt and quiet tie, was *de rigueur*. Footwear had to be of a

Figure 16. Pearls of wisdom in Belfast's High Street in the 1930s: trainees had to learn how to present eye-catching window displays.

Courtesy G. McTernan.

conventional design with hard, leather soles. Brown or suede shoes were not allowed; crepe-soled shoes and coloured shirts were unthinkable. While moustaches were tolerated and, for a while actually encouraged as having the benefit of bestowing an authoritative air, the acquisition of a beard within the ranks of management did not dare make an appearance until the third quarter of the century.

Not only was day-to-day life as a 'learner' or 'floor-man' never made easy until their increasing levels of experience brought a candidate up to the final 'ready-man' stage as an assistant or deputy manager, at which point they were in line to be given their first store, but the process would have seen the trainee being moved from location to location at random intervals. Moves often came within a few months, and at the most, did not last more than a year. It was not unknown to be moved up to sixteen times within a few years of starting on a career with the Woolworth Company.

Transfers were often given at short notice. The usual procedure was a note sent through from District Office to the trainee's manager. The call often arrived on a Thursday or Friday morning. The trainee was told, 'You are being sent to such-and-such a town. Report to the manager there at 8.30 on Monday morning – and don't be late.' For Irish 'learners', the instruction might be a move from one Irish store to another or to a branch much further afield, to Scotland or to a town or city in the north of England. The Irish psyche was not too unaccustomed to the concept of a migratory lifestyle, and although most young men made the best of fitting into a transitory lifestyle on the far side of the Irish sea, several still recall their first time away. 'I had been in different parts of Lancashire for over a year. When I got home [to Ireland] on my first holiday break my mother cried when she saw me. I'd lost about a stone and a half of weight. For the rest of that week I did nothing but eat.'[59]

In may be seen as significant that this subtle socially unsettling element was attached to the nomadic life imposed on management personnel. When a young Irish-born trainee got called to make his first move, nothing practical was organized for him. He had to make all the transport arrangements and find lodgings for himself on arrival. It was not an uncommon occurrence for a trainee, suitcase in hand, to turn up at his new place of employment, many miles from his former workplace, and find himself pitched straight away into an inventory or stocktaking session by his new manager. If he had been sent to anywhere in the United Kingdom he would be told to take off his Pioneer Pin, if he was wearing one, and, apart from being advised never to talk politics or religion, this would seem, in many cases, to have been the sum total of the advice given.[60] By 6.30 p.m., when the day's work was completed and the store was being locked up, the manager would then tell the lad to go off and find himself somewhere to stay. Sometimes, not always, there might be a list of lodging houses handed to him, but this was the most he could expect. Was this one of the deliberate tests applied to aspirants? Possibly. A favourite and often repeated axiom that could have easily tripped off the tongue of the founder himself in 1879, was for managers to remind their trainees, 'If you can't look after your own life you can't look after our business.' More than one former senior executive can recall how, when sent to a strange town, they always made a bee-line for the local police station when left to forage out a bed for the night, because police cadets were also often on the move and the sergeant on duty always had a handy list of suitably respectable landladies offering clean digs.[61]

Promotion: Accepting a Move was the Way Ahead

For such an otherwise efficiently run organization, the practice of giving short notice of impending moves with little or no regard for the health and well-being of its male employees may be interpreted in two ways; it was either a display of some flaw within the internal communications systems, or else it was a deliberate ploy perpetuated by top management to test the mettle and commitment of its personnel.

Having been broken-in by the system, a young Woolworth manager in the inter-war period was ready to accept many demanding expectations, and ambitious men on the way to the top often received what today would be viewed as less than considerate treatment. Each January brought a formal announcement of the moves that were to take place before the spring; decisions to promote managers were based on their performance in the previous year or on vacancies caused by retirements. There were times when genuine emergencies had to be catered for at short notice, but nonetheless, to receive a forewarning of an impending move was a rare occurrence.

For the young men who had reached the stage of being 'ready' for an important appointment as an assistant manager, the alacrity of their response to instructions to move at top speed was useful in furthering their future careers. One former manager who subsequently rose to a senior position in the Woolworth Company can remember how a 'blue' letter arrived at his workplace on the 4 o'clock post one Saturday, telling him to report to Bangor in Northern Ireland at 8.30 a.m. on the following Monday morning. At that time he was married and living near Liverpool. By 7.30 p.m. that same evening, he and his wife and 15-month-old baby, a couple of suitcases and the baby's pram and cot were all packed and ready to catch the boat to Belfast.[62] He was soon rewarded by a promotion to manager of a branch in Northern Ireland, but for the next five years or so there were at least four more moves to other stores in the Province; then it was back to Lancashire. On this occasion his wife was left behind to sort out all the domestic arrangements before she could follow him back across the Irish Sea. Two more moves came within the next three years, and then it was once more home to Ireland, to run one of the largest stores on the island. It is a not untypical story that could form a template for the career structure for hundreds of this company's retail store managers during the era.

The system for promotion was efficient for a firm that was expanding at a very fast rate, nonetheless. The 1920s were to see the number of Woolworth branches in the United Kingdom and Ireland grow from 81 to 375, and this rate of acceleration was to continue for many more years to come. It could be argued that the enthusiasm of the store managers became this system's lifeblood. Every Woolworth outlet in the chain was graded by size and profitability performance. (Originally Class 1 to Class 4, to which a Superstore Class was to be added later.) For the men who aimed to get to the top, there were rewards to be reaped. A move to a new store, or to one which was ranked at a higher grade, was always accompanied by a salary increase. Officially, under the terms of the contracts under which all managers operated until the latter part of the century, these moves were agreed by 'mutual consent' between the employee and the company. If a man wanted to keep a firm foothold on the upward career ladder, however, he did not refuse to accept being shifted frequently. The Woolworth strategy was ruthless. There were no second chances given. A manager's potential for promotion came to an instant full stop if the 'mutual consent' clause was cited as a reason not to comply with a directive from Executive Office. In fairness, it has to be said that in those early days the Woolworth Company had recognized that, for some men, there was a certain attraction in being able to step aside from a regime of rigorous competitiveness, and it was for this reason that the option for a manager to remain in situ until reaching retirement continued to be a valid entitlement for decades. But when major changes swept away the original corporate structures in the latter part of the century, this old-fashioned and gentlemanly 'mutual consent' clause was to become one of the first casualties (see below, Chapter 7).

Wives and Families Remained in the Background

Although it is easy to depict the world of chain store retailing as a male-oriented world, hidden away in the background were the many women and their families who gave unstinted support to the men who formed the backbone of the Woolworth Company's success. The acceleration of store openings in the 1920s and 1930s meant that bright young managers were constantly being called on to get new outlets up and running. Throughout these decades these men were shifted from store to store as frequently as they had been during their training period. As has been pointed out, there was often little or no forward notice, and men had to leave wives and families to stoically pack up home to follow in their wake.

Finding a new home was a relatively easy task in those days. White-collar service workers at this level of middle-class society in the inter-war decades were far more reliant on rented houses or lodgings than today, and it was customary for the incoming man to take over the rented accommodation being vacated by the out-going manager. One house in the Dublin suburb of Rathfarnham, for example, smoothly changed hands in this way at least four times for Woolworth men during these early days. Each new posting for a manager's family was inevitably of uncertain duration. It might only last, at best, a couple of years, but with each move, new friends, schools and familiar localities were all left behind, often hundreds of miles away. Some families thrived on this constant change of scene, others were more traumatized by being constantly up-rooted. One Woolworth wife, who moved home and children at least twelve times during the inter-war and wartime years, observed that she never expected to meet a familiar face whenever she left her house to go down to the local shops. Her husband had blazed his way from store to store while she had lived among strangers all her married life.

As for the store teams, who never moved, they had to cope with a constant stream of new managers, who, for the most part, would remain in charge of their branch for two or three years before being promoted to a higher rung on their career ladder. The concerns of a store's permanent staff centred mainly on the personality of each new manager and in emergencies it was usually the 'girls' who took the lead and held things together. Cashiers and staff supervisors all knew the ropes. They ensured the paperwork was done; counted the money; smoothed out problems and covered-up for the manager if he was caught on the hop by an unexpected raid from his superior, the district superintendent. But – like those long-suffering wives – they rarely received enough credit for this back-up.

Explaining Shrinkage

The criteria by which a good store manager's performance was measured was not only his ability to generate a large volume of sales, but also his skills in keeping 'shrinkage' to a minimum. This was the system set in place by Frank Woolworth in the nineteenth century and it remained enshrined within the Woolworth business code of practice for decades. In the jargon of the retail trade, the definition of 'shrinkage' is a stockroom inventory loss caused by shortfalls in deliveries from suppliers, mistakes in the record-keeping and paperwork, or by more straightforward stealing, either by the customers (shoplifting) or by the store employees.

To simplify explanation of how this system worked in the early days, the process was thus. All goods delivered into a stockroom were marked with a code so that every manager knew the cost price of his merchandise. However, the book-keeping for the management of each store was all calculated at the selling price of the goods purchased.[63] The total selling price of goods purchased were then set against the total of cash taken on the sales floor (counter till receipts). There were procedures for returned goods, breakages or otherwise damaged stock, and despite these built-in compensations, the difference between what was bought into stock and what was sold from the counters never balanced exactly. When inventories were taken, a discrepancy or 'shrinkage' was always anticipated.

The most important element attached to the calculation of the amount of 'shrinkage' suffered in a store was its effect on the bonus to be added to each store manager's annual salary. His bonus was a percentage based on net profits. Shrinkage was deducted from this figure. If his shrinkage was small, his bonus improved. If the shrinkage was high, it indicated his control was slack, and his bonus suffered accordingly. More crucial still, if his shrinkage was consistently higher than the average showing for the branch, the manager then risked being 'carpeted'. Demotion might even follow.

In essence, the size of his shrinkage was therefore a measurement of how efficiently he ran his store and staff. A high volume of sales across his counters counted for little if the shrinkage was also high. During the inter-war period and for a decade or so afterwards, it was a relatively straightforward procedure. But it should be noted that, in later years, this system was to be refined to allow for inflation, and it became very much more complicated when rising prices caused 'overage' instead of 'shrinkage'. Stock control was crucial. Inventories had to be strictly monitored and checked. Records were written in longhand. There were forms for everything; and everything went on up the line to the District Office and from thence to London. One former staff supervisor remembers how she hated the year-end stocktaking. It took place immediately after Christmas, when stock was usually at its lowest level.

> I had to write the book and I was not good at spelling. We had to count everything, even small things like screws. Later on we were

able to weigh them. This was before packaging came in. We went into the store on the day after St Stephen's Day and we'd not be finished until New Year's Eve. Next morning, the manager would be off to Liverpool with the results under his arm.[64]

For most managers, keeping control over shrinkage was a time-consuming obsession. How best to do this was one of the most discussed topics whenever managers gathered together. Theories abounded and views differed widely. Some were convinced that the greatest losses were brought about by internal and external pilferage. For some managers, the behaviour of customers, counter assistants, 'learners' and stockroom workers was of constant concern, and their senior girls, who worked as staff supervisors on the shop floor, were trained to have 'eyes like hawks'. Before counter service changed to cash-and-wrap or self-service in the 1960s, one popular theory within Woolworth folklore maintained that the greatest level of losses were always sustained at stockroom level. Petty pilferage accounted for most shop floor loss; regular shortfalls in the stockroom were usually more substantial.[65] A regular supplier can still recall how one successful manager used to keep his stockroom under strict surveillance:

> The staff in there never knew when he might pounce. He would have a routine like checking on everything at a certain time and then break the routine without warning. He might come back two or three times in the morning, or just before closing, or not at all for days. They never knew when, or from which direction he might arrive. He could be outside in the yard when delivery vans arrived or he might surprise everyone at lunchtime. He had eyes in the back of his head. Shrinkage in that store was kept to a minimum.[66]

Devising means to compensate for losses offered a number of temptations. The majority of managers disliked the strictures this system imposed, and a number of ingenious ways were tried out to keep shrinkage under control. Few were totally effective. The company deemed it to be a serious offence if their set rules were by-passed in any way, and over-ambitious managers were warned to be careful. They usually were. But the fact remained, how cleverly a man managed his shrinkage was crucial to his success – and his pay packet.

Ice Cream for Woolworth

Despite all the difficulties brought about by traumatic trading conditions, the 1920s saw several more pleasant elements of modern Ireland emerging from the gloom. In midsummer 1926 a long and profitable association was inaugurated between Ireland's leading makers of ice cream and Woolworth store outlets in Ireland. Three enterprising brothers, James, William and George Hughes, had taken over their father's dairy business in the tiny village of Rathfarnham, which, in those days, marked the edge of the city boundary with the Dublin mountains. By investing £4,000, they had modernized the dairy by importing American electricity generators in order to pasteurize and refrigerate the milk they delivered to households and shops in South County Dublin.[67]

The next logical step was to set up a plant to make ice cream from the surplus milk and find a reliable retailer willing to stock it. The Woolworth buyer in London had not hesitated. Both Dublin stores would be the first to carry H.B. ice cream in Ireland. On 5 June 1926 the first of a series of advertisements in a Dublin newspaper announced Woolworth as their sole outlet.

Figure 17. 'Ask for it in Woolworth's': H.B. advertises ice cream for the first time in June 1926.

Courtesy *Irish Times*.

The successful launch of this new luxury was to repeat itself almost exactly twenty years later, in 1946, when they cooperated with the Woolworth branch in Henry Street, Dublin, to set up the first retail outlet for the hugely popular American-style soft ice cream machines into Ireland.[68] The Hughes Brothers Dairy went on to become one of the Woolworth Company's longest and most loyal Irish suppliers, a relationship which lasted well after the business had been sold to W.R. Grace in 1964 and subsequently taken over by Unilever in 1973.

> ## "Bring a few Bricks to the Match"
> A few bricks of H.B. Ice Cream
> You'll enjoy them at Half-time—
> Get them at Woolworths
> GRAFTON STREET & HENRY STREET
>
> # HUGHES BROTHERS LTD.
> Manufacturers
> Hazelbrook Dairy　-　-　Rathfarnham

Figure 18. How spectators going to the match in 1927 prevented the ice cream from melting before half-time, remains a mystery.

Courtesy *Irish Times*.

CEREMONIAL INSTALLATION OF TEMPORARY MANAGER.

Figure 19. Shop floor staff members did not always take the formalities of promotion as seriously as Executive Office. A contribution from Birmingham to the Staff Magazine in 1936.

Chapter 3
A Wake-up Call for
Market Towns

1927–1939

Following the establishment of the new Irish state, a good working relationship had been built up between the Woolworth Company and many of Ireland's leading political personalities. Mutual efforts to smooth out trading difficulties were proving productive and there was a growing appreciation of the boost Woolworth had brought to the retail sector, especially in terms of creating employment. It may be a telling signpost to note that in November 1927 the Woolworth Cafeteria in Henry Street had been the venue chosen to host the Fianna Fáil Ard Fheis Ceilidh and Reception. The press reported 'a large attendance which included Mr E. de Valera T.D. and other prominent members [of the party]'.[1] Useful foundations were being laid.

By now, Woolworth had refocused its attention on its original plan for expansion in Ireland. The company's favoured maxim would soon become 'Tall Oaks from little Acorns Grow', which was usually accompanied on company literature by the exhortation that 'Progress is the just reward of endeavour'. Viewed in retrospect, this pronouncement can perfectly illustrate the level of confidence that was being displayed during the period, despite the all-pervading negativity of economic depression. Thirty years later, by which time the power of their success was unchallenged, it may be seen as significant that the slogan's description of 'Tall Oaks' had changed to 'Mighty Oaks'.[2] By mid-century this company was king of the retail forest; stronger, greater and utterly unassailable. Or so it was thought.

The inter-war years were to see what retailers today call a 'high street' presence for Woolworth spreading with enormous speed throughout the whole of England, Scotland, Wales and Ireland. This was especially so after a momentous event in 1931.

Throughout the 1920s all had been going well on both sides of the Atlantic until the American parent company's shareholders found themselves in difficulties following the 1929 Wall Street crash. The British company's ambitious building programme was already well underway, however, although, coincidently, what Seaton has called a 'knotty problem' had arisen over their acquisition of property assets. Managing Director Stephenson and his fellow directors in London had been investing heavily in real estate for their chain of stores; 'buying freeholds a dozen at a time, which they pointed out was cheaper than renting and allowed ground-up development projects'.[3] Under New York Law, however, 'public companies could not take on overseas property without first having the deeds examined in the District Court'.[4] The action of the British directors as a subsidiary of the American company had been in breach of the law. As Seaton observes, 'Something had to be done.'[5]

It was not long before a solution was found. The American Woolworth Company arranged to sell off a 48 per cent share of F.W. Woolworth & Co. Ltd on the London Stock Exchange. The British company would thereafter be governed by British Law and the legal problem of the 'overseas property holdings' was thus neatly solved as all this real estate would pass into its ownership.[6] Moreover, the move gave a measure of independence and greater freedom to Stephenson and his board. When the shares were successfully launched on the London stock market, in 1931, the fortunes of existing American investors were 'restored with a once-off special dividend'.[7]

On 11 June 1931 the *Irish Times* advertised the prospectus for F.W. Woolworth & Co Ltd. It advised that authorized and issued capital amounted to £8,750,000 and offered for sale 4,860,000 6 per cent Cumulative Preference Shares of £1 at par, and 2,250,000 Ordinary Shares of 5s each at £2 per share.[8] The following day a headline in the paper's financial column announced 'Nine millions subscribed', with the news that the issue had been an 'immediate success. The lists were closed about ten minutes after they opened'.[9] Readers were advised: 'The Preference shares are certainly an attractive investment, having regard to the extent to which their interest is covered by profits [and] it was generally held that the Ordinary shares would command a premium, even on the relatively high figure at which they were offered'.[10]

With their status now even higher in the world of business and finance, and with Stephenson's firm hands on the reins as Company Chairman, the British Woolworth directors continued to invest heavily in real estate. Booming retail sales and profits saw them awash with cash to spend on expansion. One new store was being opened every seventeen or eighteen days at the height of the inter-war building programme. By the end of 1939, Woolworth was operating out of 759 branches in these islands.

Irish Goods for Irish Counters

Any problems encountered by the firm's move into Ireland had been well smoothed out by this time. It was to their advantage that the Woolworth buyers had seen the benefits gained when American firms were encouraged by the New York Office to switch to home-produced merchandise during the Great War. Since 1922 a similar policy could be adopted in Ireland by opening up of opportunities for new business to any local Irish manufacturer who was capable of conforming to the high standards and low prices the company required. However, with the exception of a few noteworthy names, such as Jacob's Biscuits, Urney Chocolates, and some candle-makers and brush manufacturers, there was not yet a great diversity of Irish plants with large enough production lines to take advantage of the Woolworth offer to stock their products. In due course, this situation was to improve, but in the meantime the easiest solution was to appoint Irish agents who could handle imported supplies from British firms under a concessionary scheme. The Irish State issued licenses and this system of merchandising allowed the London buyers to supply Irish stores with many of their existing ranges. This method did, of course, create a precedent that went against the ordained policy of the company, since Frank Woolworth's original decision was to cut out middlemen and wholesalers. The legal, if convoluted, tactic did nonetheless provide space for remaining compliant with whatever further changes in trade directives might be brought in by successive Irish govern-ment administrations. In due course, many major suppliers to Woolworth created their own Irish-registered subsidiary company in the Free State. The Nugget Polish Company of Ireland, for example, soon had a Dublin address, as did the makers of Aspro, which although not manufactured here until 1945, advertised its products in 1927 as being 'Packed in the Irish Free State'.[11] Also, by 1927, several firms, such as Rowntree & Co. (Ireland) Ltd, had arranged to set up manufacturing plants.[12]

Moves by Irish manufacturers to secure protective tariffs were to be accelerated considerably from 1931 onwards, however. It became less easy for United Kingdom firms to set up a subsidiary branch when government legislation set-to to close off the loopholes that allowed foreign parent companies to retain effective control of their Irish operations.[13] As historian David Johnson points out, 'In 1931, eighty-one per cent of the Saorstát's imports came from the United Kingdom', adding that in that same year '68 articles were subject to tariffs; by 1936 this had risen to 281. Additionally many more imported goods were subjected to other controls … In 1937, it was estimated that no less than 1,947 articles had some sort of restriction placed on them'.[14]

Much later, when the Department of Industry and Commerce instigated new schemes that gave assistance to encourage Irish firms to concentrate on exports, a number of factories making Irish products obtained contracts with Woolworth, but these firms were constrained to operate as 'export only' concerns. This system created some curious situations. For example, a consignment of merchandise made in Ireland and ordered from London could not be directly delivered to the Woolworth branch in their local town. The goods had to be first despatched to one of the company's United Kingdom warehouse depots and the invoice sent for payment in London. The order could then be reshipped back for delivery to an Irish store that was, perhaps, only a couple of miles away from the factory that had manufactured the items.

The system carried both advantages and disadvantages. On the one hand, the Woolworth Company could legally keep tight control over the standard of goods sold in Free State stores, and some expense could be recouped by charging extra transport costs to all stores south of the Irish border. On the other hand, for these branches, the imposition of this extra cost of carriage was a distinct disadvantage. There were often grumbles. Elsewhere in the chain, a store manager merely paid the same fixed transport fee for a delivery, no matter how far or how near they were from a Woolworth warehouse. An outlet in the far north of Scotland or in south-west Devon paid the same shipping fee as one in Lancashire or Surrey.

Nonetheless, despite the shipping complications, the Irish manufacturing firms who entered into this arrangement welcomed the security of knowing that a delivery was always paid for within thirty days and repeat orders almost always guaranteed. The volume and speed at which goods could be shifted across the Woolworth counters was never anything but exceptional, and for these fortunate suppliers, conducting business with Woolworth was a lifeline for survival.

Arriving in Market Towns

The number of Woolworth stores in the main shopping streets of Ireland doubled between 1927 and 1939. It was a modest enough growth by contrast to the overall rapid expansion that was taking place throughout the rest of the chain at this time. The policy of keeping an even numbered distribution of outlets on each side of the border had continued, and locations were selected with due consideration to the all-important railway network that provided all the necessary communication links for the delivery of goods and movement of personnel (see Appendix I, Table 3).

The Dundalk store opened in 1928, followed by one in Lisburn that same year. By the end of 1930 outlets in Bangor, Kilkenny, Sligo and Waterford were all up and running. The following year saw branches opened in Coleraine and Clonmel. Within the space of the next three years there were two further arrivals in Northern Ireland; in 1934 an outlet opened in Lurgan's Market Street, followed by one in Armagh's English Street in 1935.

The selection of these outlets had been carefully thought out. Dundalk and Waterford were ports, while Bangor, in addition to its harbour, was also Belfast's nearest holiday resort, having gained the reputation of being the 'Brighton of the North' a generation or more earlier with the arrival of the railway in 1865. Coleraine was also a bustling coastal town with a riverside port. It was close to the famous Giant's Causeway, a popular tourist attraction, and not far from the holiday resorts of Portrush and Portstewart. The typical Ulster towns of Lisburn and Lurgan contained a number of industries linked to textile manufacture in addition to being the centres for their surrounding rural communities. In the Free State, Sligo was an important centre in the north-west close to the border, while Kilkenny and Clonmel were busy market towns in the rich farming areas of the midlands.

These stores became thriving outlets and the Woolworth Company was soon seeking to increase their size, sometimes by acquiring adjoining premises or by extending an existing site. For example, in 1936, only five years after its opening, it was necessary to add extra sales floor space to the Coleraine branch in response to the increasing volume of trade being conducted there.

The Power of Advertising

The Woolworth invasion of Irish market towns in the 1920s and 1930s created a ripple of excitement for inhabitants. Most towns of substance had their own local newspapers to serve every shade of opinion. Although such journals aimed to cater for a readership that stretched beyond the towns' urban boundaries and catchment of neighbouring county areas, astute editors liked to tap in to a town's business contacts and networking rumour mills whenever possible. It may be seen that there was a certain power in being able to leak hints of an imminent arrival of a Woolworth store. This was proof that 'modernity' was coming to a town; that it was worthy of the prestige so clearly being bestowed; a prize to be envied. For example, in Waterford, where Halloween 1930 marked the opening of a new store on Barron Strand Street, the 'Coming of Woolworths' had been hinted at in a number of small press columns at least fifteen months earlier, and these reported rumours of ongoing 'negotiations' for the purchase of a well-known retail property in the town put a gloss of anticipation on the story.[15]

As has been already demonstrated, the Woolworth Company continued to eschew any type of overtly prolonged advertising. The tactic of making a splash for a new store opening by inserting a large 'Important Announcement' in a local newspaper was still felt to provide sufficient publicity throughout the 1920s and 1930s. No strictly imposed template for the shape, size and layout for these notices was imposed, although conformity to a standard typeface for the name of the company was achieved on the whole. Inference of increasing confidence may be drawn from the subtle changes that took place in the language employed in these announcements, however. Up until 1921, the notices carried an old-fashioned, almost obsequious air by which they 'beg to announce' the opening of their 'new branch' or 'new premises'. By 1928, by which time the sight of a Woolworth store in a town's streetscape had become a more familiar a feature, the wording used becomes far more forthright and confident. Headings now began with the legend, 'Important Notice', before announcing with a flourish that the Woolworth Company 'will open their magnificent new 3d and 6d store' on such and such a date.

The impending arrival of a new Woolworth store in their town perked up most local newspaper proprietors and editors, not so much for the company's subsequent placing of one or two of these large advertisements in a prominent position in the paper, but rather for the frisson of anxiety that was sparked off among the local business people. When faced with the Woolworth challenge, many a town's heretofore lethargic shopkeepers were provoked into inserting a series of large rival advertisements, which were then followed by a number of incentives to improve a moribund trading atmosphere. This was no bad thing. These campaigns to boost local trade were often spearheaded by the local traders' association or town council, and every newspaper editor with an eye to improving his paper's advertising revenue was quick to lend support. Times were hard and prising money out of tight-fisted retailers for advertising was a constant battle.

When Woolworth opened for business in Dundalk on 21 July 1928, aided by the usual striking announcement on the front page of the *Dundalk*

Examiner and Louth Advertiser, business may not have been very brisk in the town at that time. Hence the paper's editorial had not missed an ideal opportunity to rouse local retail traders into more positive action to improve trade, by reminding them that,

> 'though plans for holding a Shopping Week in Dundalk were discussed last year, nothing material was accomplished. Shopping Week should be held after the harvest season, so that country people might be attracted to the town at a period when they have money to spend'.[16]

Warming to his theme of a long overdue wake-up call amid the economic downturn (one may presume the editor was male), the piece went on:

> 'When trade falls off from any cause, it does not help matters merely to indulge in pessimistic utterances. Traders need to be up and doing in an endeavour to cope with changed conditions. The power of advertising to increase trade is not yet availed of to its fullest extent by Irish shopkeepers and manu- facturers.'[17]

Between 1921 and 1934 most of the Woolworth store openings in Ireland became newsworthy events, with excitement provided in plenty. The firm's provision of a bit of additional razzmatazz to create publicity for an advertised 'preview' or 'viewing day' was one of their most successful ploys. This American-style showmanship had been introduced in 1909 when the first British store opened in Liverpool. Since then, the provision of similar publicity became a feature of most branch launches throughout the inter-war period. Local journalists loved having a colourful piece to write about, editors could wax lyrical, and the newspaper advertising sales people happily solicited Woolworth's competitors to fight back in print.[18]

In Clonmel on 19 July 1931, the anticipation of shoppers was raised when the *Nationalist and Munster Advertiser* wrote enthusiastically that not only was music to be supplied by a band on the 'inspection only' day, but that there would be a 'free distribution of ice creams'.[19] The piece went on to observe: 'Woolworth's branch should add much to our business activities, afford consid- erable local employments, and contribute to the attractions of the town, widely known as a great shopping centre.'[20]

Figure 21. Costume jewellery for 6d in the 1930s.

Courtesy 3ᴰ and 6ᴰ Pictures Ltd.

Similar opening ceremonies were held in Kilkenny, Lurgan, Coleraine, Sligo and elsewhere. Each event was organized on the same lines as stores' openings across England, Wales and Scotland. Branch managers would have received a modest budget allowance to spend on advertising and 'entertainment'. For example, in the comparable-sized town of Whitstable in Kent, under the headline 'Artists to Appear at Woolworths', a report of their arrival on this high street in 1933 declared that the services of the Roylance Orchestra had been engaged.[21] The novelty of the event prompted a local journalist to extol the talents of the star turn of this 'elaborate musical show', whom he described as 'the eminent English exponent of the concertina'.[22] One is left wondering how this entertainment compared to the musical selections provided by Boyle's Orchestra in Ballymena in 1926, or a similar offering provided by Coleraine's local orchestra, who were apparently not at all fazed by having to perform on a Friday the 13th.

Curious onlookers drawn in for the opening of a new branch in all these towns created plenty of additional free publicity, moreover. In Clonmel, the eager crowds that assembled in the town's O'Connell Street in 1930 were reported in the next morning's newspaper to have created 'so great a crush that a Guard had to regulate the traffic'.[23]

The novelty value to be had from a new Woolworth branch never faded. Five years later, speculative gossip in Armagh whipped up an even greater frenzy of anticipation. As one report claimed:

> A rumour was circulated that the first customer would be presented with a Treasury note and, as a result, a crowd gathered in front of the doors before the opening hour of 9 a.m. on Friday to surge in when the doors were open. The crowd of customers prevailed during Friday and Saturday being packed like herrings in a barrel.[24]

The event prompted the astute editor to remind his readers of the importance of advertising. A cautionary tale of the farmer who had bought two buckets in the town's new Woolworth store for sixpence apiece was featured on the same page. It related how another town shopkeeper had complained he could have sold this customer similar buckets for the same bargain price of 6d. He had plenty of them in stock in the back of the shop. But the Armagh farmer countered by asking, then, had this retailer not bothered to let people know this? The punchline of the piece drove home the message: 'Traders in nearby Portadown advertise every week and – as a consequence – draw in the custom.'[25]

The editor would have recalled that when Woolworth had opened in Portadown, some years earlier, the aforesaid traders in that town had needed no wake-up call. They had immediately struck back at the newcomer's opening day publicity by the insertion of two equally dramatic 10.5-inch column press advertisements – one of which highlighted the vision of 'slaughtered prices' for ladies' drawers, chemises and aprons, while another promised its customers 'Piles of the Cheapest Goods in Town', the result of a recent fire salvage purchase. Although claiming that 'The Bulk of these Goods are only damaged by Smoke and Water and will be sold at a Mere Fraction of their Value', it might be noted that the trader had been canny enough to add in very tiny print at the bottom, that the proprietors 'cannot quote prices or show these goods in their windows'.[26]

Indeed, it is quite remarkable how so many more 'Salvage, Fire or Clearance Sales' came to be advertised in the local papers in any town where a new Woolworth outlet opened. Almost miraculously, too, were the number of proprietors of long-established local firms dealing in drapery and haberdashery, who became suddenly inspired to recall (or perhaps invent) long-overlooked

Figure 22. Buckets and chamber pots sold for 6d each.

Courtesy 3^D and 6^D Pictures Ltd.

anniversary dates to lend excuse for a generous slashing of prices and enjoinders to remember how faithfully they had always served customers' needs.

In fairness, of course, it should be remembered that general traders, grocers, drapers and hardware merchants in Irish market towns had always thrived – and survived – on giving credit, which was a policy never adopted by cash-only chain stores such as Woolworth.[27] And there was no escaping from the hard fact that the majority of business conducted in a local farming community had no choice but to be reliant on the turn of the seasons for the ebb and flow of incomes that were based on the buying and selling of crops and animals. Such traditions created shopping patterns that did not fit easily into the business of any store dealing only in cash – even one that limited prices to below 6d.

Shoppers' Tastes

Unlike many of the chain's outlets in English towns, where there might be tramcars or a municipal bus service, the carrying home of a large number of purchases often presented a problem for shoppers in rural Ireland. To overcome this difficulty, a further incentive was offered by Woolworth in most of their preliminary advertisements in the late 1920s and early 1930s, which advised: 'Customers selecting goods to the value of 6/-d can have them Packed and Delivered Free'.[28] Six shillings was a substantial amount of money to spend in those days – possibly more than half a week's wages for many people.

When, in 1928, the exhortation 'Shop early for Xmas!' was added to the announcement for the opening of the Lisburn store in the first week of December, the management had clearly anticipated the needs of shoppers by adding a special insert telling them: 'Arrangements have been made whereby our country customers may have their purchasers specially packed and kept until called for.'[29] Noteworthy, too, was the unique offer of 'Special delivery facilities given to customers wishing to purchase quantities for Schools, Bazaars and Institutions'.[30] Apparently, this store manager would have not only had his eye on impressing his bosses by speedily shifting the bulk of his Christmas stock, he would have been thinking in practical terms of the effect on his shrinkage and end-of-year bonus.

Throughout the inter-war period the enthusiastic press coverage received for the Woolworth openings in the Free State differed very little to the plaudits given to new branches in Northern Ireland. Patterns of praise were consistent. In 1934 the editor's message in the *Lurgan Mail* was one that was repeated many times in Irish towns. Noting that the manager of the new Woolworth branch was a Northern Ireland man, the accompanying write-up comments: 'It is hoped that the new store will benefit the community as a whole.' The writer of the piece had, of course, recognized that some of Lurgan's merchants were going to suffer stiff competition from Woolworth, but goes on to point out that these local traders would be compensated eventually. Woolworth would draw a large number of extra shoppers into Lurgan. There was no longer any need for these potential customers to travel out to visit shops in neighbouring towns.[31]

Readers of local newspapers in Northern Ireland were also always reminded by at least one editor of why an allegiance to Woolworth was to be commended. Two examples can be cited. In 1928 the *Lisburn Standard* assured townspeople that 'four-fifths of the goods in this store are British-made'. More than five years later, in 1934, the *Lurgan Mail* comments how the Woolworth Company made 'every effort to support British Industry… not less than 95 per cent of the goods are British made'.[32] Loyalist newspapers, in particular, carried campaigns aimed at consumers, urging shoppers to 'Increase employment. Always buy within the Empire', and they encouraged shoppers to seek out 'locally manufactured goods marked with the Six pointed Ulster Star Quality Mark'.[33]

By contrast, newspaper editors in the Free State at this time studiously avoided any reference to the source of the goods being sold from counters when covering the opening of a new Woolworth branch in their local town. Praise was more likely to be focused on the quality and variety of the goods on offer and the welcomed amount of local employment it could provide for young people in the area.

National and/or patriotic loyalties apart, some Woolworth opening day advertisements around this time nonetheless point up several other curious anomalies which can reflect customers' tastes, preferences and lifestyles. Detailed price lists of items for sale were used on at least four occasions in almost identical half-page newspaper spreads announcing new store openings in 1928, 1930 and 1931. The *Lisburn Standard*, *Kilkenny People*, *Sligo Champion* and *Northern Constitution* all illustrate how market towns' small traders would have been forced to slash prices drastically in order to counter the invasion of competition that undercut local retailers sometimes by as much as 100 per cent or more.

Items selected for a mention in many of the advertisements that heralded the arrival of a Woolworth store in a town may now be seen to reflect many aspects of the lives and habits of ordinary people. Yet, surprisingly enough, although individual taste and popularity of certain lines were to change with the passage of time, a large number of the ranges sold from their Irish counters remained the same for decades. This merchandise was organized for administration purposes under the twenty-seven or so separately numbered department titles set in place by Frank Woolworth himself in 1909. This was a system that remained virtually unchanged well into the 1960s (see Appendix III).

In the 1930s, notices that aimed to draw would-be customers' attention to the goods for sale in a newly opened store still included materials for mending boots and shoes at home, a practice little changed since 1914. Small drapery items included children's underclothes, men's and ladies' handkerchiefs, hose,

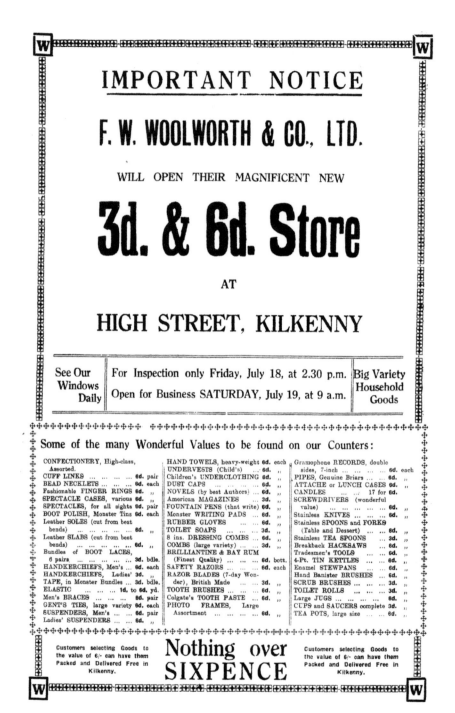

Figure 23. 'Wonderful values' included 'Fountain Pens (that write) … 6d'.

suspenders and, more inexplicably, 'monster bundles of tape'. Why the latter was required in such large quantities remains blurred. There must have been some important purpose.

At first glance, certain other sections of merchandise also provoke questions. For instance, why did 'ladies' and children's knickers at 6d a pair' appear in the Coleraine advertisement of February 1931, but not in an almost identical list for the Kilkenny opening six month's earlier? The answer may be that in the intervening period, the European owners of a family firm called Pasold (subsequently more widely known as makers of the children's clothing range, Ladybird, which was bought out by Woolworth decades later) had been encouraged by the British import control authorities to set up a branch in the United Kingdom.[34] By 1931 they were in business and had received their first order for a batch of silk 'Directoire' knickers to be sold in all Woolworth branches. It is possible this first delivery coincided with the opening of Coleraine and would, therefore, have been a useful 'special' for this and all the other stores Woolworth opened that year.

'Fashionable Finger Rings and Bead Necklets' in the Woolworth list of desirable purchases would still hold appeal for today's shoppers, but several of the essential household items, such as Hand Banister Brushes, Dust Caps, Footwarmers and Brilliantine, all of which sold for 6d, have long since disappeared from our lives. More curiously, Woolworth stationery buyers were not beyond indulging in what must have been teasing descriptions when advertising some merchandise, assuring customers of 'Fountain Pens (that write)' and 'Novels (by the best authors)'.

As the years rolled on, far more emphasis came to be placed on the sale of food and groceries in Woolworth outlets in the north of Ireland, by contrast to branches in the south. Opening advertisements in the more urbanized areas of Ulster were already featuring bottled fruits, pickles, sardines, tinned fruits, tea and cartons of cheese, a fact that points up that this trend was already underway in the inter-war period. No similar items were advertised in the Twenty-six Counties. Many decades later, when several concerted efforts were made to persuade customers in the Republic to buy groceries from both rural and city-based Woolworth stores, the results were disappointing. These outlets' profits still came from sales of sweets, ice cream, fancy goods, cheap jewellery and cosmetics.

Local traders almost always demonstrated a strident fighting spirit in challenging the arrival of a new retailer in their midst. On the very day Woolworth announced their arrival in the *Kilkenny People*, one of that town's leading retailers, Duggan & Sons Ltd, fought back by advertising a 'Monster House Sale' on another page in the same issue. Someone may have tipped them off over the items that were going to be highlighted in the Woolworth listing, because Duggan's were able to counter the competition by offering bargains in similar merchandise. They announced that their children's summer vests, at 6½ d, were worth 11d; 500 school attaché cases were priced 6½ d, 7½ d and 9½ d and 500-dozen toothbrushes, worth 1/-d, were being cleared for 3d each.[35] Some retailers even went on the offensive several weeks in advance of a Woolworth opening by announcing special promotions. In Sligo, for instance, one range of toilet products from an adversary was advertised at two for the price of one.[36] Toothbrushes and toothpaste, normally sold for 1/-d or 1/6d were being let go at half-price; soap, shaving sticks, dressing combs and vanishing cream had all been reduced in an effort to match the 'nothing under 6d' bargains on the new arrival's counters.

When it came to luxury goods such as gramophone records, the specialist music shops that sold pianos and other musical instruments as well as sheet music and gramophone records could not come near to competing with their local Woolworth store. In the early 1930s these music shops liked to advertise what they considered to be 'respectable' titles. They offered Colombia's double-sided 10-inch records with popular Irish titles such as 'The Dear Little Shamrock', 'The Mountains of Mourne' and 'Eileen Oge, the Pride of Petravore' for 3/-d each.[37] Waltzes and veletas for dancing, or the operatic arias and drawing-room ballads sung by the Irish tenor Count John McCormack, were considered 'safe' titles by these retailers.[38] By contrast, Woolworth held the edge on this competition by selling a range of modern titles on 7-inch double-sided records for 6d apiece. Their sales of 'pops' (popular music scores) also boomed, despite lingering echoes of the disapproval that saw 'modern' or 'foreign' jazz music condemned from pulpits and by athletic organizations alike. At least one national Irish newspaper headline had already thundered the message: 'Jazz Killing Athletics. Modern Dancing a Mental Disease'.[39] Not everyone agreed. At that time, such views had prompted an organist from Northern Ireland to voice regret that 'some people regarded music as the devil's best ally, luring men and women into paths of frivolity and sin'.[40] Worries like this were slow to abate. Anticipating worse was to come, the Gaelic League recommended the Cómhdháil to draft a rule in 1929, to expel members who participated in jazz dances.[41] It was all seriously strong concern. But it was all to no avail.

Eventually, fear of a Woolworth arrival in their midst died down in the Irish market towns. Having been well shaken into a more positively reactive mood, old established retail establishments smartened themselves up, held on to their long-time credit customers as of yore and stayed in business.[42] It was soon seen that, as predicted, the newcomers' novelty merchandise, which mixed the exotic with day-to-day practical items, did indeed generate increased business and bustle on formerly quiet main streets and market squares. In due course, the manager and staff of local Woolworth stores were drawn into active participation in town festivals and similar events that were often promoted by traders' associations to help raise the shopping profile of their locality or to raise funds for local charities.

Woolworth Modernizations Impress in Northern Ireland

Growing economic depression had not held back the Woolworth expansion into Ulster in the inter-war period, and the company's expectations would seem to have been fulfilled. For example, business proved so good in Ballymena that this outlet's sales floor was extended within ten months of its opening, in February 1926. The anticipated sales return for this outlet's first year of trading, which in reality covered only just over ten months, had been expected to reach £10,000. However, records show that almost half as much again had been achieved. By 31 December 1926, £14,780.3.7d had been taken in across Ballymena's counters.[43]

In the early 1920s the supply of electricity across Ireland was still in its infancy. When this Ballymena store had opened in 1926, the refurbished interior was lit by gas. Likewise, two years later, when Woolworth arrived in Lisburn, which was one of the main linen manufacturing centres only eight miles from Belfast, British-made gas mantles for 3d each were listed as one of the popular items sought by shoppers. With gas lighting still common in most of the Irish market towns on both sides of the border, any new commercial premises that enjoyed the dual benefits of modern central heating and electric light was novel enough to merit a special mention in the press coverage. In 1930 the Woolworth ground-up build of new premises in Sligo's O'Connell Street had prompted the *Sligo Independent*'s correspondent to react favourably:

> The building is constructed on most up-to-date lines with steel and brick work. It is planned and laid out in a modern style, centrally heated and, of course, electrically lighted [*sic*]. The new

store stands on the site of Messrs Sinclairs' shop and the speed with which the old building was demolished and the new one erected in its place created a good deal of interest locally.[44]

Conveying this essence of modernity was an important factor for editors to stress – and one which occasionally inspired their correspondents to create quaint turns of phrase. Writing in glowing terms about the opening of another Woolworth outlet, this time in Clonmel, in 1931, the *Nationalist and Munster Advertiser* informed its readers:

> the spacious premises in O'Connell Street, Clonmel, formerly occupied by Messrs Grubb … taken over by Woolworth's some time ago … are now an ornament to the fine street in which it occupies a central site. A wonderful transformation has been wrought. Many thousands of pounds have been spent on the building, and interiorally [sic] and exteriorally [sic] it is a credit to the firm and its staff.[45]

Buy Irish or Buy British?

Apart from established businesses' trading fears, the reception given to Woolworth in the Free State's rural towns in the 1930s was, on the whole, a benign welcome, and their coming did not provoke similar virulent anti-British protest that had been witnessed in the early 1920s. Throughout the decade, 'Buy Irish' campaigns continued to be promoted by competitors nonetheless, but the thrusts do not seem to have caused any great impact on the wider retail scene. In her thesis 'Cosmopolitanism and Nationalism', Muireann Charleton discusses how one Irish department store, Henry Lyons & Co. Ltd of Sligo, very deliberately associated itself 'with campaigns to Buy Irish in an attempt to confer consumer purchases with patriotic value'.[46] Describing how this firm took advertising to support their entry in a shop window display competition held in the town in 1930 to boost the sale of 'Irish-made goods', Charleton writes that 'Lyons appealed directly to their customers' patriotism in the *Sligo Independent & West of Ireland Telegraph*, Saturday March 8th 1930. They questioned their customers with "do you believe in supporting Home Industries? Are you sufficiently patriotic to prefer Irish-made to foreign-made goods?"' Within two months, however, as

Charleton points out, the same shop was advertising their stocks of a well-known London cosmetics firm, prompting her conclusion that this firm's 'Pleas for patriotic purchases occurred simultaneously with announcement for the latest, most up-to date products from London'.[47] Like Woolworth, they were peddling modernity and glamour, concepts that shoppers did not associate with home-manufactured wares.

For manufacturing firms in Northern Ireland, the gaining of a contract to supply Woolworth was a particularly prized achievement. Orders for the British-based chain often led to further business. One account of how a Belfast linen house owner hoped to benefit from a visit to the United States in 1930 reveals that

> Mr Samuel McCrudden, head of a well-known Belfast and Lurgan linen firm admitted that for some time his firm had been receiving orders from one of the great multiple stores … but would not confirm that his firm had secured an order for a million dozen Irish Linen handkerchiefs for Messrs. Woolworth's chain of American stores. [However, he] … admitted that his trip to America had been very satisfactory and that as a result the warehouses and factories owned by his firm would be working full time for a considerable period.[48]

It was a brave flourish of optimism. The linen industry in Northern Ireland was in for a tough time ahead.

It should be recognized that Ireland was not alone in her attempt to boost support for local industry. On the wider international stage, protectionism was rife. Throughout the inter-war period in Britain there was a spate of similar campaigns, especially as the onset of widespread unemployment increased. Shoppers were encouraged to buy locally manufactured products in favour of what were perceived as foreign-made imports. Most in evidence are the 'British Shopping Weeks' supported by retailers and suppliers, which were advertised in provincial British newspapers. For example, when branches of Woolworth stores opened in the fishing ports and market towns in rural Kent in the mid 1920s and 1930s, these locations (with urban populations of 11,000 or so) were comparable in size to some of the larger Irish market towns, such as Kilkenny or Sligo. Advertising in the press by these town's traders' associations and district Chambers of Commerce exhorted Kent readers to 'Support British Industries and provide Employment for British

Workers' and issued rallying calls to 'Follow the Flag and Buy British'.[49] Similar campaigns continued at intervals for years to come.

It may be taken that being dragged into controversies over trading and labour disputes, which were increasingly laced with political connotations, was not something eagerly welcomed by the Woolworth directors. Their focus was on building a well-run, viable and profitable retail business with an aim of serving shareholders, customers and employees to the best of their abilities. Since the foundation of the Irish Free State, a conscious effort to avoid being accused of any form of bias would seem to have been adopted. Quiet discretion was the watchword. In particular, the choice of appropriate management personnel in Ireland was addressed with care, as shall be shown. It was a rule that continued to be adhered to, even up to the late twentieth-century 'Troubles', which badly disrupted normal trading conditions in Northern Ireland.

Employment for Young Women

The coming of a Woolworth store to a rural area in the south of Ireland in the late 1920s and 1930s was of enormous benefit to young women seeking 'respectable' employment. As Caitriona Clear has pointed out, occupational tables of census returns have certain shortcomings when making an assessment of 'gainfully employed' women, whether single or married, in the decades after Independence, and 'cursory glances can be deceptive'.[50] Home duties, part-time work and the earnings of married women are blurred, although, clearly, engagement in agriculture was falling, as was employment in domestic service. In the 1920s and 1930s the number of women engaged in shop service remained around 5 per cent of the total female workforce (thereafter rising to 6.4 in 1946 and 8.6 by 1961).[51] Nursing, teaching, or a combination of both offered by the vigorous recruiting drives being carried out by visiting religious orders was about the sum total of opportunities on offer for country girls who considered themselves above seeking work as a domestic servant.[52]

A position as a sales assistant in a Woolworth store swiftly became a highly prized job for hundreds of Irish girls. The work offered security, companionship, promotion prospects at branch level, if marriage did not end employment, and the unspoken 'perk' of being able to meet and exchange pleasantries with local young men across the safety of counters while purchases were being made. Recruiting enough suitable sales staff for new branches was never a problem. When the Woolworth Company advertised for twenty or so staff members for their new Armagh store in 1935, there was an immediate response from about two hundred applicants. A correspondent in the *Armagh Guardian* in 1935 observed that 'Standing behind a counter in a uniform must have a great attraction for young girls', and the piece went on to wonder, perhaps tongue in cheek, whether 'the manager had a troublesome job making a select list for interview and final selections'?[53]

The writer may not have been aware of the hidden values behind the excellent conditions and wages Woolworth offered female sales floor personnel. In those days, this included: free uniforms and a laundry service; canteen dinners at a reduced rate; their own staffroom, sometimes called rest rooms; concession purchases of items; and a rota of 'shopping' days off. All the girls got a Christmas bonus, plus another one on their birthday, usually accompanied by a birthday card, and each employee was encouraged to feel part of the wider F. W. Woolworth 'Family'. A store would organize social events, outings and sporting activities. The girls often went away on holidays together and later sent snaps of their trips in to the company's house journal, *The New Bond*. They manned festival floats for local charity fund-raising events and organized social evenings for long-service presentations. Wages were considered good, although it would not be until the 1950s before anyone, even store managers and more senior personnel, received more than two weeks' paid holiday.

Press comment on a Woolworth arrival in a town often included editorial acknowledgement of these excellent terms and conditions of employment. When the Kilkenny outlet opened in the town's High Street on Saturday, 19 July 1930, the *Kilkenny People* wrote glowingly: 'A staff numbering thirty local girls has been engaged and adequate provision has been made for their welfare, a special rest-room being provided, in addition to a clothes drying room, kitchen, etc.'[54] The following year, a Woolworth branch in Coleraine was ready to open and the *Northern Constitution* told its readers: 'A staff of between thirty to forty girls, all local and mainly drawn from the roll of the Unemployment Bureau will attend to the wants of customers, whose pleasure it will be to shop in ideal surroundings, where every comfort is ensured'.[55]

There is evidence of only one opening that did not go as smoothly as expected. This was in Waterford, where an eruption of trouble over workers' conditions and wages required the manager to insert a special notice a week later, to 'repudiate any suggestion that our staff are not well paid and well treated', adding that the company considered 'a 46 hours' working week reasonable'.[56]

The Woolworth arrival in Waterford City had been eagerly awaited for months. This location was no rural backwater, but a busy port and thriving

Figure 24. The Woolworth store in Waterford's Barronstrand Street, which opened for business on 1 November 1930.

Courtesy Waterford City Archives.

commercial centre, and, when the branch finally opened on 1 November 1930, the appearance of pickets on the evening of the first day of trading came as quite a shock. The Trade Union protest began when the outlet kept its doors open past the usual 6 p.m. closing time. Business in the store had continued up to 8 p.m. It is possible that the novelty of this offer of later-than-usual trading hours on their opening day had presented itself as a good opportunity for activists. They could use the occasion to gain some publicity, especially as a recent visit of the area organizer of the IDWU (Irish Distributive Workers Union) had aimed to revitalize recruitment of local shop assistants working in Waterford's grocery, bar and provision trade.[57] However, as may be expected, their action did not go down well with the store's manager, who was ready to defend not only a 46-hour working week for his staff, but also the facility for customers to continue their shopping every Saturday evening up to 8 p.m. The following week's *Waterford News* carried his response in a rare, unprecedented Woolworth notice on its front page:

F.W. Woolworth & Co. Ltd wish to thank the citizens of Waterford for their support and patronage ... We regret that our efforts to satisfy the shopping public between 6 and 8 p.m. on Saturday caused a section of Trade Union members to demonstrate near our premises and apologize to our many patrons for any inconvenience caused.[58]

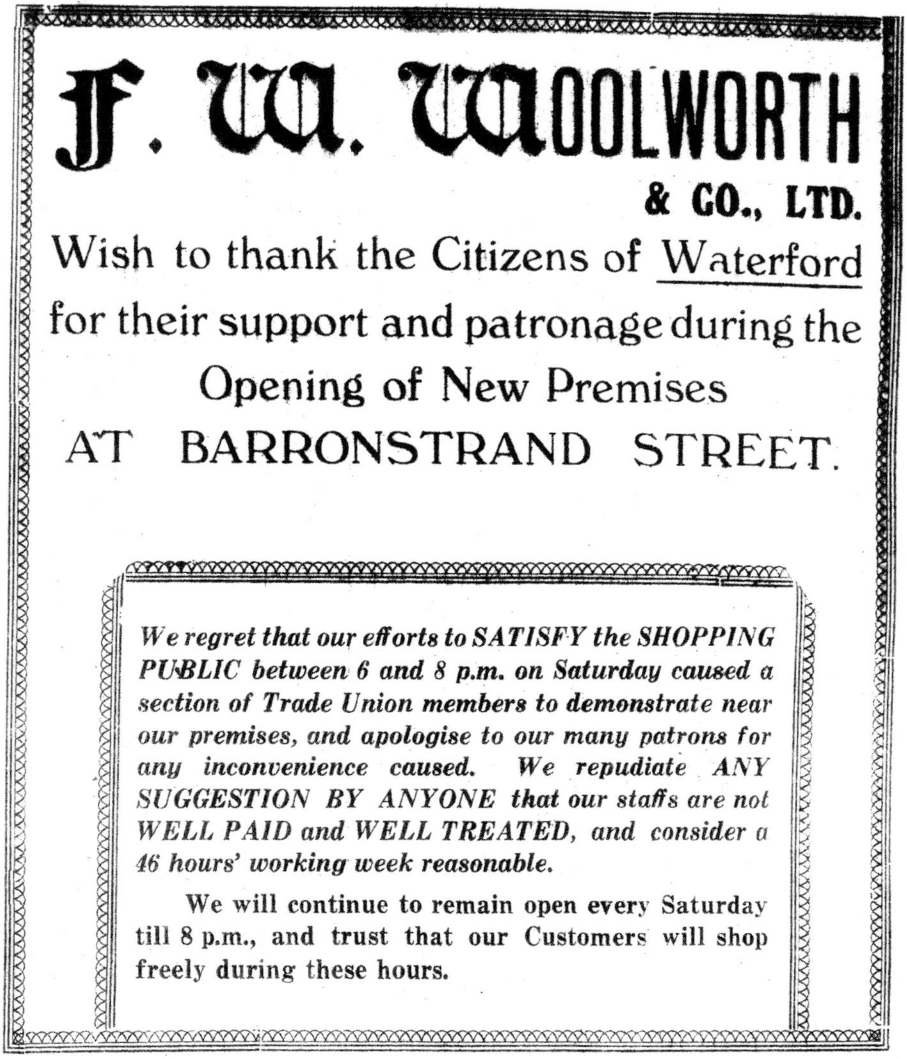

F. W. WOOLWORTH
& CO., LTD.
Wish to thank the Citizens of Waterford
for their support and patronage during the
Opening of New Premises
AT BARRONSTRAND STREET.

We regret that our efforts to SATISFY the SHOPPING PUBLIC between 6 and 8 p.m. on Saturday caused a section of Trade Union members to demonstrate near our premises, and apologise to our many patrons for any inconvenience caused. We repudiate ANY SUGGESTION BY ANYONE that our staffs are not WELL PAID and WELL TREATED, and consider a 46 hours' working week reasonable.

We will continue to remain open every Saturday till 8 p.m., and trust that our Customers will shop freely during these hours.

Figure 25. A rare riposte: ill-matched typeface and curious layout evidence the urgency of the response.

Courtesy *Waterford News and Star.*

Brought to Book

As has been discussed already, during the first decades of trading in Ireland the need for store managers to regularly attend trivial petty larceny court cases became a tiresome but necessary duty. In due course, even more time was wasted over the need to comply with the Irish Censorship of Publications Act, which came into law in 1929. As the eminent historian J.J. Lee has observed, the Act 'empowered a censorship board to prohibit any work it considered "indecent or obscene" as well as all literature advocating birth control … [and] was used to censor not only genuine pornography, but also serious work by major writers'. In Lee's view, 'The censorship legislation served the materialistic values of the propertied classes by fostering the illusion that Ireland was a haven of virtue surrounded by a sea of vice … It helped to rivet the remunerative impression that immorality stopped with sex'.[59]

From the start, cheap paperback novels and thrillers had been one of the best-selling lines carried by Woolworth stores on both sides of the Atlantic, and the avid reading habits of Irish customers saw thousands of new titles being shifted across counters every week. But clearly, the simple task of keeping counters filled with new titles for customers each week became a complicated one for store managers in the Free State. In order to comply with the dictates of this new censorship law, all Woolworth stockrooms in the south of Ireland had been given a list of officially banned books, but because the volume of business being done was so great, the task of carefully checking all new titles being delivered was an almost impossible task and one which was often overlooked in the rush to get books unpacked and out on display. Many titles slipped through the net, and vigilant supporters of the Censorship Act made sure that infringements of the law were subsequently brought to court.

One of the first of these cases to come up in the Waterford district followed a complaint received by the Gardai from a Brother J. Crean of Mount Sion, who had visited the Barron Strand Street store where he 'purchased a book and other magazines described as being of a most objectionable character which did not come under the Act'.[60] A summons was issued, and when the case came up in court, matters immediately got off to a bad start. The reporter from the *Waterford News and Star* wrote how 'Some surprise was created by the announcement that Messrs. Woolworth, who were represented by the manager of the Waterford branch, were not legally represented'. Observing that it would have been 'more courteous to have had themselves represented by a solicitor', the none-too-pleased district justice was in no mood to offer a sympathetic hearing. When the hapless store manager apologized to the court for the mistake in allowing the book to reach his counters, his regrets were witheringly ignored. The fine was hefty – £25.

The titles of such offending books were usually coyly repressed in hearings of this nature. No doubt this was to prevent any benefits to be gained from the consequent publicity. But shortly after the Waterford hearing, one such title did come to light when the manager of the Woolworth branch in Cork had to answer a similar summons for 'exposing for sale a banned book entitled *My Husband, Simon*'.[61] The author of this work remains unknown and we may assume the work was not one of outstanding literary merit, although on this occasion the manager's superiors had seen fit to provide a solicitor to defend the case. Under the headline 'A Banned Book', one national newspaper reported how the defendant told the court that he usually 'took the most rigid precautions against such books being on sale'.[62] There was a list in his office giving all the titles that were banned. On this occasion, the book had arrived 'as part of a consignment which one of his assistants had forgotten to check'. Fortunately for the manager, the local Garda superintendent was not inclined to press the case, because 'he knew [the manager] was careful in such matters'. Official approbation paid off. The fine imposed was only 40/-d.[63]

How many similar prosecutions went through local district courts is impossible to say, but by 1938 store managers were still being caught out by the censorship vigilantes, albeit by now most court appearances were being dealt with by the bench with rather more understanding.

In Sligo in 1938, when the district justice was told by the local store manager that the book in question 'had been delivered to the Sligo branch as a job lot purchased by the Buying Office and that [the manager] didn't know it was banned', the magistrate must have felt that a mild rebuke was sufficient, commenting that 'Messrs. Woolworth should be more careful how they ordered their books'. He directed the defendant 'to pay one shilling, the price of the book, as expenses' and dismissed the case.[64] It is good to report that being caught out like this had no subsequently adverse effect on the Sligo manager's career. Some years later, he was appointed as head of the Dublin Buying Office, with responsibility for all the merchandise sold from Woolworth counters in Ireland. After the Censorship Act was lifted, in 1967, his buying office bought books by the container-load for their Irish branches.[65] There was little mention of any of these books being banned by then.

Yet, how intriguing it is to find that one of the publications that Irish shoppers were not allowed to read in the mid 1930s was a book which would have been immensely popular for its title alone. American author Karen Brown's *The Girl from Woolworths* was a best-selling romantic love story. An early talkie film version of this book was made by Warner Brothers in 1929. To coincide with the film's issue in London in 1930, the publishers, Collins & Sons, brought out a new edition of the book for the British market. It sold in Woolworth stores for 6d.[66] The Irish moral vigilantes soon had it placed on the list of banned books, apparently, because of veiled references to the heroine's use of contraception.

Figure 26. *The Girl from Woolworths,* special edition for Woolworth published in Britain to accompany the talkie film in 1929.

Courtesy 3ᴰ and 6ᴰ Pictures Ltd.

The 'Poor Little Rich Girl'

By the 1930s most Irish people did not realize that an American store owner called Frank Woolworth had been the founder of the British Woolworth chain of 3d and 6d stores, but there were few shoppers who did not follow the widely publicized life of the Woolworth heiress, Barbara Hutton. In their minds, it was she who owned all the Woolworth stores and legendary Woolworth millions. Even well into the mid twentieth century, when counter assistants tried to admonish shoppers for helping themselves to sweets from an open display of confectionery, they would be told, 'Tell Barbara Hutton to pay for it – she's got plenty of money hasn't she?'[67] In their minds, the name Woolworth and Barbara Hutton were synonymous.

It had been a tragic story. Frank Woolworth's daughter, Edna, had allegedly taken her own life when in despair over her unhappy marriage to financier Frank Hutton. When she died, her daughter, Barbara, was only 4 years old. The child inherited her mother's share of the Woolworth millions, but could not come into this fortune until she reached the age of 21. Frank Woolworth's other two daughters, of course, had been left the other two-thirds of his estate. His biographer, Winkler, later calculated that by the time Barbara Hutton came of age, her personal wealth had grown in monetary terms to equal that of her grandfather.[68] She was now an extremely wealthy woman in her own right.

There is no doubt that Barbara Hutton became an icon of the extravagant living and fragile morals that marked the inter-war years. During her lifetime, she gained notoriety as the 'poor little rich girl', and her string of marriages to seven partners, most of whom offered the dubious cachet of an undistinguished European title, were all predictably short-lived and unhappy. The only exception was her remaining friendship with the British-born film star, Cary Grant, which held firm even after their three years of marriage had ended in divorce.

Odd as it may seem, the extravagance and so-called glamorous life of Barbara Hutton was not resented by thousands of ordinary shop floor Woolworth employees on both sides of the Atlantic during her lifetime. On the contrary, it was rather celebrated. Young counter assistants yearned to hear news of this fairy-tale world of unimagined wealth, flagrant excess and scandal. To feel an association, even at a far distance, with 'their' Woolworth heiress, their own 'million dollar baby', was almost a matter of pride. Impossible dreams were dreamt, and, more often than not, new baby daughters given the name *Barbara*.

Life at the Top: London Executives Live It Up

As the success of the growing chain of stores increased, the Woolworth Company began to benefit from a build-up of publicity that had commenced five years earlier. The late Fred Woolworth's son, Norman, had married Pauline Stanbury in Westminster Abbey on 9 July 1925, and the journalists of glossy magazines had taken notice that the occasion was noteworthy enough to be featured in a Pathé Newsreel. At less exalted levels, the nuptials inspired sales of a 6d pop called 'We will have a Woolworth Wedding'.[69] Employees and customers alike wanted to think they could be part of that glitzy glamour world that the name of Woolworth now evoked.

By the 1930s several occupants of Executive Office had prised open entrée to London society, and the excesses of Barbara Hutton's life at the top was being reflected in the antics of a number of wealthy London executives. To give them their due, all these men had displayed exceptional talent, and the early success of Woolworth rested on their leadership. The first buyers, in particular, had been plucked from obscure management posts by Frank Woolworth, who had the ability to recognize ambitious and innovative brains. He liked men who knew the value of risk-taking, who talked straight and who could be both kind and ruthless. Dubbed by the press in the 1930s the 'owner' of the Woolworth chain who entertained royalty on board his prize-winning ocean-going J-class yacht, *Valsheda*, chairman William L. Stephenson had always been guided by these precepts. When he took time off from running the business, Stephenson successfully competed with several luminaries of the international sailing set, including Sir Thomas Lipton, the most famous tea merchant in the world.

The men he had gathered around him in Executive Office as buyers worked hard to keep up their reputation for excellence. They also put their energies into enjoying all the benefits of life at the top. Head buyer John B. Snow, one of the New Yorkers sent by Frank Woolworth to help establish the firm in 1910, adapted himself to an English lifestyle with gusto. As the owner of a country estate, 'Squire' Snow rode to hounds in Hertfordshire, stabled a string of polo ponies and made plans to win the Grand National. He became a great racing enthusiast and shared his interest in bloodstock with his senior buyer and fellow shareholder, Wexford-born Charles McCarthy.[70] Snow was a man of great energy. Three years after his retirement, in 1936 at the age of 60, he returned to America to launch himself into a new career as a successful newspaper mogul.

When McCarthy reached his retirement age in the mid 1940s, he returned home to Ireland to breed racehorses. Although also an expert yachtsman during the Stephenson era, Mac's favourite leisure pursuit in the 1930s was rather more daring. He had been an army flying instructor during the First World War, and since that time had owned several different types of private aeroplanes which he piloted in aviation competitions. In 1937 he was one of the finalists in the King's Cup Air Race. As much a risk-taker in business as he was in the air, Mac was responsible for buying all the china and glass sold by Woolworth up to the late 1940s. He once famously placed an order with a Czechoslovakian firm for one million pieces of the Woolworth distinctive Greek-key pattern glassware. Every single piece was sold for under sixpence.

The expensive lifestyles enjoyed by the incumbents of Executive Office were for the most part maintained by the Woolworth Company's immense buying power in the commercial world. That these men were sought out by international suppliers and manufacturers, to be wooed with special attention, was seen by the firm's rank and file as proof that the business was doing well. Woolworth buyers might drive the best cars, patronize the finest restaurants and enjoy the luxury of exclusive golf courses, ski resorts and European watering spots, but these extravagances were not widely begrudged by those below them on the career ladder. Just as Barbara Hutton had been celebrated by Woolworth people as a sign of modernity and style, the excesses enjoyed by the buyers only proved their enviable skill and enterprise. It was believed the Woolworth Company was lucky to have such men at the top.

As the 1930s rolled on, times were good for the Woolworth Company. Profits continued to rise and capital investment in real estate continued with the purchase of new retail outlets everywhere. Shares were classed as 'blue chip' investments – safe, secure and popular. Share prices rose steadily. In 1936 another 100 per cent capitalization operation was undertaken.[71] This saw the company's capital raised from £3,750,000 to £7,500,000. In 1934 the British chain was operating out of 598 stores in England, Scotland, Wales and Ireland; by 1939 this number had grown to 759 branches. Only twenty stores had opened in Ireland since 1914, but these outlets were by then well spread across the island.

Figure 27. Out of office hours: Woolworth men at the top enjoyed a varied sporting life. W.L. Stephenson, C.H. Hubbard, L. Denempont, J.B. Snow and C. McCarthy.

Courtesy 3ᴰ and 6ᴰ Pictures Ltd.

Competition: The First 'Look-Alike' Store makes an Appearance in Ireland

By December 1935 there were ten Woolworth chain stores operating successfully in the south of Ireland and ten more also prospering in the northern Province. Up to this time, no competitor of any significance had emerged to challenge their presence. By contrast, in the United Kingdom, their great formidable rival from the start, Marks & Spencer, had been joined by the

British Home Stores and another newcomer, Littlewoods Stores, in a jostle to gain shoppers' attention on high streets and market squares. In Ireland, on both sides of the border, the Irish market was relatively small and population growth had been sluggish. The retail grocery trade had already been well nailed down by British incomers such as the Lipton's, Home & Colonial and Maypole outlets, and by the expansion of several highly successful home-grown grocers shops run by the Findlater and Williams families. In rural areas, individual family drapers, grocers, greengrocers and butchers formed the backbone of market town trading. Such establishments continued to be closely linked to complimentary interests in the licensed trade, cattle-dealing and farming, and these traditional family-run businesses ran in tandem with each other. Trading patterns had settled down into compliant coexistence with what was usually viewed as a Woolworth store's rather exotic novelty value. Woolworth presented shoppers with a leisure activity. Time spent in browsing was an exercise in frivolity; it offered daring cosmetics, gee-gaws and toys, books and musical entertainment, sweets and ice cream. This world of 'fancy goods' and fine china alongside natty tools for the handyman seemed far distant from the worthy dullness of purchases required for regular maintenance of bodily sustenance: food, clothing and fuel. There was no great rush by rivals to emulate that special aura of buzz a Woolworth outlet was able to create in a town. Like a circus, they were accepted for the joy and colour they brought – but there were few takers who wanted to try their own hands at being lion-tamers, acrobats or clowns.

In the autumn of 1936, two brothers from a family-run farm in Newbliss, County Monaghan, Frederick and Charles Moore, moved to the town of Enniskillen in County Down and opened a small shop in East Bridge Street. With a show of admirable enterprise, they took a close look at the Woolworth style and range of goods and, making this their guide, began to sell haberdashery, toys and confectionery from open-topped counters. They dealt only in cash, and aimed to keep prices at rock bottom. There is a well-known but possibly apocryphal tale which claims that, in their early days, the brothers would make regular buying trips to the Woolworth branch in Derry, in order to keep their own shop counters well stocked.

With the aim of becoming a Woolworth look-alike, their shop in Enniskillen bore a red and gold facia board and the elder brother tagged his initials F.A. on to the title Wellworth. Business was brisk, and the brothers were soon able to open a similar store in Omagh. In due course, after trading from a couple of different premises in Enniskillen, the Moore brothers' Wellworth operation was able to purchase a large shop in High Street, just down the road from where Woolworth would open in opposition. Their business continued to thrive and within a couple of decades the enterprise was to provide a serious threat to many of the Woolworth stores in Northern Ireland, not so much for the ranges their chain carried, but for the size and excellent location of their outlet sites and for their foresight in risking an early venture into the emerging American-style supermarket methods of vending food.

In 1938 another newcomer generated excited crowds by its arrival in Londonderry's Waterloo place. But, unlike the Moore brothers' Wellworth stores, the British-owned Littlewoods never managed to tip the scales in the competition stakes, despite it being a very obvious Woolworth copycat retail store. The use of a 3d to 2/11d description emblazoned on fascia-boards of this new retail chain strikes as having been an awkward attempt to emulate but at the same time update the 3d and 6d Woolworth slogan. It might be noted that this concept of everything being sold at a 'fixed price' was soon to come under threat. When World War Two broke out in 1939, it was no longer possible for retailers to buy merchandise in an open and free market. Supplies of goods were restricted or unavailable and, inevitably, prices were forced upwards. By the time hostilities had ceased in 1945, any notion of a return to the old fixed price limits had disappeared.

The retail arm of this new chain had begun life in 1923 as the Littlewoods Football Pools Company. They commenced catalogue retail selling in 1932 and the first of their high street stores opened in the famous Lancashire resort of Blackpool in 1937. By 1939 this company had established twenty-four outlets, which included the one in Derry. At the time, their appearance on the Woolworth doorstep in this Northern Ireland city had been nothing but a little pinprick of annoyance. By the end of July 1939 the Woolworth construction team had completed an extension to the company's Ferryquay store, confident that their larger sales floor would swiftly bring back any shopper lured away to sample the novelty of what they believed was an inferior usurper. No one then would have believed that the combined fortunes of the Moores' Wellworths and the ambitions of Littlewoods would one day come into their own as survivors.

The Role of a Superintendent in the Early Decades

Since its foundation, the route for male employees up the company's career ladder had followed a strictly structured pattern. After a few years 'on the floor', with responsibility for several departments, a trainee or 'Learner' became an 'Advanced Trainee', until reaching the stage of being a 'Ready Man' for promotion to an Assistant (later called Deputy) management post (as discussed above in Chapter 2). The first store allocated to a new manager was usually one of the small branches which ranked low on the rated system Woolworth used for all their outlets. Each branch was designated into a class or grade according to its size, location and expected sales turnover (see Chapter 2). At the top, there were several 'flagship' outlets bearing the title 'Superstore', whose managers were given a special senior status almost equal to District Office Executive because of the huge volume of sales and profitability these outlets produced. In Ireland, Dublin and Belfast each had one 'flagship'. In Dublin the honour was held by the store in Henry Street, and in Belfast it was the imposing premises in High Street.

After several years of being moved upward through a number of stores, a manager who had shown exceptional ability, having gained the experience of running one of the larger branches, would be selected for promotion to Area Superintendent. He was now firmly secure, several rungs up the ladder as part of a team reporting to one of the district offices. In the pre-war days, an area superintendent was given responsibility for 18–20 stores within a district. His job was to be a conduit between the manager and District Office. He kept a check on the performance of each of his stores, and took a lot of the credit if their managers were doing well. He sorted out minor problems and reported on every aspect of a store's operation, making sure that no rules were broken or short cuts employed to reduce shrinkage. Good superintendents acted as wise mentors to the younger men they were supervising. Their aim was to ensure that collegiate support and networking techniques were passed on to the next generation and, in this regard, there was no one to match the Irish in nurturing these skills.

One rare surviving internal memo to a superintendent reveals how a fledgling management trainee with Limerick roots, who was acting *pro tem* for his boss who was on a week's holiday leave, reported exuberantly on the increased percentages while he was in charge of the store. 'Dear Sir', he writes, 'Department 33 [Tin and Enamelware] sales percentage increase [over previous year's figure] 2.29 per cent. Department 34 [Household Goods] up 3.85 per cent. Department 35 [Crockery and China] up 2 per cent.' A contrite rider, 'Sorry about 36 [Glassware] – watch it next week!!' was a nicely attuned touch of humility.

The superintendent had returned the memo with a note on the back that did not forget a little personal touch for a young compatriot far away from home and possibly missing friends and family: 'Nice work! Time you got that D.M. [promotion to Deputy Manager],' he wrote, adding, 'Everyone at Shannon Airport are asking about you!!!'

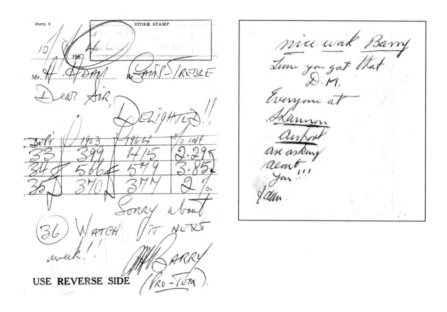

Figure 28. The Superintendent writes: 'Nice work! Everyone at Shannon Airport are asking about you!!!'

Courtesy Mike Barry.

Superintendents in those days were expected to move their home and families to live within a close distance of their district office because they had to report in every Monday morning with their paperwork. Meetings were held with their superiors and problems teased out or sent for the consideration of Executive Office in London. Stock movements and analysis findings went directly to a Merchandise Man. In Liverpool Office there was a special appointment for South of Ireland supplies, who would then report to an appropriate London buyer. The men who reached this level of management usually worked closely together. They also engaged in formal socializing. Annual dinners and golfing outings were organized. Golfing aficionados reigned supreme in the district offices, but there were private pockets of interests in other sports, including boxing, racing and card-playing. The men all knew each other very well. The company ruled their lives, took precedence over all else, and, to all intents and purposes, took on the role of kith and kin.

Examples of the closeness of their association with each other is evidenced by the in-house cartoons that were a feature of the annual dinner menu cards. The term *PC*, or politically correct, had not yet been invented, and there is little sign of any sensitivity regarding the personal idiosyncrasies of the men in middle management who were being made the butt of a joke. One popular superintendent for Ireland (an Englishman who was to return to Dublin at the end of his career to take up a senior post for the duration of several sensitively political but important years) was at one time illustrated as an anarchistic leprechaun. The superintendent for Scotland was invariably shown attired in a kilt and sporran. In the same souvenir for the 1938 annual dinner, the intimate knowledge they had of each other's drinking habits, for instance, allowed the art department to depict each man toasting a successful year with his favourite beverage. For some it was a tankard of ale, for others a wine glass, a whisky and soda or a glass of champagne; and those who were teetotal were shown with a cup and saucer.

Figure 29. All among friends: Liverpool District Office annual dinner cartoons did not worry about being politically correct in 1938.

Courtesy the late T.J. Haycock.

Being 'on the road' as a superintendent for the Liverpool District was a demanding commitment. The wives and families of superintendents usually never saw their father from one weekend to the next – especially if he was the superintendent for Ireland or Scotland. For example, until the Second World War broke out in 1939, the superintendent for the Irish stores travelled back and forth from Liverpool every week on the Monday night boat and then continued by train to do his rounds of all the stores, north and south of the border, for the rest of the week, only returning on the Friday night sailing. One superintendent in the late 1930s, bored by the tedium of long rail journeys that took him to every province in Ireland, even occasionally made the trip down the east coast by sea from Dublin to Waterford or Cork on one of the merchant shipping vessels that plied between these ports. And it must be also recognized that, apart from the unremitting drudgery of constant travel, there were many other stressful aspects to this job.

Sometimes the slower, more leisurely pace of Irish life could cause problems, especially if the visiting superintendent was new to Ireland. Inspections usually began at 8.30 a.m. sharp, half an hour before doors opened for business at 9 o'clock. But in some of the more remote Irish towns, nothing moved until well after nine in the morning, especially in the darkness of winter. Casual adjustments were made to fit into local trading conditions, such as fair days or feast days, which caused not a few newly appointed superin-tendents to have a near apoplectic fit if they were foolish enough to make an unannounced early morning visit only to find the store not yet open.

The regular supervision of a raft of managers, all with different person-alities and levels of ability, could be demanding on patience and good humour, especially when two strong personalities came into conflict. Tensions often arose. But the wisest men at this level of management were quick to tell stories against themselves to defuse volatile situations. One such story was a favourite of one Irish executive whose career ended at the top. When working as a superintendent, he and an equally strong-willed manager of a store in the west of Ireland had often clashed quite seriously over issues. If it was not an argument over shrinkage, it was a dispute over staff, displays or maintenance, or some other matter. They usually made the best of their differences and shook hands – until the next time they had to meet. But following one partic-ularly difficult session, which had left the atmosphere rather more frosty than usual, the superintendent found that the time spent on wrangling had made it too late for him to catch the local bus to the next store, some considerable distance away. In those days superintendents on a tour of Ireland had to use public transport, so he was left no choice but to request the tight-lipped manager to bring him there in his car. Off they set and drove in silence across the wilds of bogland and mountain for several miles. Neither spoke and it seemed to the superintendent that the sense of seething resentment in the air heightened with every mile. Finally, on reaching a particularly remote spot, the manager suddenly pulled the car to a stop in the middle of the road and jumped out. He said nothing, but went to the back of the car, opened the boot and pulled out a shotgun. The superintendent's blood froze in terror. Could their differences have reached such a dangerous pitch? He was a loyal Woolworth man – but was he ready to be its first martyr? Could he make a run for it? As he struggled to open the locked car door, the manager took aim and fired.

Coming from a west of Ireland farming family, the manager was no stranger to the shotgun and rarely missed his target. He was back in the car in less than a minute and threw the game just despatched on to the back seat. 'That was a bit of luck,' he said. 'You can bring it home to your missus but tell her she'll need to hang it in the larder for few days.' From then on, conversation flowed normally until the destination was reached.[72]

Several tough years 'on the road' would eventually bring a superintendent his reward. He would be in line for promotion to a desk job, either as a merchandise man or some other district office post. Alternatively, he might be offered the management of one of the 'plum' big-earning superstores. All these placements brought advancement another step higher and could be followed by a more senior position in Executive Office in London, where new challenges lay ahead. When a vacancy arose for a new director or chairman, such new appointments to the board always came from Executive Office ranks. This was the system created by Frank Woolworth for his American operation, and it remained unaltered well past the mid-century mark. With the Woolworth assurance that 'Promotions come from within and there is opportunity for all!', the company's recruitment literature continued to cite these senior positions as goals for their would-be aspirants.

In those days the American Woolworth Company still owned 52.7 per cent of F.W. Woolworth & Co. Ltd, and the ethos of 'The American Dream' continued to believe that employees who aimed to be successful should allow themselves to be owned body and soul by their company. This was the way things were in Frank Woolworth's day, and it had been adopted by the British company without question. This American concept was to be well examined by writers such as Arthur Miller and his generation in the years to come. As one successful Irish-born retired executive later commented, 'My work on the road as a Superintendent lasted for several years and being away from home every week, all week, for that length of time meant I missed out on a lot of my children's growing up years ... that's something I can never replace'.[73] There was no bitterness in this remark, only a deep sadness.

A New Anglo-Irish Trade Agreement Introduces Adjustments

By January 1938 Woolworth Executive Office were keeping a close eye on the improved relationship between the Irish and British governments. The system whereby the manager of the 76 Dublin Henry Street store had the additional task of supervising all imports of merchandise into Ireland had worked well enough when only a limited amount of British-made goods were on sale in the Free State stores and the Henry Street premises could act as a temporary depot and distribution centre. But it was known that a new Anglo-Irish trade agreement was about to be signed. This would bring the long-running economic war to an end and under its terms some preferential treatment was to be granted to British industrial exports into Ireland.[74] Would this mean Woolworth could start sending more shipments to Dublin, to be distributed to the Southern stores? The suggestion was made that the Henry Street manger should be given a special assistant to relieve him of some of the work attached to the importing of goods.[75] It was the first move in a new direction. Moreover, while not formally voiced, there must have been private worries over whether the Twenty-six Counties would stay neutral if events in Europe escalated to the point that hostilities broke out. No one could be quite sure. Support for existing Irish suppliers would have to be maintained, in any case, but the question was, how would the new Trade Agreement affect pricing? One executive pointed out that 'our aim should be to maintain the range of merchandise in these [Irish] stores as near to our usual selling point as possible to similar [items] in England'. In the meantime, one of their colleagues had been given a list of merchandise and was being sent 'to try and find factories in Ireland that would be able to supply these stores'.[76] The name of the executive being sent on this mission to Ireland was Gilbert Powers. Being held up at gunpoint by gunmen in Grafton Street fourteen years earlier had not diminished his deep interest in Ireland and Irish affairs.[77]

Twelve months later, in January 1939, the situation was still unclear but business in Ireland was looking so promising that several more new stores were being planned despite anxieties over what might happen in Europe if war could

DUBLIN 31 CELEBRATES 25th ANNIVERSARY

The Staff of Dublin, 31

Figure 30. The 25th anniversary of the first Woolworth store in Ireland is celebrated in 1939 by the staff of 31 Dublin Grafton Street.

Courtesy 3ᴰ and 6ᴰ Pictures Ltd.

not be averted. One of the logistical problems that would need to be addressed if war broke out was the fact that the whole island of Ireland had always been administered under the direct supervision of the Liverpool District Office as an integral part of the company's operation. Merchandise had settled into smooth-running shipment patterns; male personnel from Irish stores were moved frequently between Ireland and the north of England or Scotland; and visiting superintendents from the Liverpool Office travelled freely and frequently on their inspection tours of branches throughout the whole of Ireland. As September 1939 approached, the future looked very uncertain.

Figure 31. The Woolworth store on Belfast's High Street would later be extended to occupy the whole of the fine building on the right.

Courtesy 3D and 6D Pictures Ltd.

Chapter 4

Ireland's 'Emergency' and Later

1939–1948

The declaration of war with Germany was announced to the British public in a radio broadcast on Sunday morning, 3 September 1939. For the Woolworth Company, the onset of World War Two saw the island of Ireland split into two even more distinct operations, each constrained by their own set of wartime regulations. Stores in Northern Ireland were subject to British government wartime legislation which included the imposition of a strict rationing regime and other trading restrictions, whereas the twenty outlets in neutral Ireland worked within the Irish government's set of 'Emergency' laws. These included a limited amount of rationing but wide powers to control essential supplies, employment and commercial activity. As historian Brian Harrison has said, 'The war had drawn the boundary between northern and southern Ireland more firmly'.[1] For the next five and a half years the separate but parallel nature of their existence was to mark some significant changes to the way Woolworth handled management systems in the two governmental jurisdictions.

There have been experts who claim that Ireland was wholly unprepared for war in 1939 and that the 1938 Munich Crisis had exposed her utter lack of preparation.[2] For the Woolworth Company, this was not the case, however. In anticipation that the south of Ireland might remain neutral if war broke out, the board had already decided that the Dublin Buying Office would be given extra responsibility. By September 1939 a contingency plan was already in place. The manager of the Cork store had been due for promotion in January of that year, and instead of transferring him to the Liverpool Office, with a rise to the position of district superintendent – the usual career path ahead – he had been moved from Cork to a new post in Dublin as resident merchandise man for the Twenty-six Counties. By the end of the year this astute and efficient Mayo man would be given a heavy workload. He would have to ensure that all the company's outlets in the south continued to be supplied with merchandise, and to do this he would need to pull the Irish managers together into a strong team.

For the ensuing wartime years, it was not too much of a drawback for Dublin Office when the company's two-way traffic of management and trainee personnel between the south of Ireland and the United Kingdom came to a temporary standstill. A far greater problem was to keep store counters stocked. There were shortages all round, and movement of merchandise between the two countries was seriously curtailed when production lines in the United Kingdom switched to war supplies. It was fortunate that Woolworth branches in the Twenty-six Counties could continue to carry a selection of products that were sourced from local producers (partly the outcome of the boycotts and 'Buy Irish' campaigns of the last two decades). Many of these Irish factories had difficulties in keeping production lines moving, however, as many basic raw materials were increasingly unobtainable.

Supplies and Shortages, North and South

Petrol, coal and tea constituted the most crucial material shortages for citizens in the south of Ireland. Rationing of other commodities, such as flour, soap and clothing, was introduced by 1942, and as studies of this period clearly point out, the existence of 'black-marketeering and overcharging became rampant'.[3] All forms of fuel were in short supply. Petrol was rationed, and for urban households, Town Gas supplies were cut off for hours, bar a trickle to give a mere 'glimmer' for safety reasons. The severe rationing of tea is widely remembered as having hit Irish households the hardest, and the enforced use of wholemeal instead of white flour in bread was extremely unpopular. Bread supplies were kept under control by placing a ban on selling freshly baked loaves. Batches had to be two day's old before being released for sale. Nonetheless, historians agree that apart from luxury items or foreign-produced foodstuffs, 'Ireland had the good fortune to be, for practical purposes, self-sufficient in food'.[4] Rural areas were the least affected, and as a large proportion of the population in urbanized centres were less than a generation from the land, there were few homes that did not have a family connection to someone 'down the country'. This generated a steady flow of home-churned butter, poultry and eggs between private individuals. Off-the-record dealers thrived on barter and under-the-counter transactions and meat and pig producers did a roaring trade in the border counties. There was plenty of game. And there was an abundance of fish for the taking in lakes and rivers. South Wexford's market gardens began to specialize in soft fruit and apples. North County Dublin potato growers made fortunes. Moreover, as the north and south divide moved into a new dimension, the networking ability of the Woolworth Irish branch managers came into its own.

The emigration of young people from the south of Ireland to England to engage in war work and ancillary services was high throughout the war years, and as Lee observes, this volume of movement 'got rid of 100,000 excess bodies, mostly male, to Britain thus enabling recorded unemployment to fall from 15 per cent to about 10 per cent.'[5] Nonetheless, the departure of so many people from this sector of society was to have a depressing affect on shopping patterns for whatever goods were still available in stores, and general retail trading slumped into the doldrums in consequence.

By contrast, in Northern Ireland the war economy brought greater prosperity. Every type of industry con-nected to the war effort thrived, and from 1941 onwards 'unemployment virt-ually vanished'.[6] There was money to spend, and despite wide shortages of all types of merchandise, the overall effect on retail sales may thus have been more buoyant than for traders in the south.

The period 1939–45 saw every Woolworth store throughout the

Figure 32. Plenty of unused coupons remain in these Irish ration books.

Photograph: Barbara Walsh.

rest of the United Kingdom badly affected by a loss of trained personnel. In his discussion of the wartime era, Seaton describes the changes taking place.

> Running the stores was a challenge. Conscription had called most male staff to arms, cutting a swathe through the management and leaving stockrooms deserted. To fill the gap, a number of pensioners were coaxed out of retirement, often resuming control of their old store or stockroom, and many long-serving women finally got the recognition they deserved.[7]

The war years saw the introduction of another crucial change. This was the well-known Woolworth promise of 'Nothing over sixpence'. Suppliers could no longer make and deliver goods at the pre-war rates; and buyers could not travel abroad to seek alternative bargains. By 1940 the price of several items was raised by a few pence. It was hoped this was to be a temporary measure. But within a year, the concept of the 3d and 6d ranges was gone for good. Customers were soon paying as much a half-a-crown (2s 6d) for some products.[8] Fresh difficulties were also raised by the flexibility of these new price ranges. A system that carried stock selling at fixed 3d or 6d prices was easy to keep under control. Deviations or errors could be quickly identified. But with prices creeping up to odd amounts of shillings and pence, the task of monitoring mistakes was now much more onerous. Pressures increased.

Irish Shipping Comes to the Rescue

During wartime, retail outlets in Northern Ireland operated under the regulations imposed by Westminster. Ulster shoppers had to give ration coupons for many items sold by Woolworth while, south of the border, as Lee puts it, Ireland was having 'a relatively cosy war'.[9] In 1939 the Irish government had had the foresight to set up a Department of Supplies to coordinate greater industrial output. Under the direction of the former Minister for Industry and Commerce, Séan Lemass, greater efforts were made to encourage Irish manufacturing but, except for hides, woollen and cereal industries, there was a dire shortage of raw materials. Few Irish factories had production lines that did not require regular imported shipments. Moreover, 95 per cent of this trade into the south of Ireland was reliant on foreign-owned vessels. By 1940 all existing supply lines were seriously disrupted.[10] To overcome the problem, Lemass founded a merchant fleet, Irish Shipping, and contact with the outside world was once more possible. Even so, the overall volume of imports into the South of Ireland dropped considerably, which meant that the range of products that firms like Woolworth were able to carry suffered as a consequence. This turn of events was to become a positive force, nonetheless. By 1945 the drop of goods imported to the state had created a large accumulated surplus of sterling and dollars. For Woolworth, this was to put the operation of the Dublin Buying Office in a strong position in the immediate post-war era.

Looking to the Future of Irish Stores

Just how bad trading became in the south of Ireland can be illustrated by a report drawn up by the merchandiser in charge of Dublin Office, which was conveyed to Woolworth executives during a review meeting in January 1944. The meeting records state: 'The results for 1943 were nothing short of a disaster. Explanation was almost unnecessary. The previous year's sales loss of 86 per cent was due to shortages, lack of raw materials and fuel for Irish factories plus the tightening British control of exports'.[11] Clearly, the Irish stores were barely functioning in a survival mode, and while they had suffered none of the serious problems that were now affecting the rest of the United Kingdom chain, such as war damage to buildings, staff shortages and stringent rationing, the difficulty of finding enough stock to sell was still having a depressing effect. Yet, the stores had been well cared for and were structurally sound; their employees were happy and overall morale was high. All that could be hoped for was that trade would pick up again and profits from Ireland could once more move into high gear.

War Maps sold in Dublin in 1944

Throughout the Emergency strict censorship had been imposed on press reporting of war news. However, on 8 July, following the D-Day landings in France, the *Irish Times* issued a war map of Normandy. Owing to a paper shortage, only a limited number were available, but it was advertised as being for sale in 'all newsagents and principle Stationers and in Messrs. Woolworths' Stores, price 6d'. No other retailer was named.

By January 1945 the news was brighter. Woolworth executives in London met to make decisions for the coming year. One of the agenda items for this meeting was 'Policy on future developments in Eire'. The mood was positive.

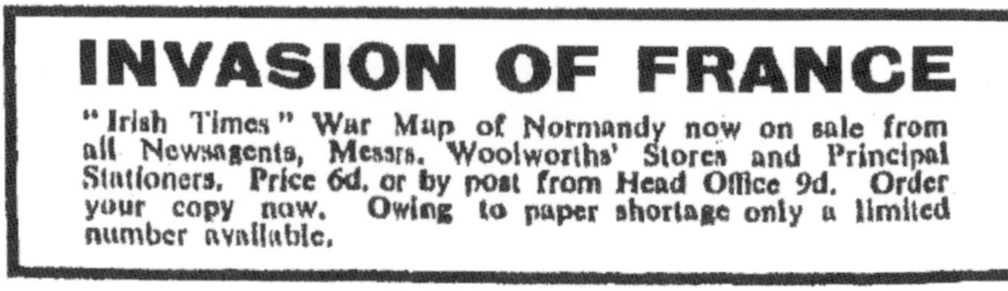

INVASION OF FRANCE

" Irish Times " War Map of Normandy now on sale from all Newsagents, Messrs. Woolworths' Stores and Principal Stationers. Price 6d. or by post from Head Office 9d. Order your copy now. Owing to paper shortage only a limited number available.

Figure 33. Woolworth stores were selected to carry some of the limited supplies of the *Irish Times* war maps in 1944.

Courtesy *Irish Times.*

Excellent news from the theatre of war in Europe had triggered speculation that hostilities might soon be over, and, clearly, those at the top were keen to revitalize ambitious pre-war plans to establish many more Irish branches. The meeting agreed that 'negotiations should continue to acquire properties in selected [Irish] towns'.[12] A factor that may have helped them in their decision-making was the necessity to appoint a replacement for the retiring manager of Dublin's Henry Street branch. Permission had been received from the British authorities to allow one of their most senior men and his family to travel from Yorkshire to neutral Ireland.[13] The new man had been selected with a great deal of careful forethought. When war broke out, he had been the superintendent for the whole of Ireland, north and south. Earlier in his career he had overseen the openings of several stores in the north of England and had managed the Grafton Street branch in the 1930s. Years of working in Ireland had given him first-hand knowledge of all the Irish stores and their personnel, including the current merchandiser in Dublin Office. If there was to be a substantial increase in the number of Irish branches, his presence in Ireland was going to be of immense value to the Woolworth Company.

On 8 May 1945 the ending of the war in Europe was announced, but it would be twelve months before any real progress was made to implement Woolworth plans for Ireland, even though several projects had been in the pipeline for years. In early 1939, well before the war, a refurbishment of Dublin's Henry Street store had been under consideration, based on a set of 1937 cost sheets.[14] These plans were put into abeyance for the duration of the war, and when it finally got the go-ahead, in March 1946, this project was already ten years old.[15] By then the directors' minds were once more seriously refocused on expanding store presence in Ireland. A list of suggested new locations had been put in front of the board, and it was agreed that sites should be sought in Galway, Tralee, Wexford, Drogheda, Omagh, Strabane, Enniskillen and Monaghan.[16] By June 1946, apart from the work to be carried out in Dublin's Henry Street store, a new proposal for improvements to the other Dublin outlet had been passed by the board, and executives were advised that 'the overhaul and alternations of the café in 31 Dublin [Grafton Street] was going ahead'.[17]

Building projects in Ireland were going to be relatively simple to organize. By contrast – although peace had returned – Woolworth had a huge task ahead to restore its shattered United Kingdom chain back to its former glory. The hostilities had brought about enormous disruption to the operation of the company's well-established and smooth-running systems that were virtually unchanged since 1909. In the past five years, well over two thousand Woolworth staff had been siphoned off to serve in the armed forces. Many employees had been lost in the conflict.[18] Destruction of property had been widespread. Twenty-six Woolworth stores in Britain's largest cities had been completely destroyed in bombing raids, and a tragic V2 rocket attack on London in 1944 had killed a store full of Saturday morning shoppers.[19] Air raids caused damage to 326 stores, and although these premises had been patched up at the time, a great deal of major repair work still remained to be done.[20] There were to be further delays caused by the shortage of building materials and government regulations, which limited how much could be spent on each project.[21] As autumn slipped into winter, it was increasingly clear that the economic and social problems that gripped post-war Britain were going to be almost as challenging as the years of conflict. People could put up with a great deal without grumbling when it was all 'for the war effort', but striving to maintain life in peacetime was a going to be a harder burden to bear. Several years of frustration were to follow.

Nevertheless, Woolworth buyers, optimistic to a man, had begun once more to seek out innovative ideas for the shopping public as soon as the war ended. Although restricted by the exchange controls on foreign currency, they wanted to be ready with an exciting new range of goods to bring a buzz back into the stores as soon as possible. The wartime gloom had to be lifted. It was important to look to the future.

Introducing the Biro Pen

During a meeting of buyers in London in September 1945, the always vocal Gilbert Powers had introduced his colleagues to a strange-looking pen.[22]

Powers had swiftly gained a reputation as a high-flyer since that incident with the Dublin gunman in 1924. He was always bursting with new ideas to streamline systems, and on this occasion he wanted to demonstrate the novelty of a special pen that had no nib but used, instead, a tiny ball-bearing. It had just appeared on the market; it could do the work of a pencil but never needed sharpening; wrote like an ordinary pen but did not need ink. This concept had exciting possibilities. Powers told them it was called a Biro or ballpoint pen.

Notes taken for this meeting reflect the high level of scepticism on the part of Powers' colleagues. One executive, commenting on the huge amount of paperwork each store had to cope with on a day-to-day basis, reluctantly conceded that to supply staff with this new novelty pen might possibly 'be a good thing to use in stores in connection with cash register reports and inventory books', but there was no great enthusiasm to replace current staff's usage of ordinary pencils or fountain pens with this expensive toy. The discussion went even more flat when Powers admitted that 'the makers could not supply any quantities of these pens until January or February 1946' – six months hence.[23] Someone may have then asked the price these marvels could be purchased for, and the answer may well have killed the idea stone dead. The minutes of the meeting merely note: 'No further action will be taken'.[24] Ballpoints were expensive. When the first models came into high-class shops in June the following year, they retailed at 55 shillings (at that time about a week's wages for a worker) and the refills, which had to be inserted by the dealer, were 5 shillings apiece. They might have been heralded as 'the pen sensation', but the Woolworth ethos of parsimony was not accustomed to indulging their employees with such luxury items for their own use.

However, Powers was not a man to let a good idea slip though his hands. He saw the products as having greater potential than merely as an aid to inventory-keeping. His powerful position as the company's Assistant Managing Director gave him the authority to cut corners, and it would seem that a deal with the suppliers was quietly negotiated. When Biro pens hit Woolworth store counters some eighteen months later, shoppers could buy them for just 9d each. By that time, the former Grafton Street manager had reached the apex of his career as the company's Joint Managing Director. Two years later, his brilliant career was to be tragically and swiftly cut short by illness. His death in 1950 at the age of only 48 left the Woolworth bereft of one of its most able men.

Figure 34. No longer a luxury: Biro pens go on display in Woolworth.

Courtesy 3ᴰ and 6ᴰ Pictures Ltd.

The Dublin Scene Dominates

Christmas 1945 saw another exciting idea put in front of a similar meeting of Woolworth buyers. London was told that that American-made 'soft ice cream machines were being considered in Éire' but that 'investigations were not yet fully completed'.[25] The method employed a gravity feed mechanism that twirled a creamy mixture out on to a cone for each customer. The cost of these machines was £250 each. This amount of money was a considerable sum at the time – enough to purchase a small motor car – but Hughes Brothers Dairy, suppliers of ice cream to the Irish Woolworth stores since 1926, had indicated their keen willingness to cooperate in the venture. They had plenty of surplus full-cream milk and were prepared to invest in equipping a new plant in the dairy to make up a special mixture exclusively for the Woolworth Company. The buyers knew there was only one Irish branch that could guarantee a high enough volume of ice cream sales to justify the expense of these machines. It had to be Dublin's store 76 in Henry Street.

The latter half of 1945 marked the beginning of the boom years for the Irish capital. The commercial climate of post-war Ireland was sunny and benign. Although coal, turf and petrol supplies continued to be in short supply, neon signs and lights blazed out on Dublin streets like a scene from a Hollywood movie. Shops had displays of produce not seen by British housewives since 1939; the windows of victuallers and butchers were fully dressed with sides of beef, lamb, pork and bacon, there was plenty of cream and milk, and the sweet and biscuit counters in Woolworth stores had lavish displays of home-manufactured goodies. The last traces of a cursory rationing system still existed, but as there was no shortage of foodstuffs, enforcement was largely ignored and was soon forgotten. Import and export routes to world markets were being swiftly reopened and the benefits soon began to roll in. Wool producers, clothing companies and small workshops thrived. Millers, breweries and whiskey distillers were flourishing, and established potteries such as Arklow and Carrigaline headed for profitable production overdrive. The years of the 'Emergency' had seen the Irish sugar beet industry continuing to gain ground, and by 1945 Comhlucht Siúicre Eireann (the Irish Sugar Company), in state ownership since 1935, was producing 89,000 tons of sugar, which was more than sufficient for the needs of public consumption, sweet manufacturers and confectioners.[26]

Although post-war economic problems had forced the British government to impose strict import controls on the United Kingdom, these rules applied neither to Irish-made products, nor to their salesmen and buyers, who were free to travel in Europe. The Woolworth Buying Office in Dublin, which had kept Irish outlets supplied with merchandise during wartime, now began to burst at the seams in an effort to keep up with demand for worldwide import/export shipments that could be rerouted to the United Kingdom under existing trade agreements. Pressure on space saw this operation expanded into a suite of additional offices above Ireland's premier store in Dublin's Henry Street, where one section dealt solely with Customs & Excise. Many new lines began to flood into Woolworth outlets via the Dublin Buying office. Stylish Czechoslovakian costume jewellery made from anodized metal, an invention perfected for military seaplanes, was an instant success, as were the return of old-style favourites such as glass Christmas tree baubles. Sales of Irish chocolate boomed. The proposal to install the American soft ice cream machines into the Henry Street store had gone ahead, and popularity of Hughes ice cream rose to even more spectacular levels.

This largely unrestricted good life offered by the Irish capital soon attracted a racy international set of revitalized tycoons and opportunists. Dublin's top hotels and restaurants, the Gresham, the Russell and the Red Bank, became the haunt of eager entrepreneurs looking for deals that could re-establish favour with the buyers from Woolworth. The long-awaited refurbishment of

Dublin's Henry Street store had been completed and the reopening of their basement sales floor was announced on 23 May 1946.[27] Executives from Liverpool District Office and London's Bond Street soon found excuses for visits to inspect – and to indulge.

The year 1946 brought promotion for the merchandise man who had headed up the difficult task of sustaining the Dublin Buying Office throughout the 'Emergency'. An important executive position in Liverpool District Office was his well-deserved reward, and his departure left the manager of Dublin's superstore in Henry Street to fly the flag as the senior Woolworth PR presence in Ireland. These extra responsibilities included welcoming and entertaining Executive Office VIPs and many of the new suppliers who were touting for business. These might range from firms in alliance with giant petro-chemical industries to overseas trade consuls. The halcyon days when the Henry Street store's cafeteria had hosted a Fianna Fáil Ard Fheis had not been forgotten, and there was lobbying from politicians and hucksters alike. Dublin's southside golf courses, race meetings and the American Grill Room in the Gresham created the backdrop. Ideas flourished. Possibilities took wing. In the meantime, back in London, Executive Office had to make do with austerity and optimistic visions for the future.

Newry Store is Launched

The Woolworth opening in Newry's Marcus Street on 26 July 1946 made a brave effort to herald a return to some kind of normality in Northern Ireland. Preparations to open this store had been well in hand in 1939, but when war broke out the final go-ahead had been cancelled and everything was left 'mothballed' until the peacetime returned.[28] Although Newry lay close enough to the border to be able to gain a few respites from British post-war food restrictions, supplies of newsprint were still in short supply everywhere, and as a consequence, no traditional half-page splash in the local press to announce the Newry opening was possible. Newspapers were mostly reduced to just four sheets per day and advertising space was at a premium, but a compromise was reached by the insertion of three small, two-column-width notices. One appeared prior to the opening, one on opening day and the final one appeared a week later as a reminder to customers that Woolworth had arrived to serve their shopping needs.

The launch of this new branch had not come about at an auspicious time, however. The worsening condition of people's lives in the United Kingdom was casting a tremendous gloom, the effects of which were spilling out across the Province. Across the water, post-war austerity had brought disappointments that bit deeply into reserves of the stoicism displayed during wartime. Food rationing had worsened. Allowances of butter and margarine were now smaller and, for the first time, bread rationing was necessary. Moreover, these rules were being applied in Northern Ireland. That summer, on the day following Newry's Woolworth store opening its doors to its first customers, the *Newry Telegraph* carried a large announcement informing citizens which coupons had to be used for bread. A normal adult was allocated 9 units a week. Children, according to their age received 5–9 units and growing adolescents were allowed 13. Expectant mothers and female manual workers were allocated 11 units and male manual workers given 15. One bread unit allowed 1/2 lb of biscuits, cakes or scones; a small loaf required 2 units, a large loaf needed 4 units and 9 units had to handed over for 3 lbs flour. Meanwhile, a few miles away on the southern side of the border, all that consumers could complain of was the continued use of 'brown' flour and the ongoing fuel shortages. It was as if they lived on another planet. Later that autumn, a great deal of this complacency was diminished by news that the unabated bad weather of 1946, a wet summer and disastrous cereal harvest might bring about the south of Ireland's own shortages of bread. These fears were genuine enough. A call went out and the people rallied to save the harvest. The Irish army lent a hand to help with transport and manpower and, despite the ferocious winter experienced that year and into early 1947, the panic soon passed. All was well and life returned to normal.

Meanwhile, in post-war Britain for many more years to come the shortage of the most basic goods created lengthening queues for everything. The food rationing regime increased its grip, and by 1948 the British government was rationing potatoes for the first time. In 1949 the allowance of milk went down to 2 pints per week per person. Sweets would also continue to be rationed for another four years, up to 1953. Severe restrictions on sales of butter and meat remained in place until 1954.

By contrast, shoppers in Southern Ireland basked in the sunshine of a renaissance. Manufacturing and industry gathered strength. The following summer saw Dublin girls sporting Parisian 'New Look' fashions; and the world's first duty free shop opened in Shannon Airport.

The First Break with the Past: Stephenson Retires

In 1948 a significant change to top management of the Woolworth Company came about when the long-serving chairman, William Laurence Stephenson, who had been personally recruited in 1909 by Frank Woolworth, announced that he was stepping down from the post he had held for the past twenty-five years. He had served thirty-nine years with the Woolworth Company, and during this time the number of stores had grown from 1 to 769 outlets. Throughout his working life, Stephenson had striven to emulate the Woolworth traditional ethos of 'an everyday store for everyone'. It was now up to the next generation to carry the torch. Notably, one of his last contributions was to chair a series of meetings held in New Bond House on 21–23 January 1948, to review the previous year's returns. The minute book noted his praise for the chain's rising star, the Irish flagship and superstore in Dublin's Henry Street. 'Mr Stephenson quoted individual Sales and Profits … and referred to the excellence of the result at 76 Dublin, which store had not only produced our highest profit, but a profit exceeding that of many companies in a substantial way of business.'[29] It would seem this Irish branch could do no wrong.

Behind the scenes, however, a little spat was being smoothly whisked out of sight. Earlier that month, it was realized that these record results from 76 Dublin also resulted in the store manager becoming one of the highest paid employees in the company. An exceptional volume of sales, high profits and shrinkage so well controlled had combined to create remuneration for that year that was on a par with, if not more than, the salaries of those at executive level. The board was shocked. It was unprecedented to have a store manager earning this much money. What was to be done?

The decision was ruthless. This manager must agree to take a cut in his bonus commission rate. He was ten years short of his retirement and there would be a lot for him to lose if he did not fall in with their wishes. This was how American-style business worked. The option was clear; take it or leave it. He had done no wrong, but the Dublin man accepted the rap on the knuckles for being too successful with as much good grace as could be mustered.

From this time on, company executives kept an eye more closely focused on developments in Ireland. It was felt that the Southern Irish branches had, perhaps, had it too much their own way during the Emergency years and needed to be reined in. At the start of wartime, the board's 'main aim was to eliminate direct contact between Dublin Office and Executive Office'.[30]

But, having put these systems into place to out-manoeuvre the strict legislative measures brought in by the British and Irish governments, the arrangements were now in urgent need of review. By 5 March 1948 the directors came to the consensus that

> the position in Dublin office is getting somewhat unwieldy… there are many items of which we have little or no knowledge which gets into the Irish stores by way of direct Continental orders … it is outside normal routine. It is our duty to set the policy and to control merchandise going into the Éire Stores from all sources. The present system of distribution whereby store 76 Dublin breaks down shipments for others stores in Éire, can hardly be regarded as being satisfactory, as the control was entirely outside the hands of the individual manager.[31]

In the end, the company took a pragmatic approach. One buyer reminded his colleagues that, 'There are a great number of firms who are now anxious to ship goods to Éire in order to help their export quota.'[32] There were opportunities to be grasped. Did Woolworth want to stay in an export/import game where the occasional creative sleight of hand required a cool head? In the end, they kept their nerve and the crisis passed. London was in no position to call any more of its Irish golden boys to heel. It would take a long time to forget that 'the gain of £25,000 made in these [Southern Irish] stores was mostly due to Czechoslovakian items'.[33]

Imports from the Far East Resume

Before the war, the bulk of the toys sold in Irish branches had been directly imported into Dublin from Hong Kong and Japan. By the middle of 1937, however, Nazi Germany had grown economically and militarily closer to Japan with the signing of an agreement that founded the 'Axis' between Berlin, Rome and Tokyo. The result was that the British Board of Trade was dissuading firms from continuing any direct contact with Japanese suppliers. For Woolworth, the break had come in January 1938 when Chairman Stephenson instructed his buyers to cease placing 'orders for direct imports of Japanese merchandise'.[34] In line with the high ethical standards which Woolworth had always prided themselves on maintaining, the buyers had been told to honour all outstanding contracts, nonetheless, whether from manufacturers or importers, and to accept all deliveries 'unless the Government issued orders that Japanese goods must not be imported'.[35] The directive was complied with and for almost a decade the door to markets in the Far East had been firmly closed.

When international trade struggled to return to normal after World War Two, Woolworth buyers in London soon had this ruling rescinded by the American parent company. Large firms with enormous buying power were being approached by the United States government to lend practical support to rebuilding the economies of the Far East. The Woolworth Company was one of the first to be asked by Congress to play its part in supporting the new policy. It was to be a commitment that remained unchanged for the next thirty years or more.[36]

Buyers Beware

In January 1948 a meeting of buyers reported: 'Woven goods are in short supply ... there are also shortages in laces. A Board of Trade licence had been obtained to import canvas shoes from Hong Kong with a selling value of £175,000 but there were difficulties to obtain licences for leather. There was also a lack of dried eggs and sugar'.[37] Later that year there was some brighter news when the production of plastic cups and saucers was taken off licence. This meant that when the buyers met, twelve months later, in early 1949, to review any improvement in supplies, one buyer could anticipate 'crested ashtrays, crested mugs and beakers, plastic cigarette boxes, gilt frame pictures, and kiddies bags were to be more available'. A colleague was of the opinion that 'there could be a great deal of increased business from plastics – good quality powders were in freer supply'.[38] In Ireland at that time, the Department of Industry and Commerce was encouraging several firms to go into production of plastic products. When up and running, these enterprises would find there was plenty of business to be done with Woolworth.

The late 1940s saw the production lines of Irish hosiery firms also thriving, whereas in the United Kingdom shortages in the home market continued to be created because of the British government's export policies. Supplies of nylon stockings were particularly limited. The drive to concentrate on export dictated that 70 per cent of British factory output had to be exported, and as one Woolworth buyer explained to his colleagues, 'This absorbs the whole of the perfect merchandise. Only sub-standard hosiery is available for the home market'.[39] It was a serious dilemma for buyers when suitable stock could not be bought. Since its foundation, the company had prided itself in retaining Frank Woolworth's high standards by never selling any of the cheap 'seconds' or flawed or damaged items that often ended up on hucksters' market stalls. Could they possibly break this long-standing rule and offer their customers 'slightly imperfect selected seconds'?[40] The meeting agreed that, if this had to be done, then the nylons must be clearly and accurately labelled as appropriate. It was a sober turning point to realize that, like it or not, reality dictated policy.

Nonetheless, Woolworth buyers concentrated on making the most of several innovative ideas that were coming on to the market. They were ready to take risks, but by late 1948 they showed particular wariness when faced with anything 'chemical'. In the post-war era, there were a lot of new cleaning fluids and washing powders called detergents that were the by-products of wartime laboratories. These products used no soap and never needed a scrubbing brush or washboard. Woolworth took a cautious attitude when asked to carry these ranges, and prior to a launch, they set up special training courses for counter staff so that they could explain to customers how these new products should be properly used.

Woolworth buyers' projections for twelve months hence were already well underway when a meeting held under the heading 'Prospects for 1949' recorded an entirely novel piece of merchandise called a 'Home Perm Set', which had been produced especially for Woolworth. It was to sell for five shillings.[41] The buyer who was introducing this new line advised his colleagues that the product 'would be nationally advertised as soon as we agreed to take up the item'.[42] Woolworth buyers tended to be collectively over-cautious when faced with utterly fresh ideas and untried concepts. The firm's standards of quality were still rigorously adhered to, and these men's training (there were no female buyers until 1974) had taught them to give even the most mundane of ordinary goods a thorough testing for durability and value. Faced with an increasing number of new inventions, previously unheard-of synthetic materials and chemical processes that had been developed during the wartime years, they took an innately suspicious approach to items which claimed to be 'novel'. A chemical kit, to be used at home and which promised to permanently wave the hair of their lady customers, was something that certainly drew a few serious doubts. Visions of possible litigation and complaints from shoppers whose hair remained uncurled, damaged or, worse still, lost as a result of using this process, were clearly in the forefront of these men's minds as they gathered to discuss the new product. There would have been a few pursed lips, despite some awareness of how ladies' metal curlers and

Figure 35. The head buyer was a powerful man: the Woolworth house journal puts its own interpretation on his role, June 1958.

Courtesy 3ᴰ and 6ᴰ Pictures Ltd.

curling tongs were used at home and of how the permanent waving of a whole head of hair required a visit to a hairdressing salon, where a large and complicated machine was used to attach clients to electrically wired curling pins. Was this buyer being too ambitious, even foolhardy, in thinking he could replace this level of professionalism by a 5/-d kit sold from Woolworth counters? The company's minute book dutifully records one executive's formal articulation of these fears: '[Mr X] made a cautionary note that we should be quite satisfied that this will do the work for which it is intended and obtained confirmation from [the buyer] that we have an indemnity to this effect from the supplier'.[43]

The Girls in Dublin Office Recall How It Was

Dublin Office in the late 1940s employed at least nine or ten girls working full time on the paperwork created by customs regulations and the liaison systems that had built up between suppliers and the Republic's merchandiser. The younger women in the typing pool were paid 50s (£2 10s 0d) a week, which was considered an excellent remuneration for a girl in her late teens.[44] With the volume of work carried by this office swollen to almost unmanageable proportions, finding additional space to accommodate extra office staff had been difficult. The upper floors of the Henry Street premises were still old and cramped at the time, unchanged since 1918, and conditions for office staff were less than comfortable. Yet, it was not untypical. In those days, hundreds of typists and clerks worked in similar conditions in the city. As one recalls:

> We came to work on our bicycles. We went into the office through the back door of the store in Henry Street, and had to carry our bikes all the way up the stairs to the back of the cafeteria on the next floor and then down some more steps to a small annex off the café where the manager and our boss ate their lunch. It was less than dignified. We all wore long-sleeved navy blue uniforms, which were buttoned down the front. Even our supervisor wore the same outfit. The boss and his secretary shared the office at the front, which overlooked the street, and our office was at the back. There were no windows in our room. It got very hot in the summer and to get some air there was a door that led out on to the roof we could leave ajar. If the boss opened the window of his office we could hear the hawkers calling their wares from the vegetables stalls in nearby Moore Street: 'get your damsons here, sixpence a pound'. He used to make us laugh by leaning out of his window pretending to shout back 'get your damsels here, sixpence a pound' … He was a very jolly man, always joking … we loved working there.[45]

Wage Rates come under Review in 1945

On the evidence of most ex-employees whose memories reach back into the 1940s and 1950s, rates of pay for Woolworth store employees in Ireland were reputedly always slightly higher than for staff in England. In 1945 wage rates came up for review in London and it may be assumed that the new rulings were passed for approval: rates for female employees aged 16–21 years ranged from 30/-d up to 52/6d, and for girls aged 22–26 from 55/-d to a maximum of 65/-d (£3 5s 0d) depending on responsibility and the grade of store. English male employees received similar rates, also dependant on length of continuous service up to a maximum of 85/-d (£4 5s 0d). The young male 'learners' who had completed several years of management training to an advanced level received £6–£7 a week. By this stage they were ready for promotion as deputy managers.[46] Store managers were permitted to draw a maximum allowance of £6–£8 each week, depending on the size of their branch. At the end of the year their drawings were topped up by the amount of bonus due. The annual bonus was a percentage on net profits. It may be noted that a different ruling applied to manageresses. Their weekly drawings were 'fixed by their store contracts'.[47]

The women in the strongly unionized Cork branch made regular requests for wage increases. In 1945 they had been granted an additional 7/6d a week, but two years later, in March 1947, they sought a more substantial raise of 12/-d a week. When the request was put in front of the company's Management Committee in London, the gathered executives were none too pleased by this demand and a rebuff was swiftly prepared.[48] However, it is likely that the Cork girls got their way in the end, although no record of the negotiations that ensued would seem to have survived. Their wages often went to supplement tight household budgets and – as important bread-winners – they were always prepared to fight their corner.

One ex-counter assistant from Cork can recall her excitement when told that her wages were to be raised by a large amount in the late 1940s. She was about 18 then and had started work with the Woolworth Company two years earlier. She remembers that her first week's wage packet had been 27/-d. 'I rushed home to tell my mother we were getting a big increase in our pay. I had a lot of smaller brothers and sisters all at home. That extra money made a big difference for her.'[49]

Despite it being a male-oriented organization at the upper levels of management, it must be conceded that the career prospects for any woman employed in an Irish Woolworth store in the post-war years was considered enviable. While Woolworth never moved their girls from store to store in the way that was imposed on male management personnel, they did present promotional opportunities for girls to take on senior positions on the shop floor, stockroom or office that few other Irish firms offered. Staff supervisors and senior cashiers were usually authorized to act *pro tem* for managers in their absence and, by the end of the 1950s, several former staff members had been appointed to branches in the Republic to run these outlets as manageresses.

From evidence provided by Muireann Charleton's thesis, it may be suggested that the Woolworth rates of pay and conditions were, indeed, more generous than those for other Irish shop assistants and apprentices at that time.[50] As late as 1965, the more substantial drapery houses in rural Ireland still used live-in apprenticeship schemes by which young employees were paid no wages but were provided free communal accommodation, food and lodgings. Juniors were allowed earn a small commission on sales for pocket money.

When the apprenticeship was complete, after several years' training, a male drapery assistant could earn £5 a week.[51]

When asked to recall their early working lives, the recollections of Woolworth 'girls' who were at one time employed as counter assistants, staff supervisors or cashiers, all echo similar sentiments. As was the custom then, the majority left the workforce when they got married, but they had all enjoyed being part of a Woolworth store team, and it was not uncommon to keep in touch with former colleagues for years to come. As one recalls, 'If I had ever needed to get another job, I would have gone straight back to Woolworths. It was such a great place to work.'[52] Others now remember that life was never dull.

Figure 36. Happy times in post-war Ireland: the cosmetic counter in Cork.

Courtesy Betty Wyse née Hallihan.

Figure 37. 'How we hated those hats!': confectionery assistants in the Lurgan branch, County Armagh.

Courtesy 3[D] and 6[D] Pictures Ltd.

Figure 38. Behind the store in Clonmel, County Tipperary: the manageress and staff take a break.

Courtesy Alice Carroll.

There was something different happening every day. You never knew what to expect. I remember this farmer was once driving a herd of cattle down the street outside. It was a hot day and the two store doors were wide open. One of the heifers skittered right into the store through the first open door. We all froze, expecting mayhem. But it was probably as shocked as we were. It just looked around in surprise and then walked calmly past the big scales that always stood between the two doors and back out into the street through the other door. No damage was done. Everyone collapsed with relief![53]

The Woolworth 'Family' Safety Net

Working for the Woolworth Company meant being expected to embrace the idea of being a part of the corporate 'family'. Colleagues not only worked and socialized together as a store team, but were encouraged to display this loyalty to every other person in the firm – and to their families. For example, in the days before mobile phones and easy contact with home, each child of every Woolworth employee became part of a guaranteed security network. If a young person ever found themselves in trouble when away from home, they were told not to seek help from a Garda or police station, but to go straight to the nearest Woolworth store. If they had had an accident of any kind, or lost their money, or were sick, or in any kind of difficulty, the safety net was always there: 'Go into the store and ask for the manager. Tell him or her who you are and which branch your mother or father works in. His staff will look after you.' And they always did. These instructions were passed down generation after generation. It was like having a member of your family in almost every town and city.

What do Shoppers Remember?

Members of Sligo's Active Retirement Group have sharply recollected memories of how the local Woolworth store was the centre of their social life when they were teenagers. 'After school we used to go in there and walk around. It was lovely and warm on a winter's day. There was a scale at the end of the shop and we used all weigh ourselves – I don't know why – it didn't matter at that age!'[54]

These pensioners can also recall the exact interior layout of the store, sixty years later: 'the open display counters were way ahead of their time. On your right on the way in you had all the sweets and biscuits. In the middle aisle you had toiletries and the far aisle had jewellery and glasses. At the end were the clothes, household goods and so on.'[55] The Sligo branch was also a favourite meeting place for older teenagers.

> Every afternoon after school, our bikes were just abandoned in the street and everyone went into Woolworth's. If you had an eye on a fella or anything like that, 'Woolies' was the meeting place. Saturday was half days from work, and we used to dress up and wash our hair and go into Woolworth's to meet the fellas from Collooney and Ballysadare – and many a date we got out of it.[56]

A similar picture emerges in the United Kingdom in the post-war era, where to spend time browsing and meeting friends in a Woolworth store was regaining its reputation as a popular leisure pursuit. There was plenty of nostalgia to recall happier times. In 1948, when a journalist in the *Shields Gazette* called for the reinstallation of some pre-war attractions for visitors to South Shields, she included 'a large Hall for skating and dancing to replace the Casino and a Woolworth's Store which trippers (as well as our townsfolk) love to walk around'.[57]

What was also still held in common on both sides of the Irish Sea soon after the war, was the way people liked to don their 'best' clothes when setting out on a shopping expedition. For example, for everyone, post-war fashion dictated that headgear be worn far more frequently than today. Women wore hats, headscarves and berets. Demobbed men sported soft American-style Trilby or Homburg hats. Children's clothes had changed very little for decades. Small boys still wore shirts and ties, short trousers and grey woollen knee socks. Girls had white ankle socks and hair in plaits or tied with a ribbon, even up until their teens. Such fashions reflected merchandise that continued to move well on Woolworth counters in Ireland in much the same way as in the United Kingdom, and this trend would continue well into the 1970s. When, in due course, the buyers began to shift their emphasis on to seeking larger items of clothing and electrical goods, this trend did not fit easily into the expectations of the Republic's customers, who were, for the most part, traditional shoppers reluctant to accept such radical changes in the range of merchandise for sale in their local Woolworth branch. For them, any time spent shopping in their local store was not a chore like the purchase of basic foodstuffs, or a serious decision-making gesture like buying clothes or a functional item for use in the house. Browsing in a Woolworth outlet was an indulgence. The goods were attractive, affordable and reliable. Treats like confectionery were for spoiling yourself. There was still a high level of customers with large families who would seek toys and children's stationery items all year round.

The Management of Staff Relationships

By the mid twentieth century most senior managers still took a paternalistic, even proprietary attitude in caring for the well-being of their female counter staff, and one of the unwritten rules was to forbid all untoward fraternization between their young male trainees and the 'girls'. There was a practical side to the issue, because, on the one hand, the migratory learners would be at most only a year or two in any location, and no manager wanted a member of his trained staff left incapable of doing her job because of a broken heart. On the other hand, the company expected managers to bear some responsibility to ensure a young floor-man's career was not thrown off-course by any romantic entanglement that might disrupt his future within the company, especially if he had shown aptitude and promise.

When moved to a new store, every trainee always carried a letter of introduction from his former manager to his new superior. The letter usually contained a short précis to give information about any particular talent or peccadillo, and Irish managers were notorious for taking a particularly strict line when a new trainee arrived, especially if his letter of introduction hinted that he might have a reputation as a lothario. One of the old-guard Irish managers had a reputation for being very protective of his young counter assistants, and his approach was never anything else but direct. As one former employee recalls, he would eye a newly arrived trainee very sternly and give each of them the same lecture, leaving no doubt as to his instructions:

> I have just one thing to tell you, Mister, and that is – you stay away from my staff. I don't want you to be interfering with them or doing anything with them. If you want to find a girl to 'court', Mister, you go outside of this store and find someone out there … in a dance hall … anyone you like, so long as it isn't one of my staff…[58]

Figure 39. All ready for the annual dinner dance: a Dublin manager and his deputy pose with their retinue of trainees.

Courtesy 3ᴰ and 6ᴰ Pictures Ltd.

Most trainees behaved themselves – the others made sure their manager never knew about it.

The 'learners' letters of introduction aimed to be useful for the manager who was about to progress a youngster's skills to the next stage, and there is at least one instance when the 'introduction' failed to be delivered. En route to a new posting, one learner, who had not fared too well under his former manager, decided to open the letter in the train while on his way there. His former boss had written: 'This is to introduce Mr X. I hope he will be of more use to you than he has been to me.' When this young man later became a successful manager, he liked to tell how, just as he was reading this message, a sudden strong draft of wind from the train's open window had caught the letter and wafted it out of his hand out and on to the track. To get on in the Woolworth Company, one of the best attributes to cultivate was the ability to take the initiative when required.

Chapter 5

Expansion Accelerates

1949–1959

The British government's easing of financial restrictions in their budget of 1949 allowed the directors of Woolworth to announce by October that they had received Treasury consent 'for the capitalisation of £7,500,000 of the company's £8,302,032 profit and loss balance and the distribution of one new 5s share for every existing Ordinary 5s unit held'.[1] As one financial correspondent explained, although 'the element of "bonus" was nil' for the company's existing shareholders, this move brought the shares to 'within the scope of a far wider circle of investors'. The 5s ordinary units would become 'available at between 40s and 45s on a 35 per cent dividend basis', which, as this commentator noted, would 'prove an attractive proposition'.[2] Woolworth was now well positioned to resume their pre-war programme of expansion and consequent growth of profit.

Ten years earlier, the directors had been planning a £2 million building programme, which was to be spent on the construction of a number of new stores and the modernization and extension of many of the chain's established branches.[3] At that time, several Irish towns were being considered as suitable locations for new branches. These plans had been abandoned when the war intervened, and since then, apart from completing the delayed launch of the Newry store and the more recent refurbishment work on the two Dublin stores, no other major expenditure had been assigned to Ireland. This was now set to change. From 1950 onwards a marathon five-year building programme was underway to establish fifteen new branches in Ireland within the next five years (see Appendix I, Table 4).

In the meantime, patience was needed in respect of the huge building programme that was due to be launched in the United Kingdom. A considerable amount of war damage remained to be attended to and the firm's efforts to accelerate progress in English cities and towns had proved to be difficult because of a chronic shortage of building materials. The British government had imposed restrictions and the company was required to obtain a building licence for each project. These restrictions were not to end until 11 November 1954, which meant that work could only go ahead when the permissions were granted.[4] As an interim measure, therefore, it made good sense to turn attention first to locations in the south of Ireland, where there were no restrictions or hold-ups. A pragmatic approach was taken over the three outlets Woolworth had planned for the province of Ulster. They would also have to wait until the need for building licences was eased.

In chronological order, the fifteen new Irish branches opened by the Woolworth Company between 1950 and 1955 had commenced with Drogheda (1950), followed by Wexford and Tralee in 1952. Five outlets were launched in 1953 – these were in Bray, Galway, Mullingar, Thurles and Ballina – and a further five branches began trading in 1954 – these were in Omagh, Tipperary, Dublin (Thomas Street), Killarney and Strabane. The new stores in Cavan and Larne were opened the following year (1955) (see Appendix I, Table 4).

Apart from Galway, a city with a population of over 21,000, the first four towns to have a new Woolworth store contained in or around 11,000 people, which was the threshold identified by the company as having the potential to support an outlet. However, drastic modification of this ideal was needed for the subsequent locations, because, excluding the well built-up area around Larne in County Antrim, the eight or so remaining towns selected for new branches held only about half the viable amount of people. Moreover, the prognosis for any immediate growth of population in these places was gloomy. Irish demographic profiles had remained volatile. Emigration from the Republic continued to rise, and this was compounded by increasing migration from rural areas into the Irish cities. Thus, trade in many of the rural communities being targeted would be unduly reliant on an older age profile. This factor was to affect the range of merchandise being carried by these new stores, as a core of conservative and traditional tastes would need to be carefully catered for. Yet, conversely, as in the previous decades, Woolworth would still be seen by locals as bringing a touch of the exotic to their town.

There was a bright note of hope on the horizon, however, and it may be viewed as significant that the stores in several of these new locations were to respond in a very positive way to the rise in fortunes of the Irish tourist industry. As Irene Furlong has outlined in her analyses and discussion of this era in *Tourism in Ireland, 1880–1980*, the flood of visitors in the immediate post-war years was to have a direct bearing on the retail sector.[5]

Tapping into the Potential for Tourism

The Woolworth choice of Drogheda as the first new location of the 1950s, reflects not only its growing importance as a port and manufacturing centre, but also its accessibility to the Boyne Valley. By 1949 a large premises formerly occupied by Messrs. A. Davis & Co., in Drogheda's West Street, was acquired and trading from here began in January 1950. Dublin was still a boom town and the stretch of coast from the capital to Drogheda was being revitalized by the expanding fortunes of the farming community and of a number of small industries. Market gardening thrived and tourists from the United Kingdom were arriving in even greater numbers to two new holiday destinations in this area – Red Island in Skerries, founded in 1947, and the Butlin's Holiday Village at Mosney, which opened in 1948. The signs were clear. The holiday-makers from Britain and Northern Ireland, as yet unseduced by offers of cheap charter flights to the Costa Brava, had discovered there was a land of milk and honey lying on their doorstep in the south of Ireland.

A concerted drive by the Department of Industry and Commerce and the Irish Tourist Board had successfully geared up the message that Ireland could provide an enjoyable temporary escape from the post-war gloom. Supported by vibrant advertising campaigns, local authorities and town councils were revved up into producing national and local festivals up and down the country. Shannon Airport boomed and golf courses in the south-west of Ireland grew in popularity. These were not misguided efforts. Tourism would come to represent over one-third of Ireland's invisible exports between 1949 and 1968, with receipts amounting to £75.7 million.[6]

Irish Souvenirs

The importance of selling merchandise linked to the Irish tourist industry cannot be overlooked. In the Republic, the Irish Tourist Board and officials from the Department of Industry and Commerce had worked closely since 1951 to encourage quality souvenirs and the involvement of craftspeople.[7] Bord Fáilte Éireann's annual report for 1958 calculated that £1million a year was spent on souvenirs, and this was followed by a survey that concluded that

43 per cent of the visitors interviewed had spent, on average, £6 on their purchase.[8] It was an expanding industry and, to achieve bulk sales, the firms to gain most benefit were those which pitched wares to suit visitors' tastes for colourful representations of leprechauns and shamrocks in preference to Celtic mythology and esoteric art forms.[9]

Figure 40. Popular taste in Irish souvenirs is timeless: tourists like leprechauns, jaunting cars and plenty of lucky shamrocks.

Photograph: Barbara Walsh.

Enormous volumes of popular-taste souvenirs were sold by the Woolworth stores' fancy goods departments in the Republic. A high level of profitability from novelty gift items for holiday-makers continued to generate excellent results for Irish branches long after sales figures for other ranges carried by this department dropped dramatically elsewhere in the chain.[10]

In Northern Ireland, historic royal occasions were always marked by increased sales of specially commissioned memorabilia. When the coronation of Queen Elizabeth II took place in 1953, store managers were not to be disappointed. The Woolworth buyers in London had put together 'a range to suit all tastes and budgets'.[11] Shoppers had a choice of 'books, china and glass, flowers and decorations' in addition to 'gold-embossed foil crowns for 3d, coats of arms for 9d' and any amount of 'flags and bunting'.[12] Business was brisk enough to draw the attention of Executive Office. A comment on the 'strong performance in Ulster' was later noted. Outside of the exceptional sales in London, the 1953 year-end sales figures for royal memorabilia in the Province were calculated to be 'double the average' of branches elsewhere in the United Kingdom.[13]

Figure 41. Coronation memorabilia from Woolworth
made a striking display in 1953.

Courtesy 3ᴰ and 6ᴰ Pictures Ltd.

Ranges of royal memorabilia did not, of course, feature in the windows and counters of Woolworth outlets in the Republic, but when it came to celebrating each St Patrick's Day on March 17, customers seeking commemorative emblems of Ireland's patron saint would find plenty of choice in every branch, while border towns like Newry, County Down, would often set up a full counter display of cards, rosettes, badges, ribbons and other shamrock-decorated merchandise for local shoppers.[14]

The large profits to be made from the tourist trade in the south of Ireland were supplemented by other Woolworth ranges catering for local visitors in holiday resorts. One former store staff supervisor in the seaside resort of Bray, who began work as a 16-year-old counter assistant in 1953, has recollections of one reliably fast-moving line of stock that speaks volumes about Irish holiday weather. 'We sold hundreds and hundreds of plastic raincoats alongside all the other regular seaside merchandise like buckets and spades.' She also remembers how, 'although we didn't sell cigarettes, people bought thousands of plastic cigarette lighters, the refill type, and one of the services we offered to customers at that time was to refill empty lighters from the bottles of lighter fuel'.[15] Plastic lighters were still in short supply in the United Kingdom, and visitors to Bray were keen to bring them home as presents for friends. No serious concern over health and safety issues appears to have been created by the handling of lighter fuel in this way, although one rule imposed on all personnel, which had always been strictly enforced in every store in the chain, was the ban on smoking, which was not permitted anywhere except in staffrooms or canteens. Notices to this effect were displayed in all key areas – especially in stockrooms. If an employee was caught breaking this rule, the penalty was instant dismissal.

The economy of Irish towns like Bray in the 1950s was very much reliant on keeping the resort's tourists happy, and the Woolworth store played its part by putting in special window displays to complement whatever novelty event was going on in the town. One former staff supervisor remembers how

> Bray used to have a designated fortnight for the different United Kingdom visitors. There was a Scots' Fortnight and a Welsh fortnight and another for the English visitors, too. Special stock would be ordered in advance and the front windows of the store were then trimmed with ranges that fitted into the scheme. They were all part of the town's festival fortnights.[16]

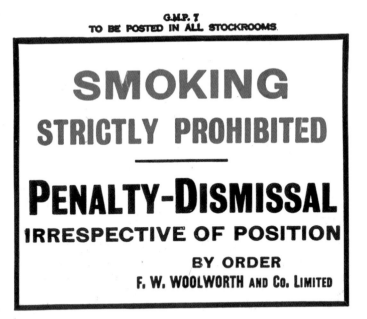

Figure 42. Woolworth rules for no smoking were strictly enforced.

Photograph: Barbara Walsh.

In post-war Ireland, side by side with this huge volume of trade in souvenirs for holidaymakers, the business done in selling Irish-made rosary beads also grew to become a reliable and profitable range for stores in the Republic. A strong revival in the practice of saying the rosary had been spearheaded in America by the Irish-born priest Father Peyton in 1947 with his slogan 'The family that prays together stays together'. When 1954 marked the Marian Year, the 'Rosary Priest' made a tour of Ireland. Huge 'Rosary Rallies' during May of that year generated even more intense devotion, and Woolworth managers were quick to tap into this popular wave of fervour. Beads of every colour and description were sold from fancy goods counters for about 1/6-d or 2/-d a pair.[17] Enthusiasm for this old religious practice had become so widespread that it became a regular routine in many Irish Woolworth stores for counter assistants to gather together to 'say the rosary' after the doors closed for business at 6 o'clock. 'Where have they all gone to?' asked one puzzled visiting superintendent from England, when Limerick branch personnel all swiftly disappeared off the shop floor at closing time. He was told the girls were all up in the staffroom, praying.[18] There is no record of how he reacted to this news, but a former sales assistant, who worked in the almost 100 per cent unionized store in Cork, can still remember how their union shop steward – a deeply pious lady – was always urging staff to remain behind to recite the rosary before going home.[19] The strong sense of solidarity with their colleagues, which Woolworth liked to translate into a 'family' atmosphere, had taken on an entirely new meaning. For these Woolworth girls, the rosary crusade motto had become: 'The workplace that prays together stays together'.

In Ireland, tourists soon discovered many more attractive destinations to visit and business in the Woolworth stores in Kerry, Wicklow and Wexford and Galway improved steadily. In the spring of 1952 a branch on South Main Street in Wexford was opened. Some months later, it was the turn of Tralee in County Kerry. The range of goods sold in each of these stores was pitched to cater for a regular stream of summer holiday visitors, as well as for fishermen, yachting and other outdoor activity enthusiasts. However, none of the new outlets quite matched a very unique attraction discovered in the Wexford outlet.

According to the local historical record, the basement area of these premises, at 41 Main Street, formerly a hardware shop called Sinnott's, clearly retained the foundation walls of one of Wexford's oldest buildings, dating back to the fourteenth century. Known as Kenny's Hall or Castle it was reputed to have been Oliver Cromwell's headquarters during his campaign in the area. There was moreover a darker notoriety. Within the thickness of its walls there was an *oubliette*, or 'murder hole', down which the body of any unwelcome guest could be despatched into an underground river, or, as was the case in Wexford, into the channelled waters of a harbour.[20] In the past, previous owners of the shop premises could be persuaded to show visitors this gruesome feature, which lay concealed but still accessible behind a section of oak panelling in the residential part of the building. In addition, down in the basement, well below street level, there was a doorway which led to a short section of tunnel cut into the hillside. Controversy has raged over the use to which this tunnel was put. Theories that it was used for smuggling, or as an escape route to the quayside and a waiting ship during penal days are now disputed. By the time Woolworth took over the building, in 1952, the furthest end of this tunnel was already blocked up and all signs of the 'murder hole' upstairs had completely vanished.

Nonetheless, following acquisition of the premises, the manager of the new Woolworth branch soon noticed that a lot of summer visitors to the town, especially American tourists, liked to visit the store, not for shopping but to ask about its history. The tunnel from the basement storeroom was still in a state of good preservation and the store manager arranged to have a string of small electric lights rigged up along its length at ceiling level, to accommodate tourists' curiosity. A counter assistant from the electrical department was given responsibility for ensuring that the lights were working properly. She was also asked to make sure that visitors who wished to view this little piece of old Wexford's history came and went in safety.[21] The task was never anything else but a welcome diversion from this girl's normal routine duties, but a problem arose if tourists offered her a tip for escorting them along the tunnel. One of the company's strictest directives laid down that counter assistants were never allowed to bring any of their personal money on to the shop floor. It was a rule devised to keep control of shrinkage. If a girl was ever tempted to dip into her till, any money found on her person before leaving the sales area by her staff supervisor provided proof for a serious enquiry and possible dismissal.

The dilemma was solved by a bit of subterfuge. The manager took charge of all the 'tips' and, at the end of the day when the assistant was leaving the premises, he would send word up to the staffroom with a request for Miss X to call into the office where there was 'a message' for her to collect. No records were ever kept, and, thus, no rules were ever broken – officially. It is not known how many people now remember this small contribution to heritage tourism in Wexford.

By June 1953 a Woolworth store was open on Main Street in Bray, and this was followed almost a month later by a branch in Galway's Eyre Square. Neither of these stores could boast of any accompanying historical secrets, but nonetheless, both locations enjoyed a huge if more conventional reliance on their local tourist industry.

Reluctance in Galway

The expansion of the Woolworth chain in Ireland in the early 1950s was for the most part a smooth operation. Town councils and fellow traders regarded the arrival of a Woolworth outlet in their midst as a welcomed sign of progress. Store managers were soon invited to join Chambers of Commerce and other active business associations. There was just one exception. This was the delay in setting up a branch in Galway. This arrival proved to be an unusually long drawn-out and difficult process, and it may be recognized that the fact of the matter was that Galway, known as the 'City of the Tribes', did not take to strangers in any shape or form.

Figure 43. The Woolworth store in Eyre Square, Galway, opened on 10 June 1953.

Courtesy 3ᴰ and 6ᴰ Pictures Ltd.

For years, a grumpy bunch of Galway town councillors, who were well supported by a number of strong-willed retailers, had prevented the advances of every new trader who wanted to enter the town's precincts. Their aim was to protect the city's historic heritage, but the result merely acerbated the decline of many already moribund areas. That said, the population of the city continued to rise and was pushing well past 20,000 by the 1950s.

Following several failed efforts to obtain suitable premises, the Woolworth property scouts finally acquired the former site of the old Royal Hotel on Eyre Square. By the summer of 1953, a new purpose-built retail store was ready for action. Local interest was intense; queues formed from an early hour on the opening day and the shop floor remained crowded for hours.[22] In the weeks that followed, the spurt of extra business being generated in Eyre Square was palpable and the shoppers that flocked to the new outlet spilled out across the pavements to the benefit of several neighbouring retailers. Most noteworthy of those whose fortunes were boosted was a newsagent's shop on the corner of the square, which was owned by one of the city's foremost councillors and one who had been, possibly, one of the most vocal of the traders opposed to the Woolworth arrival.

Nonetheless, in due course, when other chain store operations tried to break into Galway's tightly protected trading scene, its city councillors reverted to similar patterns of commercial begrudgery. It would take quite a while before all the negative thinking in this city was blown away.

Market Towns' Reaction to Woolworth Remains Favourable

Three more Woolworth outlets were launched in 1953. When a store in Mullingar's Oliver Plunkett Street began trading in August, the press coverage declared confidently: 'The fact that Woolworths have opened a branch here proves that Mullingar must be regarded as a good shopping centre'.[23] Similar sentiments were expressed when, a few months later, just before the Christmas season, two stores, many miles apart, began trading within a day of each other. An excellent position in the town's main Liberty Square had been acquired for the branch in Thurles, County Tipperary, while an outlet in Ballina's Arran Street, in County Mayo, held the promise of good business.

Worth noting, is that none of these openings created anything like the level of public awe and excitement created during the 1920s and 1930s. There was no panic among established retailers, no protests, pickets or other unruly receptions. The sight of the Woolworth red and gold fascia-boards were now being received by communities as if a great honour had been bestowed on them. Not only was this firm welcomed as a provider of employment, it signalled that viable commercial progress was being made at local level. When the Drogheda store opened its doors on West Street in 1950, the press had written how it 'will make [Drogheda] a popular shopping centre for townspeople and the many visitors who patronise the town,' while adding rather optimistically that 'almost everything from a needle to an anchor' was among the varied goods that could be purchased.[24]

Three years later, a similarly warm reaction awaited Woolworth in Ballina. A week ahead of the store's official opening, on 27 November 1953, an enthusiastic headline bore the message: 'Woolworth's are Coming! Mammoth store for Ballina'. The paper's editor gave considerable space to commentary on the building work, observing that 'the opening was to bring to a close one of the biggest reconstruction jobs ever seen in Ballina.[25]

Woolworth's are Coming!

MAMMOTH STORE FOR BALLINA

LARGE LOCAL STAFF TO BE EMPLOYED

Opening date – November 27th

When tall, fair-haired manager Ian Gardner throws open the doors of Messrs. F. W. Woolworths new stores at Arran St., Ballina at 9 a.m. on Friday morning, 27th November next, the town's biggest and brightest store will come into official operation. The opening of the twin doors to the public will

premises, formerly occupied by Jas. McConn and Son, were stripped to a virtual shell including the removal of 9,000 cubic feet of earth which had to be excavated before the actual job itself could proceed. To give some idea of the mountains of materials called for in the course of the work, foreman Preen pointed out that 4,000 square feet of Jap-oak flooring were laid, 200 tons of gravel, 50 tons of cement, 60 tons of sand and 13,000 concrete blocks went into the work. The steel work alone accounted for 8 girders each weighing 15 cwt. and the erection of 5 steel columns. Plastering was spread over 1,500 square yards of wall; 8 cwt. of nails

ped rest room. Highly commendable feature will be the provision of a special water-filtering plant which will allow only pure water to be used throughout the stores. The colour scheme upstairs is green and primrose matched by an excellent floor covering in harmonious tones. In the public stores cream and brown will predominate.

THE STAFF

The present staff have all been appointed following an interview and during the first opening week will be augmented by trained personnel. Manager Gardner is a native of Harrowgate, Yorkshire, and has spent many years in the

Figure 44. Mammoth store for Ballina, 1953.

Courtesy *Western People.*

Having further extolled the facilities for the twenty-five local girls recruited by the new store, the local press report also noted that the newly appointed manager from England was married to a girl from Dublin – clearly seeing this as a bonus. People's intense interest 'was creating a mounting anticipation … coming so close as it does to the usual Christmas activity, the opening has caused the postponement of many shopping expeditions to see what lines the new store will bring'.[26]

In the meantime, another journalist sent to cover the opening of the branch in Thurles displayed new levels of enterprise and good PR by containing gossipy details of local interest for readers, writing that

> Early this year Woolworths purchased adjoining premises in Liberty Square, owned by Mr W. McKenna and Mr M. Carroll for £4,500 and £3,500 respectively. Possession changed hands on 31 March. The work of demolition and erection of the new premises has been proceeding for some time and a large number of city and local tradesmen have been employed at carpentry, plastering, painting, electric wiring, etc.[27]

The Woolworth expansion into the rich farming lands of the Irish south midlands during the 1950s targeted towns that enjoyed a reputation of being good commercial centres. Thurles was a renowned centre for sporting events, – a factor which kept it a busy place all year round. By this time, county councils' planning permission regulations had become much stricter and store designs were required to merge quietly into existing streetscape vistas. Nonetheless, it was always a good reflection on the Woolworth Company when extensive building work had had to be carried out in a town. Although these projects were directed by the company's construction division, who would put in a foreman to oversee the project, it was their policy to offer contracts to local tradesmen, labourers, timber merchants, stone and gravel suppliers and others in the construction industry close to the area.

Steady Expansion in Northern Ireland

By 1954 a start was made to expand in the Province of Ulster. New stores arrived in Market Street, Omagh and Castle Street, Strabane. Omagh was a busy market town with a number of manufacturing firms, and Strabane was famous for flax spinning. By July 1955, on the east coast, the long overdue outlet in Larne finally opened its doors. A branch to serve shoppers in this area had been approved by the board since 1946. It had been a long wait.[28]

In addition to creating brand new outlets in 1950–9, the volume of business being done by Woolworth in Northern Ireland throughout the 1950s had justified the expansion of a number of older and more long-established stores. Improvements were carried out either by building extra sales floor space on an existing site, or by the purchase of neighbouring retail premises. Whenever an abutting retail unit came up for sale or looked ripe for negotiation, the Woolworth property department would make an approach. For example, in February 1950, only four years since its opening, the store in Newry increased its shop floor size. The Ballymena branch was also made larger in June 1954. In Bangor, the Woolworth outlet received extra sales floor space in February 1958, and by the end of November 1959 an extension was ready for the Christmas trade in the Portadown branch.[29]

Cavan or Navan?

The choice of Cavan Town's Main Street for a Woolworth opening in 1955 has a curious tale attached.[30] Their arrival here, it is believed, came about because of a simple enough mistake. Some time after 1946, a person in London's Executive Office with scant knowledge of Irish geography had misread, mistyped or in some other way mixed-up the name of Cavan with that of Navan. The suitability of the latter town for a new store was clear. Navan lay on one of the major routes north out of Dublin. Although of comparable size to Cavan Town in terms of population (both carried in or around only 4,000 people), Navan enjoyed being in the middle of a rich belt of farming land and was not too far from two other thriving stores, in County Louth, Dundalk and Drogheda. A new Woolworth outlet in Mullingar, opened two years earlier, was also conveniently close. By contrast, Cavan Town was relatively isolated and was surrounded by a depressed area where farms were small and the land of indifferent quality. No one ever found out who was to blame and the error remained undetected until someone asked why tradesmen from Mullingar were being used for the work on the new store in Cavan, fifty miles away? By then it was too late.

The Woolworth branch in Cavan Town opened on 27 May 1955 and the store here went on to serve the town well for the next thirty years. Steady business was conducted, possibly better than expected, and in due course all traces of this little piece of corporate embarrassment was buried. However, there is a parallel factor that cannot be ignored. This is the reality of life in the border counties. It may be held that, in trading terms, there were three Irelands being operated in cooperative coexistence; the South, the North and that swathe of territory from east to west known as 'the Border'. Movement of goods and money in this area was known to be fluid. Economic anomalies existed that could be exploited by the people and the businesses in the region.

A Boon to Small Manufacturing Plants

What may be seen as strikingly significant about the arrival of the fifteen additional Woolworth outlets in the five-year period following 1950 is that, unlike the panic that spread through market towns in the 1930s some twenty years earlier, there were no slashing of prices, fire sales or concerted efforts by rivals to 'match' what Woolworth had to offer. By then, the chain stores had earned a special niche within local arenas that gave room for comfortable coexistence with the more established traders in main shopping streets. This became especially so when increasing numbers of small factories and workshops gained contracts to supply Woolworth with goods under the 'export' licence system. Having this steady and reliable market for their goods undoubtedly increased employment in several Irish provincial towns and cities which had no previous long-term history of manufacturing, and the press coverage of openings very often pointed out the 'high proportion' of Irish-made merchandise being carried. In Mullingar, for example, the writer of the publicity article on its opening day had stressed that 70 per cent of the goods sold by the new store were Irish-made.[31]

For Irish manufacturers, the support received from the Republic's Department of Industry and Commerce was crucial. By 1955 the Irish Industrial Directory list had grown to more than 3,000 firms, and many more thousands of products were now being made within the state.[32] Irish factories were now benefiting from a British 'Imperial Preference' concession, whereby tariffs on certain raw materials produced in Britain were not imposed. For example, the production of goods made from plastic was flourishing. This increasingly popular new material had emerged after the Second World War to replace items made from Bakelite. The Irish Industrial Directory for 1955 lists no less than seventeen headings related to the manufacture of plastic products, and many of the items were sold from Woolworth counters. These include household products and tableware, toilet articles, religious goods and electrical fittings.

Woolworth in Thomas Street

Not every newly opened store in Ireland in the 1950s proved to be a subsequently runaway success. The location of a third Dublin store in a rundown area of the city centre was later seen as having been a bad decision. In times gone by, when Woolworth sought to expand into a new area, the procedure was to negotiate for only the best and most sought-after high street site. By mid-century the British chain had already acquired and occupied most of these prime locations and the policy now being embarked upon was to open new branches in less prestigious shopping areas. Side streets and areas peripheral to a town centre, or in the suburbs of cities and towns, were now considered acceptable. Those in favour of this strategy argued that if the Woolworth Company was to continue to grow and if prime sites were hard to find, then they had no option but to go 'down market' in the search for premises. It was to their advantage that lower-grade sites were cheaper to buy and owners were happy to enter into the security of long leases with a firm as solid as Woolworth. Since the retirement of Stephenson's strong leadership, the men who made decisions at board level had to contend with conditions that were very different to the pre-war era. Most of the directors were due for retirement in the 1950s, and by their own admission, they were not too worried if radical changes in strategy brought about a few mistakes.[33] It would be the next generation who would have the responsibility of keeping the profitability of the business on course. Greater emphasis was being put on fiscal matters and the voices of the company's accountants were now more often heard and more acted upon in the boardroom than the opinions of the company's buyers or managers. However, senior men among the management ranks were uneasy at the signs of new policies. They still believed that a top-class location reflected status. It also mirrored the high standard of merchandise stocked. They put their faith in stores that were surrounded by other retailers of equal reputation for efficiency and style because this spread the message that Woolworth counters offered similar but more affordable quality.

When the Woolworth Company's real estate executives from London chose to locate a new store in Dublin's run-down Thomas Street, several of Dublin's senior men advised caution. It was, at best, a risk-taking move. The new site was undoubtedly a low-cost acquirement and there may well have been rumours the authorities in Dublin City Council had plans to undertake major work to upgrade and reinstate the status of the area. But could anyone say for sure when this urban renewal programme was likely to begin? Surrounded by decay and poverty, a new store here would have a struggle to survive, warned the Dublin men.

Nonetheless, the project went ahead. The premises had been a pair of tenement houses up to 1940. A building here had then been occupied and used for five years by the Bloomfield Laundry, but since their departure, in 1945, it had lain vacant for almost ten years. When Woolworth took over the site in 1953, what was left of the laundry premises was completely demolished and replaced by one of the firm's ultra-modern post-war design structures. Surveyed thirty years later as part of an architectural street study in 1986, the verdict of the survey team deemed it 'built in an aggressive style, although the scale of the street was maintained'.[34]

The Thomas Street store opened for business on 27 May 1954. From the start, the premises were under siege from some of the roughest elements of Dublin citizenry. It was sited in the middle of a street on which many of the neighbouring shops stood derelict and boarded up. Hoardings on either side masked its two adjoining sites, where ruined buildings had been abandoned or demolished. Apart from the stalls of street traders who filled the area with noise and colour once a week, the only signs of activity in the street were the comings and goings of unemployed men attending a nearby local labour exchange. The Thomas Street store soon gained the dubious, albeit probably

Figure 45. The Woolworth branch in Dublin's Thomas Street,
which was opened on 27 May 1954.

Photograph: © RTÉ Stills Library.

exaggerated, reputation of being broken into every night; and would-be
assailants did not confine themselves to darkness, either. The story is told how
one manager here was once strongly upbraided by a seriously annoyed visiting
superintendent who had spotted some men engaged in work on the outside
wall overlooking the vacant site. A major breach of rules had occurred. He
reminded the young manager that any major repairs had to be submitted for
the senior man's approval before going ahead. Explanation was needed.
Mystified by the ticking off, the manager went outside to take a look. By
then, the busy but uninvited 'workmen' who had gained access across the
adjoining empty site had already spirited away a large section of the outer
skin of bricks from his exposed side wall.[35]

Faced with daylight robbery of this nature, the ultimate fate for a store like
Thomas Street was not hard to predict. The store was one of the first casualties
to be closed down during rationalization in the mid 1970s.

Alternative to a Mouse Trap

For the average Irish shopper in the 1950s, memories of the 'best buys' on Woolworth counters rotate around the sweet and biscuit counters, the soft ice cream, the cosmetics and the toys. Some unexpected and bizarre recollections can now reflect household practices that are long gone. One elderly lady remembers how her mother bought the Woolworth range of cheap eau de cologne to use as a mouse repellent! A small amount of the liquid would be set on fire in an old metal saucepan on the kitchen hearth of their inner-city Dublin home before the household retired to bed. The pungent scent of the defused cologne, described by the teller more colourfully as 'the stink', repulsed any rodents on the prowl that night. Having to keep mice and rats at bay in old houses was a fact of life in those days.[36]

The same large bottles of cheap eau de cologne were also sold in great quantities in the city of Cork. As one former counter assistant recalls, 'We often suspected they were being bought by the men who came up from the docks. We had a lot of rough-looking foreign sailors, deckhands or whatever coming into the store. We wondered could they be drinking it? It was very cheap'.[37] On the other hand, perhaps they were merely seeking to get rid of ocean-going rodents.

Clearly, not everything on a Woolworth counter came to be used for the purpose for which it was intended. In later years, one former staff supervisor remembers reporting one unusual and puzzling situation to her manager when a brand of cleaner for suede shoes suddenly started to sell in unbelievably large quantities. Day after day, the counter in front of her was being cleared of stock. She was instructed to keep a careful watch and it did not take too long to discover there was a problem. The range was promptly withdrawn; local schoolchildren were buying up this cleaning fluid to use in orgies of 'glue-sniffing'.[38]

Everyday Life in the early 1950s: England v. Ireland

In respect of the ranges of goods that were available for sale from Woolworth counters in Ireland, these had quickly returned to normal after the wartime 'Emergency' years. By contrast, life for shoppers across the water had remained grim. The British government's drive to improve the economic crisis by concentrating on exports meant that availability of the most ordinary items for personal or household use was still heavily restricted. Shortages ensured that wartime queues remained. On 25 November 1950 a crowd of 10,000 queued overnight for the reopening of a war-damaged Woolworth store in Plymouth, in the south of England. What these customers sought to purchase in order of priority were: a prized pair of nylons, a can of tinned fruit or some crockery. All were scarce luxury items. When the doors opened at 10 o'clock, the first eighteen to enter were rewarded for their vigil with two pairs of nylons and a half-tea set. By the afternoon the queue still reached around the corner into the next street.[39]

In Ireland, shortages on this scale did not exist and the counters of Woolworth stores were full of merchandise. One former manager remembers how an English visitor in the early 1950s was awestruck by a huge display of Cadbury's chocolate bars on one of the sweet counters in his store. The holidaymaker wondered if it was possible to buy a bar without a ration coupon? He was told that no coupons at all were needed. His next question was even more tentative. 'Do you think I might be let have two bars?' The reply had puzzled the sales assistant. She told him he could buy as many as he liked. There was no restriction. The customer immediately left the store only to return shortly with a suitcase, which he filled to the top.[40]

Equally as popular and profitable as the confectionery counters, the Woolworth Toilet Goods department in all outlets carried a huge range of Hollywood-style cosmetics. Styles had changed little from the wartime emphasis on bright lipstick colours, mascara and permanently waved hair, and the home perm kits that had gone on trial in 1949 had proved successful. Meanwhile, on the drapery counters, luxury items such as nylons, which were by now being manufactured by several Irish firms, were plentiful.

Serious shopping trips for leisure or entertainment were to the major city centres, such as Dublin, Belfast, Cork and Limerick, where stores had large music departments. Among the most pleasant memories of this era is the popularity of sales of sheet piano music. Customers who went into the Woolworth store in Dublin's Henry Street could ask for a piece of music to be played by Peggy Dell, a well-known and popular pianist, who performed on the baby grand piano that was installed on the mezzanine floor.[41] At this time almost every home still had an upright piano in the 'front room' or parlour, and a 'musical evening' of party-pieces and sing-songs for friends and family continued to be popular entertainment long after it had gone out of fashion in the United Kingdom.

Since the late 1940s there had been greater emphasis on entertainment provided by radio programmes and gramophone records. (Television was not to arrive until New Year's Eve 1961.) Meanwhile, whilst sophisticated radiograms that played LP records were slowly making an appearance, the popularity of portable 'wind-up' or electric gramophone record players remained high. Recording artists were often also film stars or radio stars, and Woolworth had reintroduced sales of popular records in the early 1950s. Stores could now have an electric gramophone installed on a sales counter so that customers could request to have a record played before purchasing. Later, some of the larger stores installed listening booths. One ex-employee recalls the immense power wielded by the record counter sales assistant who operated the gramophone. 'She had her personal favourite records and played these over and over all day long until we (the rest of the staff) were sick of hearing them.'[42]

Working for Woolworth as a shop assistant continued to be regarded as a glamorous and desirable job for a girl well into the post-war years. Film magazines were a popular selling line, and the cosmetics counters were full of brands of lipsticks, mascara and face powder that reflected associations with the Hollywood film world of make-believe. In 1957, when screen actress Virginia McKenna starred in the Rank Organization film, *Carve Her Name with Pride*, the role re-enacted the life of an ordinary Woolworth girl recruited by the French Resistance to work behind enemy lines in World War Two. The storyline was authentic. Thousands of Woolworth sales assistants were thrilled by the scenes which depicted this film star serving customers from behind a faithfully replicated Woolworth counter. When the film was issued, several illustrations appeared in the Woolworth staff journal.[43]

In the 1950s the ownership of a private car was still a relatively rare luxury for many urban-based Irish people, and long before the advent of garden centres, which catered for car-driving customers, keen gardeners liked to patronize their local town's Woolworth store to buy spring bulbs, seeds and bedding plants. Each branch's horticulture counter was one of the few departments for which the company allowed a manager to buy in stock directly from a local supplier. An arrangement with a nearby plant nursery or seedsman for seasonal items on a year-round basis would be set up and, from time to time, a Woolworth store would sponsor local competitions or events aimed at encouraging gardening pursuits. For many years, a Woolworth Cup for the best vegetable garden was presented to winners in the Dublin Garden and Window-Box Guild and National Garden Guild competitions.[44]

A horticultural department in the 1950s offered shoppers several new ranges of goods including the latest pest control DDT and other emerging chemical fertilizers, while hosepipes, buckets and other equipment were now

Figure 46. Virginia McKenna in the 1957 feature film *Carve Her Name with Pride* (Rank Organisation), was publicized in the Woolworth house journal.

Courtesy 3^D and 6^D Pictures Ltd.

being made of this new material called *plastic*. However, all in all, apart from other goods that used synthetic materials in their manufacture, the merchandise carried by Woolworth stores in the south of Ireland in the 1950s had changed little in style from what was being sold in the 1930s. There was still a marked contrast, however, between the ranges and brands of goods sold by Woolworth on either side of the border. Not only were there different suppliers, but emphasis had shifted considerably. Northern stores had always carried a greater range of grocery items and they were now poised to move forward in this direction to a much greater extent.

Having Political Pull to get a Job in Woolworth

A decade of the post-Emergency years saw the number of Woolworth outlets in the whole of Ireland approaching thirty-five stores. These stores created a fresh influx of locally recruited Irish management 'learners', and many of the young men who started off their career within the Woolworth Company at this time were to go on to reshape Ireland's retail business world, either within the Woolworth Company, in business on their own account or as an employee of one of the powerful competitors that were to emerge in the coming decade. To have achieved a foothold on the Woolworth career ladder was still held up as a desirable position within Ireland's commercial world in the mid 1950s, and there were many instances of strings being pulled to get a promising youngster accepted as a trainee. The late Pat Quinn, of Quinnsworth fame, liked to recall that he 'got into Woolworth' as a stockroom boy because of his family's long friendship with Éamon de Valera.[45] When asked for help, 'Dev' obligingly wrote in to the Woolworth Company. This letter may have gone to the Dublin Office, to the manager of the Dublin store in Henry Street or even into the Limerick branch, which had a reputation of having the best networking system. The request was responded to positively. The ambitious youngster was given a job and Quinn worked his way through the various stages of training in several branches, including Limerick and Dublin, until he was promoted to the post of deputy manager of the Galway branch in 1957. A short time afterwards, driven by an entrepreneurial streak that could not be contained any longer, he left for Canada. Quinn's training in Woolworth stood him in good stead. He built on the Woolworth experience to learn more about how the grocery trade worked in North America. On his return, he set up his own firm, Quinnsworth. It soon became a formidable player in the battle that was to begin between Ireland's retail supermarkets.

The Distraction of a New Horizon for London Executives

Although it made no impact on developments in Ireland, the focus of London's executives had become distracted in the 1950s by the rather more exotic possibility of establishing a Woolworth presence in a number of Commonwealth countries. It could be speculated that the advantage of having a separate import/export office in the Republic of Ireland in the post-war years may have prompted the investigation of similar advantages elsewhere. But notwithstanding the reasoning that lay behind their decision, the establishment of several overseas branches in the British colonies went ahead with a great deal of enthusiasm. They commenced with a store in Kingston, Jamaica, in 1954 and in the following year an outlet on the island of Trinidad was opened. For legal reasons, separate subsidiary firms were registered: F.W.

Figure 47. A staff charity event, 1957, organized by the deputy manager
of the Galway branch, the late Pat Quinn (front row).

Courtesy Peter Carr.

Woolworth & Co. (Trinidad) Ltd and F.W. Woolworth & Co. (Jamaica) Ltd.
In 1956 the company opened stores in Barbados. The subsidiaries went on to
expand for another twenty years, in Jamaica, Trinidad and Barbados.
Woolworth also opened in Salisbury, Rhodesia (known today as Harare,
Zimbabwe), in 1958, and six years later a second store was built in Bulawayo.[46]

Irish stores and personnel were unaffected by the overseas expansion
strategy, although during the setting-up period, one of the brightest up-and-
coming trainee managers from Ireland was selected by Executive Office to
take a post abroad. He can now recall his dismay at receiving instructions out
of the blue to get himself a thorough health check, some 'shots' for yellow
fever and a suit of tropical gear, because he was being sent out to Africa to
open and manage a store there in two weeks' time.[47] It was not to be, however.
When his boss learned he was on the point of getting married, the enforced
deportation order was swiftly withdrawn. Only single men were suitable for
posting abroad. Apparently, the company wanted no one out in foreign parts
who was encumbered by a wife or a family.

The overseas adventure was interesting but not sustainable in the end. Within a decade, the tide had turned in Africa and sweeping changes were on the way. Woolworth subsequently sold out all their overseas subsidiaries during periods of rationalization from 1987 to 1990.

Fifty Years Old and Never Had It So Good

Events in London held the key to what lay ahead. Celebration of the British Woolwoth Company's golden jubilee took place in 1959. The directors were determined to make the most of the firm's fiftieth birthday and an elaborate convention was hosted in London for all management personnel. It was the British company's first ever gathering of this nature. Over 1,300 delegates and guests attended, and the speeches were both nostalgic and rallying. The latter rhetoric reveals how the company saw itself at this pivotal moment in time. Executive Office was in a self-congratulatory mood. Throughout the day's proceedings a number of directors and buyers aired their views on past successes and future plans. With the gloom of the difficult post-war years now lifted, the fortunes of the Woolworth Company looked bright. The firm now conducted its business from more than 1,000 stores; there were 25,000 items on the stock lists, none of which was priced over £5 10s.[48] Moreover, some of the addresses confirmed that many of the old basic tenets had not yet vanished. As one speaker put it: 'A District Manager can be likened to the father of a great and growing family. As new stores are opened each year, I can assure you that they do take a fatherly interest in the welfare and progress of all staff in their Districts.'[49] Yet behind the scenes, there were others who would not agree with such altruistic sentiments; who recognized that the paternalistic management style and high ethical standards that heretofore had sustained the ethos of the company were on the way out. In a break with tradition, the current chairman and managing director of the British company had neither started his career on the shop floor nor gained experience through the usual retail management rankings. Recruited into the Liverpool District Office thirty or so years earlier as an accountant, he had been transferred to Executive Office in this role after the war and, more recently, had become the company's secretary. His expertise was centred on finance, not on the skills of clever shopkeeping and customer care. A new era was on its way. Already the message had filtered through to a few fellow directors. One board member told the assembled audience: 'We may talk of the Art of Salesmanship [but] we are not in business to express our creative personalities or to uplift the cultural standards of the public. To be quite frank, we're in the business to make money for F.W. Woolworth and Co. Limited.'[50]

The convention's delegation from Ireland included all the current store managers or manageresses plus a future incumbent of a new branch in Northern Ireland to be launched later that year. They were accompanied by several of their retired colleagues and a number of influential people from Liverpool District Office who had started their careers as trainees in Ireland and progressed through the management promotion system to reach positions of authority.[51] One of the last survivors from the earliest days of the company's arrival in 1909, the former executive buyer for china and glass, now living in retirement in Ireland, Charles McCarthy (Mac), was also in attendance. Notably, the delegates from branches in Thurles, Ballina, Omagh, Tipperary, Killarney and Cavan were all female. This, in itself, was exceptional. Women holding any form of senior management role in Ireland were almost unheard of and it should be explained that the appointment of a manageress was usually reserved for smaller stores that might be thriving and profitable, but with little potential for expansion. As was normal practice in those days, these ladies were employed on a different basic salary base and, although given a bonus on results, they did not enjoy the normal contractual arrangements or career prospects held by their male counterparts.[52] Promotion to the post of superintendent was not an option open to them because the company still did not deem it appropriate that female employees be subjected to the stresses and inconvenience of constant travel. However, as analysis of the attendees at this convention shows, it is remarkable to discover that the percentage of women at this level of store management in Ireland was considerably higher in proportion to that found across the remainder of the chain in the United Kingdom. In 1959 only 29 (or just under 3 per cent) of the company's 978 stores in England, Scotland and Wales were being run by women.[53] By contrast, the 36 Irish branches included 6 outlets with a manageresses at the helm (or around 17 per cent). This would seem quite remarkable.

Another notable feature of the convention, which drew comment during the proceedings, was how very few of the company's retired personnel were still around to enjoy the occasion.[54] Even the retired long-serving chairman, William L. Stephenson, who had just turned 70, was missing because of serious illness, and only a handful of the men he had recruited in the early 1920s had lived much beyond the retirement age of 60. By 1959 the dangers to health brought about by constant stress and over-rigid disciplinarian regimes was starting to be recognized, however, and it was know to all in that assembly that a successful career within Woolworth revolved around a tightly prioritized schedule of work and responsibility which carried high levels of stress. In the old days, successful careers depended on a man's performance in serving the company, their store or district, to which was added how he cared for the well-being of his staff. Personal family concerns and commitments had been barely tolerated by the men at the top in those days, and any other outside interests that might involve business contacts and friends had been actively discouraged or even seen as disloyal.

However, the Woolworth firm had gained fifty years of wisdom. The more senior colleagues, who had discussed this matter privately and frequently, were therefore not surprised to hear the chairman making a formal reference to this concern in his address to the assembly. Warming to his theme that not enough managers developed outside interests to which they could turn on retirement, he urged:

> Get yourselves on committees … join in your local activities. You must have diversion of thought and action away from your respon-sibilities in the Company, so that not only do you return to your store or office in the morning fresh to take up your work, but in your retirement you can develop these hobbies and enjoy your leisure. To be suddenly bereft of responsibilities and duties and to be without a hobby can be deadly…[55]

The 1959 Woolworth jubilee convention had been an extraordinary event, but despite the speeches and warm conviviality that had marked the day of celebration, the golden glow it had created did not have a happy ending. The highlight of the evening was to be the formal congratulations offered by the American parent company in the person of their president, Robert C. Kirkwood, who had travelled from New York to make a special address to the gathering. The relationship between the American parent company and their British subsidiary was a delicate balance of mutual respect and independent thinking. The parent company's greater shareholding allowed them complete control of their British subsidiary, should they care to use it, but since the early 1930s the New York Office had wisely left the British company largely to its own devices. By the end of the 1950s, however, a new regime was running the New York Office, and they were eager to prove themselves to be in the forefront of the most modern business strategies and methods. To their minds, many of the firm's traditional values and systems were outdated and would have to go. Their wish was to see American marketing techniques leading the way. The British company must follow suit.

When the company's president rose to his feet to speak, he was greeted with warm applause. He complimented the company on their golden jubilee and expressed admiration for the British board. He then went on to talk about the future. Adopting a low and serious tone, he began to outline the picture of a desperate struggle on the far side of the Atlantic.[56] Changed shopping habits in the United States and ferocious competition had cut their gross margins to the bone. To combat this threat, the American board had spent $320 million on capital improvements. As a result, half of all the shop floors in their stores were by now switched over to a completely new layout system to provide shoppers with self-service. They had started to open many more outlets in locations he called 'Malls'. If stores in the United Kingdom did not follow suit, he warned, the British company, too, would soon see profits slashed. An apocalypse loomed.

His audience was stunned. As the speaker wrapped up, a chilly silence fell across the room like a dead hand. His message had been clear. They must follow the American company's example to survive. Having urged them 'most earnestly' to 'take action as indicated', he was telling them to throw out Frank Woolworth's tried and tested formula and replace it with this new customer self-service idea.[57] When he sat down there was no applause. The golden bubble of celebration had burst.

For those in the audience, the gloomy prognosis was perplexing. They knew the British company had been skilled in creating a far more buoyant, cash-rich and successful business than the American operation, and it was no secret that, in percentage terms, the profits made by the London board of directors was far superior to the American parent company's returns on capital. So why would the American president want them to emulate the American retail system – and what did he mean by 'shopping malls'? Nobody in the room had ever heard of such things. It was a confused and deflated gathering that packed up to go home. A lot of puzzled managers would return to their stores in a much less confident mood. What now lay ahead?

The Irish contingent's reaction to the night's momentous speech is interesting to relate. For the more senior members of the group, warnings of difficult times ahead were nothing new. The Irish stores had already experienced years of strife. They had survived the Anglo-Irish War, civil war, the Economic War and the Second World War 'Emergency' years, and yet were still trading successfully. Several of them had taught the men at the top table the rudiments of the Woolworth business and were unimpressed by a long day of speech-making. One of the youngest managers brought over for the event still remembers how the evening ended. When the rest of the convention delegates had gone home, everyone from Ireland got together in one big group. 'We made a good night of it,' he recalls, 'and ended up having a sing-song.'[58]

Later that year, arrangements were made for every store in the chain to mark the fiftieth anniversary for more lowly levels of personnel in some special way. Most of the managers organized a special outing for their counter and stockroom staff. The girls from the store in Tipperary donned their summer finery one Sunday morning, gathered up husbands and boyfriends and went off for a day's outing to Ballybunion. Fifty years on, the occasion is still remembered by one of the 'girls': 'We worked as usual all day Saturday and went off in the coach first thing on Sunday morning. We were all back into the store as usual on Monday morning.'[59]

Figure 48. Staff from the Tipperary outlet take an outing to
Ballybunion to celebrate the 50th jubilee, in 1959.

Courtesy Alice Carroll.

Could Anyone Compete with Woolworth?

In the early 1950s the Woolworth Company's chain of 'variety stores' still had the field practically to itself in the Republic. Unlike the company's expansion into the high streets of England, Scotland and Wales, there had been no serious rivalry from other retail chains in Southern Ireland since 1914. No Penny Bazaars, Marks & Spencer, British Home Stores, Boots or others hoping to emulate the formula had appeared on Irish Main Streets. Admittedly, stores in Ulster had been challenged by the Moores of Enniskillen since the late 1930s, but the strongest competition from this firm's provocatively named Wellworths chain was yet to be faced down. These battles lay ahead.

It must be pointed out, nonetheless, that in the 1950s the overall standards of retailing in Ireland, especially in regard to shopfittings and layouts, were still at least thirty years behind America.[60] In particular, the grocery trade was poised for a huge shake-up. The next few years were to see a lot of fierce competition over price cutting and other issues between rivals in this sector, and it would not be long before the Woolworth presence in Ireland would find itself in the firing line. Battles were soon to be fought over the introduction of additional food items such as groceries, fruit, vegetables and supermarket-style sales floor layouts. Rough times lay ahead.

Embracing Self-Service Shopping

By mid 1959 the planned batch of new Woolworth outlets in Ireland had almost reached completion. Each branch was designed to be run in the style of their traditional store layout – unchanged since 1914. However, before the decade ended there was one more unit yet to open. This was located in Ulster, and it would be here that the company would introduce its version of self-service shopping to Ireland.

In post-war Britain the concept that shoppers could be persuaded to serve themselves to goods from aisles of open display shelving had been brought back from America by a grocer called Alan Sainsbury in 1949.[61] The following year his firm opened their first store using this system. In Ireland, however, a similar retailing concept had already been up and running on a small scale in a number of Payantake shops in Dublin since 1936. A young man called Eamonn Quinn, son of a Newry grocer, had seen the idea working in America, but on returning home to Ireland had been unable to persuade his father John to try out the idea in the family's Dublin shops.

Eamonn was determined to go ahead nonetheless, and the new Payantake shops, whilst not technically self-service, introduced Dublin customers to a cut-price form of grocery shopping that challenged the existing grocery retailers who continued to offer the more expensive credit and home delivery form of retailing. Eamonn and his brother Malachy Quinn had the backing of their father, John, and during the 1940s had built up a chain of Payantake outlets that were innovative and offered a lower cost form of retailing.

This family's enterprising streak was not to end here. By 1947 Eamonn Quinn had moved on from running a chain of self-service stores. With unerring instinct he had launched into another, equally novel experience by opening Ireland's first holiday camp in Red Island, Skerries, with the aim of encouraging more English and Scottish tourists to holiday in Ireland. Business circles in Dublin were small. There were very few players who did not know one another, either as mutual non-combatants or as adversaries. Informal consultation and advice was often exchanged and a fluid stream of practical assistance was always available for enterprising ventures that could contribute to the country's economic growth. It is worth noting that the Quinn family's penchant for innovative business moves lasted well into the next generation. Almost twenty-five years later, Eamonn's son, Feargal, set new standards with his successful Superquinn Supermarket chain.

In Britain, Alan Sainsbury's new style of retailing was swiftly copied by his competitors. Within five years, 2,500 self-service outlets had opened and by mid 1957 more than eighty supermarkets were up and running.[62] However, the British Woolworth Company's response to this challenge had been sluggish. Their own first self-service outlet in Cobham, Surrey, did not open until 1955, and as one of their executives admitted four years later, while 'self-service is the selling medium of the future … we have not proceeded as fast, or as far [to convert stores to this system] because of our inability to control the shrinkage figure within reasonable proportions'.[63] Devising new methods of stock management continued to be difficult to work out and refine. Consequently, by 1959 only 57 of the 1,014 F.W.Woolworth outlets had been converted to self-service stores, and these outlets were mainly concentrated in the south-east of England.

The challenge could not be held back, however. It was inevitable that the new style of retailing would have to be introduced into Irish stores, but it would need careful handling. The war years had seen many specific differences developing between the ranges of goods sold in Northern Ireland and those carried in their Republic of Ireland outlets. The citizens of the smaller but more densely populated and industrialized province of Ulster had grown used to shopping for a large number of packaged grocery items in their local Woolworth branches, and many of these ranges would transfer easily to a 'self-service' system. However, the Woolworth stores in the south of the country had always tried to avoid carrying grocery lines, especially in the market towns where family grocers, greengrocers and butchers thrived on a customer base reliant on the provision of credit. Most rural town's retail systems were firmly attuned to the seasonal ebb and flow of income generated by agricultural production. It would be almost a decade before Woolworth would risk introducing a cash-based self-service outlet to the Republic.

Other retailers in Ireland in the 1950s were not so cautious. The players in the grocery trade were keeping a close watch on the swiftly growing self-service and supermarket developments across the water. Taking their cue from the impact made on British household shopping habits by these changes, several independent Irish firms had already launched cash-only cost-cutting shops. An organization for independent grocers, RGDATA (Retail Family Grocers, Purveyors, Dairy Proprietors and Allied Traders), had been set up by a number of traders in 1942 with the aim to provide mutual support during the war years. They soon became a major national organization which by September 1949 could boast 5,602 members and eighty-nine branches nationwide.[64] Moves were soon underway to devise ways of facing down the possible threat of UK-based self-service and supermarket concerns moving to Ireland or, indeed, the expansion of similar enterprises by Irish firms.

Little documentation remains of some of the earlier innovative attempts to bring this new style of trading to other parts of Ireland. There was a small family grocer, originally from Leitrim, who fitted out his shop in Galway's Shop Street as a cut-price self-service market outlet called GTM. He pared down his margins to the minimum and shoppers throughout the west of Ireland flocked to his store. This style of trading was only to be found in Dublin at the time. However, this demonstration of entrepreneurship caused ructions among fellow traders and a bitterly fought price war ensued. The smaller man eventually gave up. It had been a brave try.[65]

Woolworth introduced its first self-service outlet in Ireland in the summer of 1959 and the province of Ulster was chosen for the launch. This new-style store opened in Newtownards on 28 August (see Appendix I, Table 5). The manager was a Dublin man, one of the bright post-war Irish trainees recruited by Dublin's Henry Street store in the early 1950s. His subsequent career would see him rise to the topmost senior management position in Ireland as head of the Dublin Buying Office.

Mindful of the unadventurous and conservative nature of Ireland's shopping public, who might need some explanation of self-service, the Newtownard's opening announcement advertisement offered 'speedy, convenient shopping' and also included the instruction to customers to 'Use our baskets and serve yourself'; 'pay as you leave – at one time – at our new speedy cash desks'. The local press was enthusiastic. Commenting on the variety of merchandise carried, it observed that those British manufacturers who had made the 'wise decision' in 1909 to become suppliers to the Woolworth Company had subsequently 'made big fortunes from small beginnings'. Quoting from PR material, the piece went on to note how Woolworth 'has dealt with 899 of its suppliers for more than 20 years, with more than 405 of them for more than 30 years, and with 113 for 40 to 50 years', ending with the observation that 'These figures speak for themselves.'[66]

Meanwhile, in the south of the country, competition was gearing up to this perceived new challenge to traditional main street shopping in Ireland. Within weeks of the Woolworth arrival in Newtownards, a flourishing Irish grocery chain, H. Williams, opened a 5,000 square-foot supermarket store directly facing the Woolworth flagship store in Dublin's Henry Street. This firm had previously attempted to open a fully self-service grocery store on the site in 1947, but their attempt to introduce the concept was too far ahead of its time and proved to be too novel for conservative-minded Dublin customers; Williams had been forced to revert to their regular counter service within a few months.

The reopening day of the Williams supermarket is still clearly recalled by a former Woolworth trainee. Flanked by his boss, who was an experienced and successful store manager, the learner had watched this demonstration of up-to-the-minute American-style competitiveness opening its doors across the street from the front entrance of the 76 Dublin store. He remembers being gripped by a sense of excitement by the event. Was this where the future lay in retailing? The Woolworth manager beside him had been ominously silent. As they turned to go back into the store, the older man delivered a confidently dismissive observation: 'It won't last,' he said, 'This supermarket idea is just a gimmick. Just a flash-in-the-pan! It won't ever amount to anything.'[67] The Dublin manager was not alone in taking this view. Everyone in the Woolworth Company from the chairman down to the newest recruit had come to the same conclusion. F.W. Woolworth & Co. Ltd was a household word; a well-established and successful operation. They believed the firm's dominant position in the marketplace was too entrenched and too powerful to be seriously challenged by an entirely different trading formula. Only a few recognized that the tide had turned.

Chapter 6
Head-to-Head Competition
1960–1969

Since their arrival in 1914, Ireland's chain of Woolworth Outlets had remained under the control of the Liverpool District Office. Regular inspections of all Irish stores, north and south, came under the responsibility of a single superintendent until the Second World War intervened. In the earliest decades the Woolworth Company required the Superintendent for Ireland to have his home base in Liverpool, so that he could attend district office meetings held every Monday. He would then catch the evening B&I (British & Irish Steam Packet Company) boat to Dublin. His family would not see him again until Saturday morning.

Ireland's neutral status during the Emergency brought about radical changes to this routine. Throughout the war years and for the following decade the supervision of the Ulster stores continued separately. By the 1960s another readjustment had become necessary. The number of Irish stores had been increased, and in order to even-up the amount that could be handled efficiently by one man, five east coast Irish stores were attached to the 'Cheshire' District, which was the area around Chester and north Wales. The superintendent here now had the responsibility of also overseeing the operation of Drogheda, Dundalk, Dun Laoghaire and two Dublin stores, Grafton Street and Thomas Street. The other east coast Woolworth branch, Ireland's flagship store in Henry Street, was not included; it qualified as one of the company's twenty or so elite 'superstores' which had a separately designated superintendent based in England. Meanwhile, while the remainder of the Irish outlets continued to be supervised by the superintendent for the Republic, the Woolworth branches closest to the border areas still formed a subtle, unofficial substrata, where managers might often make the most of all mercurial situations dictated by shifting tax regimes, shortages and surpluses.

Advertising is Something Entirely New

Since its foundation in 1909, apart from a press announcement for the opening of a new store or public-spirited displays giving sponsored help to town festivals or local charities, the Woolworth Company had traditionally eschewed other forms of media advertising. Policy dictated that a striking window display was sufficient to stimulate passing shoppers. To have a good knowledge of window-dressing techniques was part of a manager's training programme. Each store had a number of female sales assistants who acted as window trimmers under the manager's guidance, and the company encouraged a competitive spirit by giving prizes for displays that were particularly spectacular or imaginative. Photographs of prize-winning windows were then circulated for other stores to copy. Seasonal changes or special promotions were frequent, and it might be said that Woolworth windows became a colourful art form that enlivened every town's main shopping street. To have a full effect was dependent on having a prime position on a well-thronged thoroughfare, however. Even the most excellent display could not increase footfall in the same way as a striking advertisement in a widely distributed local paper.

The first cracks in entrenched principles appeared during the 1959 jubilee convention, when one of the directors indicated that the London board's old-fashioned 'no advertising' policy was about to be scrapped. This speaker reminded his audience: 'Advertising for the Company is something entirely new ... as an institution in this country we believed we did not need to tell the mass of the British public about Woolworth's and were content to let our values, our variety and our displays more or less speak for themselves'.[1] He then went on to announce to the assembly that things were about to change. A launch of special bargain lines for customers to celebrate the fiftieth jubilee was to be backed up by a national advertising campaign called 'Walk into Woolworths'. Advertising spreads would appear in Sunday newspapers, supported by 'a TV film on all stations'. The production and costs had been covered by the American Woolworth Company as a 'fiftieth birthday present' and might be seen as marking the British company's first move into modernity.

However, it would seem that this initiative sparked very little enthusiasm from the men at the top. A few concessions over press advertising during the autumn and Christmas seasons were introduced, especially in places where local rivals were considered more than usually strident. As for the concept of running nationwide TV campaigns in the United Kingdom, more than a decade was to pass before this idea was to be fully embraced.

The Trend to Sell Food

Meanwhile, in Ireland as well as elsewhere in the chain, competition from a number of emerging supermarket chains had gathered momentum. These rivals concentrated on food sales. They also advertised regularly in local press outlets.

For some time, all the Woolworth stores in the United Kingdom had countered the supermarket competition by expanding existing ranges of groceries, frozen food, fresh fruit and vegetables. For Irish branches in the south of Ireland, this was not a viable option. Woolworth outlets in the Republic had always considered their main competitors to be a town's drapers, stationers and hardware merchants, together with chemists, sweet shops and record and music stores. No branch had ever set itself up in direct competition to a market town's grocers, butchers or greengrocers. For at least three decades, a trading niche for everyone had been developed that allowed for a comfortable balance of commercial interests. By contrast, Woolworth stores in the more tightly urbanized Province of Ulster had always stocked substantial amounts of groceries, vegetables or meat products. As the 1960s advanced, they were therefore well placed to follow trends in British stores. It is likely that the Woolworth buyers in London may have entertained a misguided expectation that Irish stores in every part of Ireland would be just as successful in following their example. It would not be so.

Irish Grocers go into Battle

The struggle for supremacy among grocers in the Republic was already well underway and gathering momentum when the H. Williams branch in Henry Street, Dublin made their second attempt, this time successfully, to switch to a supermarket format in 1959. Almost twelve months later, in November 1960, a similar style store was opened in Dundalk by a young Feargal Quinn. In the same way that many of the young Irish trainees in Woolworth had benefited from childhood formative years dominated by a shopkeeping family lifestyle, this independent-minded entrepreneur had all the advantages that could be drawn from an experienced family business background. Hugh Oram tells how, in 1968, Feargal's father, Eamonn, liked to claim that 'his late father, John, and himself and his son Feargal between them had nearly 100 years in the grocery business'.[2] Known at first simply as Quinn's Supermarket, it would later be renamed Superquinn.

The 1960s witnessed many more similar changes taking place in Ireland's retail grocery trade. A Five Star supermarket had begun operating in Limerick, and a Cork-based wholesale firm, Musgrave Brothers, had set up Ireland's first cash-and-carry wholesale warehouse. This enterprise has been described as a revolutionary concept that allowed independent small retailers to overcome delivery costs from individual suppliers by collecting stock as needed from a central warehouse.[3] Musgrave went on to found their own franchise chain, which traded under the VG symbol group. Other wholesalers were quick to follow suit. The Dutch-based Spar franchise operation was introduced into Ireland in 1963 by Dublin wholesaler AWL (Amalgamated Wholesalers Ltd) and Cork wholesaler MUM (Munster United Merchants). In 1966 Mangan Brothers acquired the Mace franchise and, very much later, ADM (Allied Dublin Merchants) secured the Londis franchise in 1970.[4]

The Dunnes stores chain, founded in Cork in 1944 and already in Dublin since 1957, had moved far beyond their drapery base by 1965. Their venture into selling mainstream groceries was flourishing while in Northern Ireland the ubiquitous and increasingly powerful Enniskillen-based Wellworths was getting ready to launch a far more serious challenge.

Throughout the 1960s and later, the Republic's self-service stores and supermarkets fought it out amongst themselves. In due course, serious casualties were caused within many former family-owned grocery firms. Tony Parker, in his chapter entitled 'The Changing Nature of Irish Retailing' in *Ireland: A Contemporary Geographical Perspective*, points out that 'In the Republic there was a 35 per cent decline in grocery outlets between 1966–1977, while in Northern Ireland there was a 27 per cent decrease between 1965 and 1975'.[5]

Woolworth goes ahead with Refurbishments and new Openings

Despite evidence of increasingly frenetic activity within the retail grocery trade throughout the whole of Ireland, the board of F. W. Woolworth & Co. Ltd remained relatively unworried. It may have been felt that the company's position in Ireland was secure. Woolworth was the most widely distributed and well-established chain of variety stores and there was no serious competitor. The population of towns and cities in the Republic had remained either stagnant or in decline, so there was no need for any increase in the number of stores in the south. If there was to be any further expansion, the built-up urban areas around Belfast held more promise. Consequently, some new outlets in Ulster were planned and, in the meantime, all that was needed in the Republic was some refurbishment and improvements to the older branches.

Figure 49. Limerick's Woolworth store gets a new look in 1963.

Courtesy Sean Curtin, Limerick, A Stroll Down Memory Lane.

In 1963 the Limerick store received a complete facelift while still keeping its doors open for business. Previewing the formal reopening on 5 April with a salvo of publicity, the press wrote: 'The whole world is Woolworth's customer and Limerick people are no different from their counterparts anywhere else; they stop, they go in, they wander around; then buy.'[6] The writer goes on to comment on the type of customers passing through its doors, observing that

> Within an hour or two, the furs of distinguished lineage rubs shoulders with the plainest of cloth coats. The plain cloth coat may spend 10/-d, the splendidly-bred mink a mere 6d; it is all one to Woolworth's, and all part of a policy based on value for money; no matter how much of it you have or how little.[7]

Worth noting, too, is the immense change of attitude towards the source of merchandise, which is reflected in a second article on the next page: 'in the Irish Woolworth's there are goods which came from all over the world. For all this, however, we hear that a very high percentage of sales are registered on goods bought in this country, so that, in fact, the public has the best from every part of the world.'[8]

Shopping in a Woolworth store in the 1960s was done for pleasure as much as for economy. It was a world away from the mundane business of buying basic foodstuffs or day-to-day necessities and this would hold true for the future. When supermarkets eventually lost their novelty, the weekly loading up of a car-full of groceries would become a dreary chore. A visit to a Woolworth store was never that; the counters still offered small indulgences at modest prices.

Although no longer lambasted for selling 'foreign' goods, by the end of 1963 Woolworth managers in the Republic had to face into a new problem. Despite enormous levels of protest from retailers in the Republic, the Irish government had announced the imposition of a Turnover Tax on Sales (later to become VAT or Value Added Tax). Its introduction was very unpopular and the legislation only scraped through the Dáil with a majority of one vote. The Turnover Tax came into force in November. All retailers with a monthly turnover in excess of £750 a month had to register. Its implementation had been intended to assist the Irish application to membership of the European Economic Community (now the EC), but when the British membership was vetoed by President De Gaulle that same month, Ireland's entry was also blocked.[9] However, the new Sales Tax was retained.

Figure 50. A familiar appearance is retained on the shop floor
after refurbishment, Limerick, 1963.

Courtesy Sean Curtin, Limerick, A Stroll Down Memory Lane.

This tax impacted on F. W. Woolworth & Co. Ltd in two ways. On the one hand, for shoppers in the border areas it encouraged them to take advantage of the cheaper prices to be had in the Ulster stores. This brought about a boost to their sales. On the other hand, the situation brought about a reduction of turnover in those few stores lying on the Republic's side of the border. In the meantime, tax or no tax, local access to 400 unauthorized crossing points ensured that goods in demand continued to move back and forth at will.

In the United Kingdom, a programme of modernization was accelerating the switch from counter service to self-service stores. There were confident expectations that this strategy would eventually pay off. Many additional ranges of groceries were being carried in the English, Scottish and Welsh branches, and there had been a push to increase drapery and electrical goods. The Woolworth intention to improve their presence in Northern Ireland commenced with the opening of a new self-service store in Dungannon on 8 November 1962 (see Appendix I, Table 5). This branch was the company's 1,068th outlet in a chain that now stretched from the far north of Scotland to the southernmost counties of England and Ireland. The newly built premises replaced Matt Johnson's hardware store in Scotch Street, Dungannon, County Tyrone, and the event was conducted with the usual flourish of publicity.

The local *Courier and News* carried two full-page spreads of advertising with photographs emphasizing the ranges of grocery and frozen foods being stocked. Clearly, in this store, the policy of placing importance on the sale of foodstuffs was being pursued to the full. A specially written feature highlighted the optimistic views of the chairman of Dungannon Urban Council in regard to the district's increasing industry and population.[10] The main building contractors and suppliers were all Ulster firms. Light engineering, plastering and granolithic contractors, electrical, brick, sand and gravel merchants, timber merchants and fuel oil and interior decorators took large and splendidly supportive advertising, which was only marred by the unfortunate and embarrassing blip made by a firm of plumbers who announced their work had been carried out for the closely named rival Wellworths. Did any of the local shoppers notice the gaffe? Probably not.

The Dungannon's *Courier and News* sales team had also made good use of a call for improved car-parking facilities in Scotch Street, with a headline 'Traders aim to make Scotch Street the Shopping Centre' on the following page.[11] This gave them the opportunity to sell a lot of additional advertising to a number of small firms who offered items in competition with many Woolworth ranges. Urging Dungannon shoppers to 'let our experience be your guide', these rivals promised 'keenest prices' or 'unrivalled value'. Significantly, the reaction of established traders here was rather more strident than had been seen throughout the 1950s in the Republic. The appearance of a Woolworth branch in Dungannon was giving the business community a good shaking up. Moreover, when the next new Woolworth branch opening came about, two years later in Banbridge, County Down, major competition from the Moore Brothers' Wellworths was waiting with rather more serious intent. These big guns would be primed and ready for action. Woolworth would need to be well prepared.

The Woolworth Company's impressive new premises at 33–39 Newry Street, Banbridge commenced trading on 30 July 1965. Whether by design or accident, the Woolworth strategy was not confined to a preliminary announcement in the press either prior to, or on the day of, its opening. Instead, the advertising took the form of a slow but striking 'drip–drip' of news, which was staggered across three following weeks of half-page features in the *Banbridge Chronicle*.[12] The first notice, one week later, on 6 August, carried the building contractors' congratulations. Everything possible had been supplied by local building suppliers. The next appearance, a week later on 13 August, was a half-page advertisement carrying the formal announcement that F. W. Woolworth & Co. Ltd were 'Now Open – come and see for yourself the excellent range of special bargains'. Curiously, there was no immediate emphasis on the grocery department, but, instead, 'Extra Special Big Values in Toilet Goods'. Finally, on August 27, another half-page advertisement urged shoppers to 'note the address!', adding the slogan: 'Make the One and Only Woolworths Your New Shopping Centre'. In the list of twenty or so of their twenty-five departments, the 'Delicatessen and Big Value on All Foods' had been highlighted. No hint was given to competitors as to which departments would be carrying the best bargains. No prices were quoted. The focus was merely on generating increased footfall into the new store. Shoppers had to come and see for themselves. This tactic gave the Moore's Wellworths opposition very little leeway to mount any of their own 'special offers' in selected departments to lure customers from checking out what 'specials' might be found on Woolworth counters. It was a cat-and-mouse game.

It was not long before several other traders in Banbridge were also keen to challenge Woolworth. In mid September one of the neighbouring retailers in Newry Street, Finney's Fancy Goods Shop, concocted a snappy slogan, 'You'll Fare Better at Finney's', and mounted a one-week sale by advertising bargains in the *Banbridge Chronicle*. 'Cups, Saucers, Plates at a penny each and 10% off all other goods including jewellery, kitchen equipment, etc.'[13]

Finney's Fancy Goods Shop

SALE

Starting this Friday, 17th September for 1 Week including Sat., 25th Sept.

Cups, Saucers, Plates, at A PENNY each!

Special Value in Dinner Plates, Salad Plates, and all sorts of oddments; Big Reductions in Dinner Sets, Fruit Sets and Companion Sets

10⁰/₀ (2/- in the £) off all other goods including:

Costume Jewellery, Waterford Hand-Cut Crystal, and a wide range of beautiful Ornaments, Pictures, Kitchen Equipment, etc., etc.

"You'll Fare Better at Finney's"

S. FINNEY (BANBRIDGE) LTD.

Newry Street Phone 2210-2291 **Banbridge**

Figure 51. Finney's of Banbridge, advertisement, 1965.

Courtesy *Banbridge Chronicle*.

The Finney advertisement was a significant challenge, but the Woolworth manager was well positioned to return fire. The Woolworth marketing team had recently introduced an innovation. A new pricing system had been tried out which allowed managers who were facing serious new competition to offer a selection of products at very competitive prices. Used extensively in Banbridge as well as by the other Ulster stores under pressure from Wellworths' competition, these price-cutting campaigns were supported by eye-catching fluorescent signage, which was colourful and impressive.[14]

Within a week of Finney's salvo, the Banbridge manager was advertising a Woolworth autumn sale to run from 24 September to 2 October. The half-page notice in the *Banbridge Chronicle* listed their range of departments and reminded shoppers of the new mantra: 'Make the one and only Woolworths Your Shopping Centre'.[15] Meanwhile, the big guns, the Moore brothers' Wellworths Stores, remained silent, waiting for the most apt opportunity to begin a barrage.

MAKE THE ONE AND ONLY
W O O L W O R T H S
YOUR NEW SHOPPING CENTRE

Figure 52. The Woolworth Mantra.

Courtesy *Banbridge Chronicle.*

Two weeks later, on 8 October, the Moore brothers fired their first salvo. Their advert was headed 'Wellworths Announce an Autumn Sale for 8 days only – genuine saving', and the half-page layout detailed eighty-six special sale items in their grocery, drapery and household goods departments. Each one was priced to show the exact reduction being made.[16] Shoppers were told, 'A visit to the sale will repay you – see windows'. And, when the Christmas season arrived, the Moores sneakily pre-empted the arrival of Santa Claus to Woolworth by advertising, on 3 December, that he was already installed in their Wellworths store down the street surrounded by 'bumper parcels for 2/-d and 1/-d'.[17]

Figure 53. Rival Wellworths advertises the arrival of Santa in 1965.

Courtesy *Banbridge Chronicle*.

Throughout the Province, Wellworth's advertising campaigns were relentless and effective. For the first time ever in Ireland, Woolworth managers were feeling it increasingly difficult to hold their own against a competitor. The Moores had cannily acquired some of the largest and most prestigious sites in Ulster towns, and, for the most part, their sites were superior to anything the Woolworth real estate team was able to negotiate. The Moores' stores were usually more spacious and better located to attract passing trade. Their floor layouts made clever use of space, and they displayed all their food at the very back of the shop floors, which meant customers always had to pass through tempting arrays of other merchandise en route to buying groceries.[18]

A Corporate Identity Programme: Out with the Old and In with the New

The 1960s brought other radical changes to F. W. Woolworth & Co. Ltd. Ever since the warning issued by the company's American president at the fiftieth jubilee convention, the British board had been coming under increasing pressure from the New York-based parent company to make use of American-style marketing techniques. A new image was needed to match the self-service style of selling and they were urged to seek the advice of marketing consultants, whom Seaton calls 'the brand gurus, who argued that a widely recognized own-brand was a must-have for every retailer'.[19] On their recommendation, the British company chose the name 'Winfield' – taken from the founder's largely unknown and unrecognizable middle initial – the *W* in the half-century-old, widely familiar F. W. Woolworth & Co. Ltd.

The Woolworth Winfield brand was finally launched in 1963. One of the company's own in-house pieces of literature later explained to its employees how

> the new Winfield symbol ... has been designed as part of a corporate identity programme, and its use in packaging, décor stationery, wrappings etc. will assist in creating a new positive identity for the Woolworth Company and for the Winfield brand name, which can only be used on top quality exclusive Woolworth merchandise.[20]

Selling this idea to shoppers was not without its difficulties. Seaton comments how 'Customers struggled to understand the concept of Weedkiller and Sherry or Talcum Powder and Ant Powder with the same brand name'.[21] Indeed, this is an important point, which may be seen in hindsight as a grave oversight on the part of the 'experts' advising the company, and one has to wonder at the extent and results of the market research carried out prior to its launch. Irish shoppers at this point in time would have been even more puzzled, because they were unaccustomed to the idea of an 'own brand'. The Irish Dunnes Stores' St Bernard range, launched seven years earlier in 1956, was still in its infancy and confined to clothing labels. Firms like Marks & Spencer, which had used their own St Michael branding on merchandise for decades, were still not trading in the Republic (they did not arrive until 1979, another sixteen years hence), and it would be almost twenty years before competing supermarkets Superquinn and Quinnsworth adopted their own versions of 'own-brand' cut-price ranges, respectively Thrift and Yellow Pack, in 1981.[22]

Only a very small number of the Winfield-branded products were ever carried by the outlets in the Republic, and their performance would seem to have been unremarkable. Nonetheless, across the water, Winfield items filled Woolworth counters for the best part of the next two decades.

Success and Failure

1965 saw F. W. Woolworth & Co. Ltd making plans for an expansion in Dublin city centre. The negotiation for the purchase of one of the city's largest department stores, Pims of George's Street, had been completed by the end of the year, and by mid January 1966 planning permission was lodged for

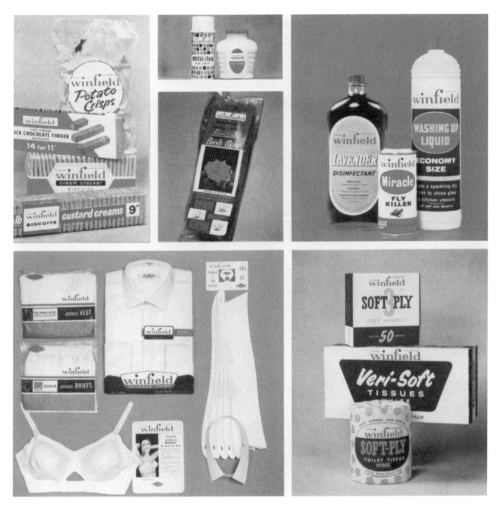

Figure 54. The Woolworth 'own-brand' Winfield
was to last for about twenty years.

Courtesy 3D and 6D Pictures Ltd.

modernization. Whatever intention they had in mind for this building never came to fruition, however. The planning application was unsuccessful and the premises were subsequently sold off.[23]

Apart from this venture, and in conjunction with an understandable level of uncertainty in regard to what membership of the EC might bring to future trading conditions, planning to improve their presence in Northern Ireland was seen as a better bet. By April 1965 the Woolworth store in Coleraine had been extended and the outlet in Lisburn received a similar increase of its sales floor in August 1966. One month later, an elaborate modernization and extension to the branch in Ferryquay Street, Derry, reached completion.

A Case of Mistaken Identity

It could be said that growth of the Woolworth Company during the 1960s brought the disadvantage of a widening gap between London's Executive Office and Liverpool District Office. A good way to illustrate how head office knowledge of the Irish store chain suffered, is the case of 'mistaken identity'. Here was another alleged glitch that was never officially acknowledged.[24]

A vacancy had arisen for the post of Merchandiser for the Republic of Ireland in the early 1960s. It was a key position. There were special privileges and power wielded by the holder of this post. Its incumbent was required to liaise with Irish semi-state organizations and local manufacturers, and this meant that some of the most astute and able men in the Woolworth Company were always chosen for the position. Wide knowledge of the particular trading conditions affecting the Irish chain was needed together with personal acquaintanceship with every member of the close-knit circle of Irish managers and their senior staff. Understanding of the tastes and habits of Ireland's customers and the alternative ranges and suppliers for Ireland was also a necessary attribute. The man chosen was always Irish.

As was usual on such occasions, Executive Office had asked Liverpool District Office to recommend a candidate to fill this vacancy. They named a man with a record of excellent service both as a manager and as a superintendent, who had inherited a bank of good connections from his long business and social association with the Irish stores, including everyone attached to the Dublin buying office – a vital element. Word soon leaked out of the impending appointment via the Irish networking service. The candidate was well known and well liked; it was to be a *fait accompli*. Everyone was very pleased. Word was sent from Liverpool to Executive Office to convey the news of this promotion, but, apparently, it was not noticed by the office staff in London that their list of company personnel at this level of management carried two similar surnames, with different initials. A secretary was instructed to contact the successful candidate. She selected the first name on the list. It was the wrong man.

The senior men in Executive Office never noticed the error. A puzzled but pleased superintendent who had enjoyed only one brief posting as a manager in Ireland in the inter-war period before being called up to British war service in 1940, was duly summoned by the chairman and congratulated on his new responsibilities. By the time the mistake was spotted, nothing could be done. The new man was an excellent administrator and, of course, Dublin Office did not subsequently fall apart as a consequence. Life went on. The company compensated the disappointed Irish candidate by promotion to the Republic's highest-earning superstore, but this attempt to right the wrong was never quite accepted by the Irish network. For them, this incident had proved two points: those at the top in London were not as infallible in their judgement as they always claimed to be, and since passing the 1,000th store mark, Woolworth had grown too big to function as efficiently it had in the past. Was the Woolworth system in danger of becoming too impersonal, and, perhaps, too indifferent? It may have been a lesson learned. In 1967, Liverpool Office made sure that there was no similar mistake in appointing the right man to the right place when two new branches were due to be launched within a week of each other.

In the Republic, the midlands town of Carlow had been chosen to launch the company's first self-service outlet in the south of the country. A similarly modern store in Northern Ireland was ready for business in Enniskillen, not far from the border. Both openings took place in mid October 1967. A profile of these new store managers and their careers within the company was included in the publicity for both outlets. Each man had been carefully chosen.

The Right Man in the Right Place

A press release which added a few personal details about a Woolworth store manager to brief local journalists was not a totally innovative tactic, and the company must not have been unaware of the importance of passing on this knowledge in locations where close-knit commercial and social networks carried a great deal of influence. For towns in Ireland, this was certainly true. In places as distinctly different as Carlow and Enniskillen having the right man in the right place would go a long way to ensuring success.[25]

In Carlow, the manager being installed was described as 'A native of Limerick, he joined the firm in 1958 as a trainee in Cork and was subsequently transferred to the Henry Street Branch in Dublin.' The piece went on to list how he had worked in various Woolworth stores in England and added that he was a keen golfer, had been educated at Clongowes College, where he had been a Leinster schoolboy inter-provincial, and that he was now a member of the Dolphin Rugby Club, Cork, where he played in the First XV.[26]

By contrast, in Enniskillen, County Down, the details supplied in the press write-up informed townspeople that this young man was a native of Carlisle, in Cumbria, which lies near the Scottish border with the north of England. He had worked for Woolworth for seven years and followed in the footsteps of his father, 'who recently retired from the managership of the Ayr Branch in Scotland'. The hobbies of this newcomer to Enniskillen were given as 'out-door sports, including shooting, boating and golf', adding that he was 'formerly interested in the Boys Brigade'.[27] Clearly, both men's private interests set them firmly on the right course to be welcomed into each of these very different local communities.

Two Openings, Two Outcomes

When the branches in Carlow and Enniskillen commenced trading in 1967, no one could have foreseen that the fate of the two outlets would be so different. The decision to open in Carlow became a disaster. The move into Enniskillen was a triumph.

When the Carlow store opened on 24–25 Tullow Street on 17 October 1967, there was no indication that they were only going to survive here for four years. Yet, by Christmas Eve 1971 its doors closed for good. What happened?

The Carlow branch was positioned in the town's foremost shopping street and the Woolworth arrival here in October 1967 was well publicized in the usual way by a striking full-page advertisement in the *Nationalist and Leinster Times.* Under the headline 'Woolworths Comes to Carlow', a report claimed this outlet was the firm's 'first self-service unit in the Republic'.[28]

While the advertising announced 'frozen foods and groceries, fresh fruit and vegetables' and reminded customers that this branch was 'Everybody's store for quality and value!', it is strange to find that the written piece failed to highlight the novelty of a greater range of groceries now being offered, but, instead, noted bargains in some of the more familiar ranges shoppers expected to find: gloves, rainwear, head-squares, nylons, razorblades, paper hankies, baby pants, shampoo and toys.[29]

On the face of it, the selection of Carlow Town for the first self-service in the Republic would have seemed a wise move. The Woolworth scouts would have been aware that Carlow's Chamber of Commerce had been very active

Figure 55. Woolworth introduces self-service to Carlow in 1967, but optimism was short-lived.

Main image: courtesy 3ᴰ and 6ᴰ Pictures Ltd.

in the drive to attract new industries into the town since 1960. By 1967 hopes were still high that the drop in employment could be staved off by an influx of new ventures. Earlier that year, in March, the big event had been the Heinz–Erin merger, which 'put the industry on a very secure basis', and this news was expected to 'increase the acreage of vegetables grown by the farmers'.[30] That same year a draft plan for the development of Carlow had been published and the town had also seen the setting up of two new manufacturing plants.[31] There were hopes, too, that the introduction of a new one-way traffic system, albeit controversial, would free up the flow of traffic in the town. All augured well for the new Woolworth store.

As had always been the case in the past four decades, the coming of a Woolworth store continued to be seen as a beneficial addition to an Irish town's commercial amenities. In the December issue of the Old Carlow Society journal, a contributor supplied a flattering, if slightly inaccurate, reaction to the firm's arrival, writing that, 'Facing the Ritz is the immense block of Woolworth's, indistinguishable of course from its counterparts in Shanghai or South Bend, Indiana, but impressing by its very cosmopolitanism'.[32] Alas, no branch of the British F.W. Woolworth & Co. Ltd ever graced a high street in Shanghai, but the observation is worth repeating because the image created by a Woolworth store in rural Ireland in the 1960s still epitomized the concept of affordable exotic glamour and, as this unknown writer recognizes, a sense of shopping 'cosmopolitanism'.

Four years later, when the company abandoned their Carlow branch (the first time such a failure was witnessed in Ireland), why had their hopes been so badly dashed so swiftly? There are several factors to consider.

First might be the location of the Carlow store, which at the onset had a serious drawback by being on a narrow market-town street with little or no parking facilities for vehicles. At the time, it may have been argued that private car ownership, although rising slowly, was still limited and the existing on-street parking was therefore adequate. Yet, the provision of public transport continued to be non-existent within Carlow's urban area and at best skeletal in its rural hinterland. In the 1960s bicycles remained very much the popular mode of getting around the town. Furthermore, what may not have been considered was the forthcoming construction of a one-way traffic system. The disruption to trade in general in Carlow caused by this work was to become nothing short of a disaster.

Second, as has been demonstrated, a Woolworth store, with its wide counters of toiletries, small drapery items, hardware, ice cream, biscuits, sweets and stationery, was still regarded by shoppers in towns like Carlow as palaces of affordable pleasure and indulgence. A place for treats. Unlike busy urban towns in Britain, where shoppers might dash in on the way home from work to grab a few urgent necessities before catching a bus home to a suburb, the Woolworth store in an Irish small town was still a place in which to dawdle over little luxuries; people wanted to chat to the sales assistants about the merits of the latest cosmetics, gramophone records, costume jewellery or toys. Home dressmaking and knitting was still in vogue. Wools and needles, trimming and notions could all be selected with the help of the girl behind the counter. A self-service format did not offer this entertainment.

Finally, it may be worth suggesting that the introduction of a self-service format to support new ranges of fresh and frozen food into a small and deeply conservative rural community was a mistake. Customers from these areas were still accustomed to buying on credit for staples such as groceries and meat, and the most popular vegetables – potatoes, cabbage and carrots – were often grown locally. Family sizes in the Republic were large by British standards, and for households with limited budgets that had to be stretched to feed up to six, seven or more, frozen food was considered an expensive luxury. More to the point, most household refrigerators only provided a very limited storage facility.

Within two years of their arrival, far more serious drawbacks were looming in Carlow. Unemployment continued to rise and there were disappointments in the efforts to bring more industry to the town. In 1969 the arrival of a Swedish industrialist to open a big clothing factory was abandoned because of financial difficulties. Moreover, the preliminary work to reroute the traffic from the town centre soon started to cause havoc. It was to get worse. People from outlying areas began to avoid the town. Those with cars could travel to alternative venues. A supermarket called DKL had opened in Athy and a large shopping complex was planned for this town centre. The nearby town of Portlaoise was also to have a shopping centre, and it was rumoured that one of the big players, Powers Supermarkets, was to take up a lion's share of the space there.

In 1970 the Irish government doubled Turnover Tax. Prices went up. Trade went down. But the setback to increasing consumerism was only temporary. By the start of 1971 there was confirmation that the rumours had been correct. Power's Supermarket and Penneys were joining forces in what was to be described as a 'Great New Food and Drapery' store in Portlaoise. The complex would be open by the end of the year. This news came as a fatal blow for the struggling Woolworth branch in Carlow. It closed for good on 24 December 1971. Today few townspeople remember it has been ever there.

In October 1967 the Carlow store had been heralded as the company's first-ever self-service outlet in the Republic, but it should be noted that the claim to fame was swiftly and discreetly forgotten when the experiment failed. The town of Carlow received no mention when a publicity campaign was mounted in June 1971 to boost buoyantly successful branches such as Clonmel and several Dublin outlets, describing them as 'the first Woolworth outlets to offer self-service' when they switched to 'cash and wrap', or as the press called them, 'a half-way house between over the counter sales and supermarket check-outs'.[33] At that time, the Woolworth Company's rocklike durability continued to be widely admired as unassailable. 'While [other] Irish stores change hands at dizzying speeds, Woolworth goes marching on'.[34]

The Woolworth arrival and survival in the border town of Enniskillen was a very different story. This store was launched on 26 October 1967, one week after the Carlow opening.

It had taken the Woolworth Company a lengthy spell of time and persistence to establish a branch in the town. Several frustrated battles had been conducted over planning permissions, but eventually a suitable site on the town's High Street was obtained. It was a splendid location. A short distance away in the same street lay the premises owned by the company's most formidable rival in Northern Ireland, the Moore brothers' Wellworths shop and headquarters. That Woolworth should challenge the Moores in Enniskillen, their opponent's home ground, was akin to throwing down the gauntlet. It was not going to be easy.

Nonetheless, their arrival received an auspicious start. On the afternoon prior to commencement of business, the mayor and members of Enniskillen Borough Council were entertained to a private preview and conducted on a tour of the new building. On the following morning at 9 o'clock, the formal opening ceremony was performed by the mayor, Alderman Richard Barton. The occasion was marked by the attendance of the Woolworth Liverpool Office Assistant District Manager, who presented the mayor with the gift of a cheque for the Fermanagh Society for Handicapped Children.[35]

On the opening day, full-page advertisements pointed up the new branch's large frozen food department in addition to offering 'Smart Clothes for All the Family'.[36] Local journalists had been well briefed. Unlike the Carlow store, the Enniskillen branch had not offered self-service to shoppers, but instead emphasized the message given by the attending district manager, that 'personal

Figure 56. The branch in Enniskillen challenges Wellworths on home ground.

Main image: courtesy 3ᴰ and 6ᴰ Pictures Ltd.

service is our motto – not self-service', making it clear that a member of staff would be in attendance 'at every counter or display gondola to assist the customer in his or her choice and advise where necessary'.[37] Despite the modern display fixtures and new-style shopfront windows which 'allowed customers to look directly into the store at the counter displays', it seems clear that this branch of Woolworth was to be run on traditional lines.

For decades, the often repeated assurance that a new store was providing plenty of local employment was one of the positive elements the F.W. Woolworth Company never failed to emphasize in its press releases. Thus, it was dutifully reported in Enniskillen how 'The store employs a staff of about fifty, mostly girls when fully in operation. A number of key personnel, recruited locally, have been given special training in the operation of a modern department store'.[38]

Figure 57. A rare picture from behind the scenes: the manager and office staff on
Enniskillen's opening day, 26 October 1967.

Courtesy *Impartial Reporter and Farmers' Journal.*

Unlike the previous week's press write-up for the opening in Carlow, which
told shoppers only about well-known and uncontroversial ranges of goods, the
introduction of several innovative features picked out for journalistic comment
in the Enniskillen store clearly indicate how much more this town was attuned
to British shopping habits. For one thing, the food department had 'impressive
refrigerated cabinets – the second largest in Northern Ireland'. There was also
'a full range of groceries at very competitive prices' and 'fresh vegetables
counters'.[39]

Worth noting, too, is how the correspondent from the *Fermanagh Herald*
stumbled over explaining the name of a new range of sweets being introduced,
writing that

> A novel feature of the confectionery counter, where there is a
> mouth-watering array of sweets and chocolates, is the 'pick 'n'
> price' [*sic*] arrangement. On the counter are 64 trays of different

varieties of confectionary and customers can select as may as they wish from any of the trays and then have them weighed and priced by an assistant.[40]

The necessity of the explanation begs the question whether the year 1967 marked the arrival of pick 'n' mix into Ireland? It was to become almost synonymous with the name of Woolworth.

It goes without saying that their arrival in Enniskillen received some serious attention from its rivals. Moore's Wellworths Stores' first broadside had been launched a month earlier by offering shoppers an autumn sale in September. This was followed almost immediately, on 7 October, by a three-column seven-inch high announcement that Christmas was only eleven weeks ahead. 'Join our Christmas Club now,' they urged, 'and provide for a Happy Christmas.' Their aim was to get customers signed up before the Woolworth opening, which was sure to include the announcement of their own Christmas savings club. Meanwhile, another trader, Wilson's of Enniskillen, had also launched a solid broadside by announcing a ten-day anniversary sale to commence on the Woolworth opening day, 26 October. This shop's notice, on the front page of the *Impartial Reporter and Farmers' Journal*, not only offered bargains but clearly aimed to catch the eye of their long-standing customers with the claim they were 'for 28 years the family store for all the family with the best value at the keenest prices'.[41] Could this have been a veiled euphemism to convey credit terms were still available as heretofore? Possibly. However, as with all the other appearances of a Woolworth in an Irish town, the local traders soon settled down to coexistence and the Enniskillen store never succumbed to competition.

Resistance to Change

When it came to pushing forward new ideas, it could be still difficult for younger men coming up the ranks to shift many of the views of the Woolworth old guard. For example, having to resort to a press advertising campaign to generate an increase in sales was a knotty problem for the older managers. For many, it was almost like being asked to worship a false God.

One ex-employee, who had been a young man in a great hurry in the 1960s, can recall his impatience with attitudes adopted by his superiors. Their reluctance to take on any change was frustrating and his observation forthright: in his view, 'Those old guys regarded Woolworth as if it was a religion. They believed nobody could go to Heaven in the retail business unless they kept to the straight and narrow path of how Woolworths did things. It was the One True Way'.[42]

In similar vein, there was little regard for intellectual pursuits beyond anything that was organized by the company. A Dublin store manager once berated a young trainee when he discovered his floor-man was spending several evenings a week studying for a part-time Liberal Arts degree at the local university. The much older man was genuinely shocked that a 'learner' was entertaining ambitions beyond the Woolworth fold. The young man's bundle of books and seminar notes had been enough to prompt a stern lecture. Ushering him into his office, the manager indicated the racks of Woolworth Company folders stacked on the shelves behind his desk. They contained hand-written detailed data analysis for every department in his store. There were folders for counter sales, for stock movements, for stockroom order sheets, returns and damaged goods, for shrinkage figures, for data on 'try-outs', for seasonal ranges and suppliers. There was also a heavy, ring-bound 'Manager's Store Manual', several inches thick, which contained instructions for every protocol attached to the running of a branch down to the tiniest detail. The first page warned: 'This book must not be taken from the store. Persons entitled to reference to its contents are: the Store Manager, the recognized Assistant Manager and the First Cashier'. 'Do you see all these?' the trainee was asked. Then he was told: 'That's your University, Mister. Everything you'll ever need to learn is on them shelves'.[43]

Such sentiments, inherited from Frank Woolworth's own beliefs, remained at the core of the Woolworth Company's ethos for decades. Cited by his biographer, one of his most repeated declarations had been: 'I prefer the boy from the farm to a college man. The college man won't begin at the bottom and learn the business.'[44] Nonetheless, by the end of the 1960s there were several at the top of the management hierarchy who were beginning to argue that the old-timers, who held on to their beliefs and put their trust in such traditional Woolworth precepts, had forgotten that their illustrious founder had thrived on being innovative. In his day, Frank Woolworth had been a young man with ideas that were fresh and untried, and he had been proved right. Top management were now beginning to ask whether, in keeping strict adherence to old-style rules, the Company had lost the knack of giving younger men with fresh ideas and drive the chance to be innovative? Several believed moves must be made to change all this.

By end of the 1960s Executive Office in London was worried at the lack of suitable applicants coming forward for management training. It was proposed that a big recruiting campaign should be launched. Strict preference was to be given to trainees who were university graduates. The announcement subsequently generated a mixture of opinion as to its ultimate success.

One tale that is told relates to how, when the scheme had been underway for a year or two, a meeting was set up to review some of the first results. The splendid performance of one exceptional trainee from Limerick was cited as an example to prove the point that the recruitment of young men with third level qualifications was producing the right results. The candidate had been sent off to England, where he subsequently made swift progress and filled a couple of management posts very successfully. What the top men at the meeting did not know was that the young man's excellent 'third level qualifications' on his application form had been filled in for him by his Irish store manager with a certain amount of creativity. The local manager had recognized the young man's potential and, being of the old school who firmly believed the best and only attributes a good trainee should demonstrate was the ability to use 'native cunning and common sense', had awarded this applicant enough 'qualifications' to see him safely on to the bottom rung of the career ladder.[45] The 'graduate' went on to fulfil his mentor's highest expectations. No one was ever the wiser until years afterwards.

Life on the Shop Floor in the 1960s

Former employees who worked as counter assistants in the sixties still remember that fifty years or more ago the regimentation of staff in that era was as rigorous as it had been in much earlier decades. Assistants were still lined up and inspected before going out on to the shop floor. Uniforms and general appearance had to conform to the rules – hands and nails were checked – and anything untoward got a reprimand or a reminder: 'You're wearing too much lipstick, Miss' or 'Where is your duster?'[46]

Part of the assistant's job was to keep the stock on her counter spotlessly clean and tidy. Supervision that this was done properly was the responsibility of the young trainee floor-man in charge of her department. Dust was a big bogey. Many a former trainee or 'learner' remembers his manager's habit of holding up a finger that he had just run along the edge of a counter to detect some lurking dust and asking, 'What's that?' Any attempt made by a trainee to joke in response, 'It's your finger, sir…', at best received a withering look, but usually triggered a tongue lashing.[47]

Old cash registers were still in use in some of the stores. Each till had a small pad and a pencil beside it for assistants to calculate multiple purchases or work out change. The older and more experienced girls were able to tot up everything in their heads faster than they could write it down. Part of their training also entailed being taught the right way to hand back change to customers, by counting the coins back into their hands.

Keeping an eye out for shoplifting customers was an important task for everyone working on the sales floor. If a well-known practitioner entered the premises, a number of warning codewords were called out from counter to counter. Announcing 'General Shillings' was one code still remembered by former assistants.[48] Floor-men also had to watch for any unusual behaviour by staff, who might be tempted by the easy access to cash. On one occasion, an elderly male shopper was seen browsing among the birthday cards. He would select one, pay for it, and be handed the card back in a paper bag. Half an hour later he would be back again to browse and select another card. Some time after, he returned once more and the same procedure of selecting and paying for a card was conducted. A floor-man and a staff supervisor began to keep a closer watch on this performance, and later that day, the customer came back into the store. The same routine was repeated, but this time the scam was caught. On each occasion when he had handed his money to the counter assistant, she opened the till and put a bank note inside the card before she handed it back to him with his change.[49]

The specific instructions for a manager who had to deal with cases of proven larceny were set out in each store manual. When stores were very crowded, mistakes did happen on occasion and outraged innocent customers who pursued restitution often benefited quite considerably. One former manager recalled how easily an error might arise. A lady customer in one of the English stores was seen putting handkerchiefs into her shopping bag, but, as it was later proved, she had merely been comparing the size, quality and price of the Woolworth stock on the counter with similar items just purchased from Marks & Spencer next door. The incident was many times repeated as an apocryphal tale to warn all managers to be careful. This false accusation of stealing had prompted the lady's solicitor to threaten the company with court proceedings. Apologies and suitable compensation were being sought. In the end, the lady graciously accepted a gift of a grand piano.[50]

Most stores insisted that staff adopt a thrifty attitude towards waste and long-standing traditions continued to be enforced with the same rigour as in the founder's day. Every scrap of waste paper and packaging was collected up and tightly baled for collection by one of the waste paper companies under contract to Woolworth. Every light switch had a notice with 'SOS' pinned underneath it. This was to remind staff to 'switch off and save'.[51] Saving money sometimes became an obsession. Managers who needed to make a bit extra sold off flattened cardboard boxes locally for 2d each, while counter staff were told to turn their till rolls when they got to the end so that they could be used a second time by printing out receipts on the unused blank sides.[52] And yet, gold leaf was still being used to refresh the fascia signs. When the painters were in, the manager had to keep their supply in the safe.[53]

The Troubles Erupt North of the Border

By January 1969 the number of Irish Woolworth stores had reached its peak. A total of forty-one branches conducted their business the main shopping streets of towns and cities on each side of the border (see map, Appendix IV and Appendix Table 8). Twenty-three branches operated in the Republic and eighteen branches in the North of Ireland. All seemed well.

By the summer of that year, however, the resurgence of civil disorder in Northern Ireland brought violence back to levels not seen in Ireland since the 1920s. The observation made by historian Eunan O'Halpin, reiterated more recently by Christopher Andrew, holds that even those in the highest echelons of power in Westminster had little inkling of the problems that had been bubbling along for years under the surface in Ulster. O'Halpin has neatly described how Irish society was regarded by the British authorities at that time: 'Northern Ireland in 1969 might as well have been North Korea, so sparse was the reliable information available.'[54] This comment could not be applied to many of the men at the top of the Woolworth Company. Liverpool District (later Regional) Office had handled delicate situations in the Province for decades with commendable sensitivity. Their knowledge and under-standing was based on the practical experience of the two generations of superintendents and managers who had worked hard to keep harmonious relationships and viable trading conditions working smoothly in each of the two jurisdictions, North and South, since 1922. As has already been demonstrated in Carlow and Enniskillen, care was taken to ensure that appro-priate branch managers were appointed in different regions.

To present an adequate commentary on the extent of disruption to retail shopping in the Northern Province brought about by the impact of the Troubles, would require a whole volume to itself. For the retail trade, one of the most immediate effects was the threat of similar violent acts spilling out across the border into the south of Ireland or across into England. There was the need for greater vigilance within stores, shops and supermarkets everywhere. For shopkeepers, several new routines were introduced into their administrative protocols. One former Woolworth assistant recalls the drill.

> Every night we had to search the store very carefully for incendiaries. We checked all the displays – especially in handbags or in anything in which a small device could be hidden. Security was very tight. During the daytime the back entrance was always kept closed in case anyone tried to slip into the store that way.[55]

Brian Feeney, in his compressed but useful précis entitled *The Troubles*, writes how, by 1976,

> Every sizable town in the North and many smaller ones now had barriers manned by soldiers to prevent car bombs being driven in. The centres of larger places, like Belfast and Derry, were protected by so-called Gated Areas, comprising 2.5 metre high fences with gates at all major entrances. Civilian 'searchers' frisked anyone entering through the gates. Within the Gated Areas all shops employed searchers. Long queues formed at the gates and at the entrances to shops. In the early evening the gates were locked and the centres of Belfast and Derry became ghost towns. Outside the towns, random military vehicle checkpoints delayed travellers and disrupted business. People became resigned to the queues, the detours, the bomb scares, the increasingly intrusive security measures.[56]

For retail outlets in main shopping streets, car bombs brought about indiscriminate carnage and damage; incendiary devices, if not detected in time, could destroy stock and interior fittings with fire, smoke and water damage. For personnel in every type of retail outlet, from the small shop to the large department store, their workplace became a place where danger might strike suddenly and without warning. In-store training now included razor-sharp alertness and well-rehearsed tactics to combat an 'incident'. Stress levels soared.

No Woolworth store in Ulster escaped an attack at one time or another, and several locations underwent multiple incidents. But they were not alone. The company's most serious long-time competitor, the Wellworths store chain, was targeted on many occasions and they, too, suffered badly from bomb and incendiary damage. The year 1972 is now considered to have been 'the most disruptive year in the history of the Northern Ireland Troubles'.[57]

Throughout the 1960s and for some time after, every Woolworth outlet in the North of Ireland was refurbished. Sometimes they were repaired, rebuilt and refitted out several times. Work was carried out in Belfast, Derry City, Portadown, Newry, Dungannon, Ballymena, Lisburn, Bangor, Coleraine, Lurgan, Armagh and Strabane. When a significant rebuilding was needed, this might allow for an extension of sales floors and modernization, but not every bomb-damaged store was subsequently rebuilt. When the outlet in Omagh closed because of damage, it lay idle for five years before being eventually sold off because the company was unable to acquire adjoining premises for an expansion of its sales floor. Belfast's store in North Street suffered the same fate. It closed in 1975, following bomb damage, and was never reopened.

Belfast's flagship store in High Street suffered regularly. As one of its former managers recollects, 'It was endless. We had six security guards for our three entrances but it couldn't be stopped. We had four floors in that store and the incendiary devices were nearly always on the top floor, hidden in pillows, or clothing or near paint.' Water and smoke damage were common occurrences. 'I remember going into the store one night, the sprinklers had been activated and we were completely flooded several inches deep. Staff came in to help and we swept all the water away into the elevator shaft. It was like a swimming pool down there.' Car bombs caused structural damage.

> I remember a colleague and I going into Lurgan after an incident. We could only go into the town with permission from the authorities and for health and safety reasons we had to be very careful. We knew the town well, but the destruction of it was so bad that we didn't know which side of Market Street we were on. We had to try and find a bit of red sign or similar recognisable piece of the façade to identify the Woolworth site.

Security ring breached: big store blasted

By PETER McKENNA

DESPITE the "intensive security" precautions in Belfast city centre bombers yesterday evaded police, troops and security men, and planted nine devices which set fire to the huge giant Woolworth store in High Street.

In just over an hour five fire bombs exploded in various sections of the building and thousands of pounds worth of damage was caused. About 60 firemen with 10 appliances fought the blaze which followed the explosion and prevented it from spreading to nearby buildings.

At one stage it was believed that the fire would reach Burtons tailoring shop on the junction of High Street and Cornmarket, but after more than two hours, the firemen began to get the flames under control.

An R.U.C. spokesman said that at 4.07 p.m. a Belfast morning newspaper received an anonymous call saying there were nine devices in Woolworths and warning that they would explode at 30-minute intervals.

Meanwhile, a box with wires leading from it was spotted on the second floor of the building. Security guards evacuated staff and customers and the first device went off at 4.21 p.m.

A minute later another bomb exploded and as firemen and troops rushed to the scene explosions followed at 4.32 and 4.55 p.m.

As troops and police cordoned off the area and city centre traffic came to a standstill, firemen fought the blaze, but at 5.19 p.m. another bomb exploded and the fire began to spread.

Bombers struck for the third time in 24 hours at Catholic-owned bars in Belfast early today when a car-bomb wrecked a public house at the junction of Union Street and Donegall Street, injuring seven people.

They were taken to hospital, but released after treatment for cuts caused by flying glass.

NOT ENOUGH TIME

A police spokesman said that a two-minute warning of the bomb—estimated at 200 lb—had been given, but the security forces had not enough time to alert passers-by.

On Thursday morning, an 82-year-old pensioner, Mr. Hugh Devlin, was killed instantly when the Ulster Freedom Fighters planted a bomb in the Spa Bar on the New Lodge Road.

A barmaid, Mrs. Maureen McStravick, received severe back injuries and is said to be "seriously ill" in hospital.

Firemen fighting the blaze in Woolworths Store, High St., Belfast, yesterday evening after a series of explosions occurred in the building.

Figure 58. Firemen fighting the blaze in the Woolworth store in Belfast's High Street, February 1974.

Courtesy *Irish Independent*.

Store managers were regularly called out at night if a bomb warning had been phoned in. They were the only people who could open the premises to check it out. There were plenty of hoax calls, but no chances could be taken. For this ex-manager, the memory of those days is still very clear.

> If the army weren't able to use a remote control, an army bomb disposal man had to go into the store. He would be tied to a rope and they would put him into a metal suit and a hat with a camera set into the front. His movements were then directed from outside from a control van. I once asked one of these men if this metal suit would save his life. His answer was 'No, but my wife would have a body to bury.'[58]

For the Woolworth Company, full compensation was received from the British and Northern Ireland authorities to cover structural damage, replacement of stock and staff wages while repair or rebuilding was taking place. Moreover, all staff members were given a guarantee that their jobs were safe. Following a report of an incident made by a store manager, insurance claims were signed by the company's area manager and agreed by the Northern Ireland Office. For repair or rebuilding damaged by terrorism, 100 per cent of costs were received, followed by 100 per cent stock replacement and full closure pay for colleagues while the store was shut. 'The bigger the incident, the more money we got,' one manager recalls.

> We might get £1 million paid for merchandise, but if that store was not rebuilt straight away the stock might not go back into that branch but into another one. Some stores which usually carried about half a million pounds worth of stock would suddenly have to carry three-quarters of a million pounds. Fire and smoke damaged stock also had to be moved around a great deal.[59]

Belfast's impressive building in High Street was eventually sold off to Dunnes Stores. 'It had been bombed so often it had a lot of structural damage. All this had to be made good before it could be sold.'[60] The total cost of the repair work on this premises was more than adequately covered by the compensation received from the Northern Ireland Authority. The balance went into the company's coffers for other projects.

In official eyes the status of the Woolworth Company remained high. Westminster saw the firm as an integral part of the commercial life of Northern Ireland. It was a well-respected firm and one that could display an excellent example of a business concern whose employees, while drawn from both sides of the sectarian divide, worked in harmony with each other.

Keeping up the spirits of his team was a priority for all store managers in the Province. Everyone tried to make the best of things, but sometimes it was felt that the disruption endured by their people was not fully appreciated. In those days, the importance of post-trauma counselling was only beginning to be recognized, and Woolworth staff had nothing special organized in this respect.[61] However, during the height of the Troubles, the editor and assistant editor of the *New Bond* were sent to Belfast by Executive Office in London. They were to write a special feature on the Northern Ireland stores. The visitors were brought around to branches struggling to stay open for their customers despite having been damaged. They were shown how the staff cheerfully managed without adequate heating, food or lifts. Many premises were reopened for customers before a lot of the basic facilities were restored. Staffrooms, rest-rooms and canteens were often the last section of the building to be repaired, but the girls soldiered on, making do with a small Superser heater, a kettle and a few mugs for a brew of tea. Photographs were taken and interviews conducted. When the visit was completed, the pair from London went back to their office, impressed by everyone's cheerfully positive attitude, promising to write up a thoughtfully sympathetic piece. Time passed. When the article failed to make an appearance in subsequent issues of the journal, enquiries were made. The answer received revealed why. Someone more senior in London had decided the story was 'Too political'.[62]

Chapter 7

Challenging a 'Fuddy-Duddy' Image
1970–1979

Although the 1970s continued to be dominated by the Troubles in Ulster, a number of events brought fresh challenges to be faced within commercial life in Ireland. Retailers, wholesalers and suppliers were all affected.

First up was a nationwide bank strike in the Republic in 1970, which lasted for over six months. The doors had closed on 30 April and had not reopened to the public until 17 November.[1] Woolworth stores always paid the staffs' wages from the takings, so they had no great concern at this level of their operation. But their Irish suppliers were badly hit. These firms soon became strapped for cash. They were accustomed to payment for deliveries within thirty days by cheque. Contingency plans were set up in a hurry. Arrangements were usually reliant on the existence of a 'gentleman's agreement'. With no banks to take in their daily lodgements, Woolworth surplus cash was ferried by security vans to suppliers all over Ireland. In return, these firms wrote cheques for the amounts received and as long as these businesses stayed solvent all was well. Cheques could be honoured when banks reopened. It was argued at the time that companies that did business with Woolworth were inevitably solid and dependable concerns, and as anticipated, no serious defaulters emerged at the end of six months. (A number of other firms offering similar 'Good Samaritan' aid were not so lucky.) But, as someone later pointed out, the Woolworth Company lost out in this exercise. Apart from the additional cost of laying on security measures and transport, there had been no charges or interest levied on the cashflow that they supplied to manufacturers and agents.[2] It was only a small slip-up in the hastily arranged system and London felt it to be an insignificant matter. But this was not the view of the Irish store managers. They took collective pride in their enterprise. It worried them that Executive Office was taking an indifferent attitude.

Three months later, Decimal Day, 15 February 1971, brought further challenges throughout the whole of the chain. Despite fears of confusion, the decimalization of the pound sterling and Irish punt went ahead smoothly. Querulous shoppers asking 'How much is that in old money?' gradually faded away.

The Cost of Modernizing Stores

The change-over to decimalization had been costly. It entailed the scrapping or conversion of thousands of cash registers. To make savings, Woolworth accelerated the switch-over of United Kingdom stores from individual counter service to a centralized 'cash and wrap'. This tactic cut down the number of tills and counter assistants needed for each branch and helped to reduce overheads. More expense lay ahead. By the start of the 1970s the modernization of stores in the United Kingdom had gathered momentum. Company literature describes the extra work as 'extending male, female and children's clothing departments, fitting rooms, sports departments, music and record departments and extended hardware and household departments'. The updated British stores now had 'extensive food departments, selling delicatessen, fresh fish, fresh meat, fresh fruit and vegetables and frozen food; everything from lobsters and smoked salmon to varying breads and patisserie'.[3]

The cost of all this work was enormous. To help pay for it, money was raised by a sweeping rationalization programme which sold off and closed many of the chain's less profitable branches in the United Kingdom. Forty-four stores had gone by the end of the following year.[4] In the south of England, fourteen outlets in the London Metropolitan District had been disposed of, together with seven stores in the Kensington District. The English Midlands lost six branches attached to the Birmingham District, and the Liverpool District Office saw seventeen of their stores also gone for good. Two of the latter were in Ireland. The demise of the Carlow store, in December 1971, has been discussed already. Its closure was followed three months later, on 1 April 1972, by the shutting down of the Woolworth outlet in Liberty Square, Thurles. This branch, which had opened in 1953, was sold to Heaton's, a well-established Irish chain of drapery and sports stores. The new owners reopened the premises for business almost immediately and have continued to trade from there ever since.[5]

The cost of expensive store refurbishment was not the only reason the Woolworth Company had to raise cash from outlet closures. A serious amount of money was being funnelled into an entirely new venture, the Woolco Department Store Division. This was a concept copied from similar outlets opened by the Woolworth Company in the United States and Canada. The Woolco stores were huge out-of-town shopping complexes with vast car-parking facilities. The first had been built in 1967. A further two followed shortly after, and by 1970 there were plans for several more.

In the meantime, in Ireland throughout the 1970s every branch was being brought up to date as economically as possible. Instead of disposing of all the old mahogany counters and replacing them with completely new metal mesh display gondolas, many of the store counters were merely reduced in height by being cut down by a foot or so.[6] At this height they could then be reused as the base for the upright display stands that were needed to hold increasing amounts of pre-packaged goods. These lowered counters with high displays built up between the aisles were not always popular with store managers. As one recalls, 'the high displays prevented us from keeping shoppers under observation. When the full self-service was introduced I had small square marks painted on to the floor tiles and instructed my staff to stand in these positions so that they had a clear eye-line of the customers. Very little was stolen.'[7]

For the branches that were given a total overhaul, the term used was 'crash-modernization programmes. These stores would close down on a Saturday and reopen on the following Friday fully modernized with new fixtures and fittings.'[8] Irish customers and staff alike had mixed views over the introduction of new shop floor layouts in the 1970s. One Cork lady was emphatic: 'I did not like it at all when they changed the store. They started to sell large items of clothing like dresses. It did not seem like a Woolworth store any more.'[9] Another long-time employee, when asked for her reminiscences ten years after the changes, explained to a journalist how 'the atmosphere changed forever when they did up the old store and switched to self-service a decade ago. There used to be two or three girls to a counter'.[10]

One of the less popular modernizations also introduced at this time was the replacement of many of the stores' old pitch-pine floors. The routine of caring for the floorboards by oiling them regularly had been stringently applied since the firm's foundation. When a branch closed on a Saturday night, the last task for the trainee floor-men was to spray all the sales floors with linseed oil. It was then left to soak into the wood for the weekend. On Monday mornings before opening, a proprietary substance called Felspar was sprinkled on to the surface. This procedure was not to ensure all the oil had been absorbed, as was often thought, but to add a fine dusting of grit which made the floors safe to walk on.[11] The oiling of floors was a regular chore that kept the pine in good condition for decades, and the method had become so entrenched that, during the years of the Emergency, when supplies of linseed oil ran out in Ireland, it was not abandoned. Instead, a mixture of waste engine oil was used. It was dirty and smelly but fulfilled the purpose, albeit with one disadvantage. As one ex-floor-man still remembers, 'it wrecked our shoes'.

The replacement of old pine floors was one of the first modernizations to be introduced when the refurbishment of the store chain was underway. The concept had been first mooted in 1944 by the company's London executives when eagerly anticipating exciting post-war improvements. Back then, they had already agreed to modernize the lighting systems in each outlet with a new type of fitting called 'fluorescence [*sic*]', which they would be receiving from America, having noted that 'whilst [it was] more expensive to install, [it] halved the running costs and gave much more candle power'.[12] The next item on the agenda at that meeting had been an equally revolutionary proposal to replace all wooden floors with a concrete-based terrazzo or terrazzo tiling.

A point worth noting is that the suggestion had not met with immediate and total approval. In the opinion of the company's newly appointed architect, the old-style wooden floors were warmer, and he warned that 'much more heat was required in a building' when terrazzo was installed.[13] His view was supported by at least one of the executives. Minutes for the meeting carefully note his observation, that 'Tiled floors were also more dusty and had to be cleaned by washing', adding that 'there is a lot to be said for pitch pine which is warm, absorbs oil and is resilient and dustless'.[14] The latter knew what he was talking about. He was one of the old-timers who had been put to 'sweeping a stockroom floor' in his early days. In due course, the dissenting voices would seem not to have borne any weight, however, and the plan to go ahead with the installation of terrazzo flooring was later passed for approval.

Counter assistants for decades came to mourn the loss of the old wooden floors. They missed the pliable comfort of pitch pine underfoot, and complaints are still remembered: 'putting in all that new tiling was so bad for our legs'.[15]

There were new ideas for image improvements being introduced that affected all aspects of the business. For example, by the 1970s more stylish uniforms for sales assistants and office staff were being regularly reviewed. Instead of being issued with a lightweight buttoned-up overall-style 'shop-coat', worn over their own clothing and hardly changed at all since the 1920s, staff supervisors and cashiers now sported air-hostess-style pinafore tops and skirts, complemented by long-sleeved blouses with fashionable kipper collars.

Figure 59. Marking a momentous day in 1974: senior staff in their new uniforms are in attendance when a young Irish manager takes up his duties in his first store.

Courtesy Alice Carroll.

Looking after shoppers in a self-service store obviously required less personnel than heretofore. In the 1930s to have a staff of thirty or forty girls in an average-sized branch was considered just about adequate. By the 1970s, smaller stores that could have employed over twenty women, could now be run efficiently with just seven or eight people. Part-time seasonal work and more regular Saturday work was always on offer, nonetheless, and recruitment for extra help in Irish stores continued to be reliant on word of mouth or family connections. Such was the case at every level of personnel, from sales floor up to the ranks of management.

Irish Grocery Chains vie over Wider Ranges

In 1972 the Irish supermarket chain Powers bought out all the Pat Quinn outlets and their brand name. By 23 May this firm had switched over to trading under the name of Quinnsworth.[16] Although essentially a grocery chain on the lines of H. Williams, the new owners of Quinnsworth were now able to sell a much wider range of goods, and they began to nibble away voraciously at some of the most traditional and popular merchandise stocked by Woolworth, such as stationery, cards, household goods and seasonal toys. Woolworth branches were also coming under more pressure from Dunnes Stores, which by then had also made substantial inroads into their sales of small drapery items such as socks, scarves, gloves and ladies tights. The Dunnes chain was in the ascendancy. It was launching a serious challenge to H. Williams and Quinnsworth by expanding its food, toiletries and hair care product ranges. The extent of the combatants now selling the latter may be illustrated by a beauty contest campaign called Ireland's Supergirl '72, which was sponsored by the *Evening Herald* and a big toiletries firm, W. Hampshire Ltd. This campaign aimed to boost sales of a brand of shampoos and hairsprays called Supersoft in the midsummer season of 1972. The entry forms were available from chemists and independents in addition to the sixteen multiples that stocked their products, which were named as: Dunnes Stores, Five Star, Golden Goose, MACE, MNC, Lipton, Londis, NWGA, Piggybank, Power Supermarkets Ltd, SPAR, Superquinn, Quinnsworth, H. Williams & Co., VG and F.W. Woolworth & Co. Ltd.

As 1972 drew to a close, all Irish retailers had to be ready to face a new tax regime being brought in to replace the existing wholesale and turnover tax. It was called VAT (Valued Added Tax). The legislation had been postponed three times, but it finally came into effect on 1 November 1972 as part of the state's application to join the EEC.[17] Two months later, the United Kingdom and the Republic joined the European Economic Community. By 1 January 1973 the Woolworth board had to be ready for whatever lay ahead.

At that time, Executive Office in London was abuzz with activity. Since the appointment of a marketing director, a spate of innovative ideas had been launched. But, as the focus was resting entirely on shopping trends in Britain, some of the new concepts brought little or no benefit to sales in Ireland. For example, in 1973 the introduction of Woolworth catalogue shops, 'Shoppers

World', which were run on similar lines to Argos, was a new experience for the company.[18] By the end of the year, fourteen of these outlets were up and running and they might have proved successful in Ireland if either this style of retailing or their 'Woolworth by Post' had been tried in the Republic. But nothing was done, and it would seem that the new VAT charges and Customs & Excise duties presented too many stumbling blocks. Moreover, no equivalent catalogue-style promotional material was provided for any store in the south. The gap between what was available in Ireland and what was being developed in the British outlets was widening further. As one former branch manager remembers,

> Customers would come in with catalogues they had got when on a visit to England. They wanted to have our versions of the goods on offer with prices over-printed in punts. But we never had any such thing to give them. So shoppers did not have the details of the ranges we stocked and the value we could offer. It was a great mistake. Thousands of pounds worth of extra sales were lost to us.[19]

On 19 March 1973 a headline in the business section of the *Irish Times* read 'Changing Woolworth's "fuddy-duddy" image'. When interviewed for this piece, the company's newly appointed chairman explained: 'Previously we were a buyer-oriented retail group … now we are market oriented'.[20] His statement neatly sums up the wave of new thinking that was sweeping through the Woolworth Company. The long reign of the powerful buyers in London had been challenged.

The chairman reminded his interviewer that the Woolworth Company had appointed their first marketing executive two and half years earlier. 'We made an analysis of what people thought of Woolworth's and its branches … upgraded the traditional lines … and have moved into the higher priced market – audio equipment, lawn mowers, casual furniture, carpets, high priced electrical goods and so on'.[21] What he did not say was that the company's United Kingdom branches had become increasingly reliant on selling food. Within twelve months, financial commentators reckoned this section accounted for about a third of Woolworth business.[22] Only their branches in the Republic of Ireland had remained outside this trend. The Irish managers had stood back and let the grocers fight it out between themselves.

1974: New Faces and New Ideas

By 1974 the diverse range of merchandise now being handled in Woolworth stores triggered a shake-up among top management personnel. Its profile was changing. In an unprecedented move, six young lady buyers and a female press officer had been appointed to Executive Office. Up to this time, the only women at this level of management had represented the company's Bureau of Staff Relations, which later became Training and Staff Welfare. The four regional offices, Liverpool, Birmingham, Metropolitan (London) and Kensington, had also appointed women to take responsibility for their signs department. By then, also, two men sporting beards had been admitted to the Kensington Office. Their qualifications in architecture and construction engineering must have allowed for some leeway. Here was evidence indeed that a new era had arrived.

There were other revolutionary changes. By 1975 a new logo had been designed and optimism rode high as the promised advertising campaign took off. It was cleverly steered by a London agency, who received the board's permission to use the colloquial term for the chain, *Woolies*, as a brand name to catch the shopping public's attention. A number of well-known entertainment stars were rounded up to feature in advertising campaigns aimed at the British market. All this effort culminated in the later claim that within five years Woolworth became 'the largest retail advertiser dominating TV schedules'.[23] Yet, significantly many customers in the Irish midlands or in the south and west of Ireland at that time could not benefit from all this razzamatazz. Woolworth did not advertise on the Irish RTÉ (Raidió Teilifís Éireann) television channel. Excluding shoppers living along the east coast or in border areas who could pirate television reception from Wales or Northern Ireland, television viewing in the Republic was still limited to one single black and white RTÉ nationwide transmission. When colour television was fully adopted, in 1978, a second channel, Network, was subsequently launched (later called RTÉ2).

In due course, some benefit to Irish store sales was generated from press campaigns being run in the United Kingdom. A number of British newspapers had a steady readership in Ireland, and Sunday newspapers were particularly popular; fortunately, Woolworth's use of display advertising did not give details of any prices.[24] The Christmas season usually saw traders' associations being drawn into supporting special shopping features in Irish newspapers, and Woolworth managers would take advantage of this by briefing journalists. Any accompanying press advertising was modest, however.

An Irish Experiment

On 15 June 1976 the first and only Woolco store in Ireland burst on the scene with a big fanfare of publicity. Some commentators later dubbed it 'an Irish experiment'.[25] The British Woolworth Company had begun building the huge Woolco outlets in the United Kingdom in 1967. The giant shopping complexes were designed to be 'under one roof and on one floor. [They] offered a complete range of quality branded goods, from food to furniture, clothing to cameras and records to refrigerators, jewellery, radio and television'.[26] Seaton describes how the new-style stores were not only a 'vibrant new division within the firm, with 200 office-based jobs', but had also 'absorbed the lion's share of Company investment, too'.[27] A telling point. By the end of 1974 nine Woolco department stores were being run by a team of sixty-one men ranking from executive level down to managers and divisional managers.

There is uncertainty over whether or not Woolco had ever originally intended to open one of these monsters in Ireland. At least one of the retired Dublin senior men had been called in by a political figure in the late 1960s for advice on the feasibility of giving planning permission support for a Woolco in the environs of Dublin. Subsequently, following other consultations and a wider discussion of the proposal, the idea came to nothing. By the mid 1970s, however, trading in the British Woolco outlets was no longer working out as well as had been intended and, apparently, alternative formats were being considered. It was around this time that a hybrid version, described as a Woolco Hypermarket, made an appearance in the Ulster province in 1976 (see Appendix I, Table 6). It was to become a run-away success.

This arrival of an experimental Woolco Hypermarket as the anchor tenant in the Ards Shopping Centre in Newtownards, would seem to have been brought about by a combination of unusual circumstances. Some years earlier, following negotiations to acquire a presence in this proposed new shopping centre, Woolworth entered into a rental agreement for the largest unit in the still to be built complex. The site for the Ards Centre was located about nine miles outside Belfast and the new Woolworth store was to occupy 30 per cent of the whole retail area. Under the planning permission requirements at the time, it was announced very clearly that this branch would be specializing in food. But, apparently, the opening of the Ards complex later suffered a number of delays, which, it would appear, may have included the difficulty of getting tenants for the other larger units. Eventually, the Ards people signed up an

NEWTOWNARDS SEES FIRST WOOLCO HYPERMARKET

A first for Woolco and a first for Northern Ireland —that is the new hypermarket that the company opened three weeks ago at Newtownards.

The store which is in the town's new Ards Shopping Centre is the largest single floor store in Northern Ireland and the first hypermarket the country has seen.

Newtownards is a residential area some nine miles east of Belfast.

What makes this Woolco store a hypermarket? Firstly there is its size and the way in which the merchandise is displayed. All the gondolas and shelves are much higher than in a coventional Woolco or Woolworth store. The main gangways are up to 13 feet wide compared to the normal five to six feet. This is to allow for the fact that everyone is shopping with trolleys.

On opening day there were 900 trolleys neatly lined up outside the store at 10.00 a.m. Within minutes they were all in operation.

The first customer Mrs Elizabeth Bittle had been waiting outside the precinct entrance since 7.35 a.m. and was very impressed with what she saw in the store. The Wizard of

Woolco's first petrol station has six high-speed pumps and a 16,000 gallon tank capacity.

Figure 60. The Woolco hypermarket in Newtownards, which opened in June 1976.

Courtesy 3^D and 6^D Pictures Ltd.

agreement with Stewarts Supermarket, a leading chain in Ulster that had a well-established reputation for food sales. Stimulating competition had been created.

It is at this point that the story becomes blurred. Comment made over six months later in the press hinted of some untoward behind-the-scenes activity, and although the possibility of speculation in this report cannot be overlooked, as one journalist put it, 'Rumours had it that the delays in opening experienced by Stewarts were not all of accidental origin'.[28] The value of this observation is difficult to assess. Nonetheless, the journalist's curiosity had also been whetted as to why the new outlet's fixtures and fittings had been suddenly switched from being a regular store fit-out to one which could accommodate an additional Woolco-style layout.

Although substantially larger than one of their normal town premises, it would appear that Woolworth had, indeed, originally anticipated that their new branch in the Ards Shopping Centre would be run as a regular store in this shopping mall. The new complex was to serve not only what was undoubtedly one of the most urbanized areas in Northern Ireland, but also customers from further afield. It seems odd, therefore, that this journalist later suggested that 'quite a number of the firm's store managers in nearby towns were discommoded at the prospect of having a super-sized branch on their door-step'.[29] It was a provocative statement. When the correspondent asked, 'Would the new monster swallow up their customers? Would it have too many unfair advantages?', the theory put forward as an answer suggested that Woolworth was 'keen to avoid dissent among the town managers, yet equally keen to exploit what it saw as a distinct position of advantage' and, consequently, the company had 'sought to change the name and style of its Ards store'. To back up this argument, the journalistic eye of the observer had pointed to the evidence, calling it 'the skid-marks of a sudden swerve'.[30]

This claim of a last-minute decision was correct – but it had been right for the wrong reason. Apparently, the writer had been not been fully briefed and was therefore unaware that the changes being made to create a Newtownards Woolco Hypermarket were a clever experiment prior to the introduction of similar self-service formats at Woolco outlets elsewhere.[31] In Britain, the performance of the Woolco stores was flagging. They provided a personal service only up to a point, and it was being suggested they be adapted into fully self-service hypermarket operations to copy a style then being introduced into Europe. The large, almost ready branch in the Ards Shopping Centre offered the opportunity to carry out a trial run.

When the Newtownards hypermarket opened its doors on 15 June 1976, shoppers discovered wide aisles and high merchandise stacks that were a feature of the British Woolco outlets, but, in addition, the sales floor carried all the normal island displays of food and goods found in regular Woolworth stores. The huge branch was entirely dedicated to self-service.

The experiment was a success. From the day it opened, Ards Shopping Centre became not only a popular venue for people in the area, but also attracted thousands of shoppers from the Republic. Serving a catchment area of 315,000 people, the Woolworth hypermarket in this complex had twenty-four checkouts, 900 trolleys, a petrol station and late-night shopping two nights a week.[32] Sales soared and the business went from strength to strength. For the record, it can be said that the profits returned by the Newtownards Woolco Hypermarket more than justified the investment. The press reported that 'The store cost £1.25 million to equip and fit and a further £0.5 million to stock';[33] meanwhile, the company anticipated an annual turnover of £5m in its first year.[34]

A month or so after the opening, the Woolco manager was able to grab additional publicity in the *Irish Times* when a short-lived but intense price-cutting war waged over the Stewart's Supermarket launch of their 'own-brand' loaf. Bakery workers and bread delivery-men alerted their unions, a disruption of supplies was threatened, but Woolworth and Crazy Prices between them fought off the challenge successfully. Claiming that his outlet's weekly sales targets since the opening in June 'have all exceeded expectations by at least 10 per cent',[35] the Woolco manager gave a Belfast journalist a glowing report on progress when he came looking for an interview about bread sales.

Forthcoming years saw trade consistently buoyant, but nonetheless, despite the success and record-breaking performances (in one famously recalled week this outlet alone had generated higher sales than the whole of the London Metropolitan Region), Ireland's first hypermarket was not fated to survive. Almost exactly ten years later, in the summer of 1986, it became a casualty of the radical change of direction being taken by the Woolworth board. Why this goldmine was sold off to a strong rival probably carries as many alternative opinions and mysteries as does its opening. What may be recognized with some certainty, however, is that by the mid 1980s attitudes towards the Irish retail scene had altered to a great extent.

Shopping in a Woolworth Store in the 1970s

Tightly organized Irish communities in the Republic like to regard their local Woolworth as an integral part of their town's commercial life. The stores were accepted for their role in sustaining a town's economic well-being, and store managers grew used to a level of independence that often circumvented the rules as to what could and what could not be sold from their counters. Woolworth had come a long way since the days when wartime shortages and the dangers of black market dealing prompted directives from Executive Office that insisted 'No store manager or staff are permitted to write direct or contact suppliers. Any query or request must be taken to your district office. Only exceptions are Departments 2 (Café and Ice Cream) and 32 (Horticulture).'[36]

One former manager of a rural branch remembers how a local poultry-man once approached him to see if he could take supplies of pullets' eggs off his hands. He quite often had a surplus that were no use to his regular customers, but, if sold loose, they could be retailed at a rock-bottom price; an absolute bargain. The Republic's stores had long abandoned carrying any significant stock of grocery items by this time, but a deal was done. Deliveries were organized and the eggs subsequently brought benefit to both parties and to local shoppers. Shortly afterwards, the manager was given promotion and moved to a more prestigious Irish city branch. The man from the hatchery made a fresh approach and the lucrative arrangement was re-established for deliveries to the new outlet. All continued successfully until the day someone forgot to remove the unorthodox display prior to an inspection visit from the store's superintendent. The eggs were spotted as the visitor did his rounds with the manager. He stopped in his tracks. 'Tell me I am seeing things? Who said you could sell chickens' eggs?' he asked. They both knew there was no Woolworth store in the world selling loose pullets' eggs from its counters. But when told, 'I took in £1,000 on these last week', the reply was swift, 'I don't care who told you. Keep them'.[37] The superintendent was a wise and experienced man. He knew when to look the other way.

For some shoppers, bargains could backfire, too. At that time, a currency restriction of £50 was still imposed on goods brought into the Republic from England, but day-trippers on the ferry services to Wales discovered they could bring in the portable televisions sets Woolworth had for sale in the United Kingdom for £49.99. They were a wonderful bargain – half the price of the similar item in Ireland. But very soon, the Dublin store in Henry Street was being inundated by shoppers returning their sets and asking for their money back. The Woolworth Company had always retained a policy that offered customers their money back for items purchased in any branch of a Woolworth store 'anywhere in the world'. This was now being put to good use. These little portables had been built to British specifications and could not receive transmissions from Irish TV channels. The customers' money was always refunded. The sets they returned were packed up and dispatched back across the Irish Sea to Wales. The company bore all the costs.

Throughout the 1970s the larger and more impressive Woolworth outlets such as the Henry Street and Grafton Street branches in Dublin and the Cork and Limerick stores remained meccas for shopping pilgrims 'up from the country'. Making a beeline for the Woolworth 'Aladdin's cave' was the highlight for these shoppers' days out.[38]

For customers, Christmas in a Woolworth store was a world in itself. A newspaper feature about shopping in Grafton Street in December 1978 captures an age of greater simplicity. There were plenty of presents costing less than £1. The writer begins by assuring her readers that 'Woolworth has all kinds of goodies'.[39]

Figure 61. Henry Street Christmas lights outside matched the sparkle
on the Woolworth counters inside.

Photograph: © RTÉ Stills Library.

For little girls they have little leather purses, the kind to hang
round your neck and not lose your bus fare, at 75p. A box of Prices
scented candles with glass holders is 49p and these are enough to
split up between two stockings if you like. Artificial flowers are
30p … Leather key rings with names are good for children – those
that are too young to have keys might like to wear them around
their neck on a rawhide thong, good value at 59p. Small mirrors,
plastic backed at 45p. On the make-up counters there are Miners
eye shadow mates, two colours and applicator for 80p. Kohline
and crayon at 45p …

The list goes on. She talks about 'iron-on patches', 'bubble blowing stuff' and
'autograph albums'. 'Miniature Raggedy Ann dolls cost 75p, Ladybird and
Enid Blyton books from 17p to 55p.'[40] It would seem that Dublin children
were more easily pleased in those days. Computer games and mobile phones
were still a generation away.

Mixing Work and Play Supported Many Charitable Causes

In every store, the Woolworth Company ethos expected management and staff to contribute in some way to local charity fundraising. When the late Pat Quinn worked as a trainee manager in Galway in the mid 1950s, his role as a showbiz impresario was already emerging. One of his ex-colleagues remembers his organizational skills with admiration.

> One of the store's counter staff had been sent off to a sanatorium with TB and we were raising money to send her to Lourdes. Pat would go up down the streets of Galway with a loudspeaker: 'Don't miss Woolworth's First Ever Charity Ball in the Hanger Ballroom – compared by Mick Meys of BBC fame'. Meys was another of our trainees who had once been interviewed on the radio in London. Pat also went around the pubs selling tickets to predict the winning score at the All-Ireland Final. We got in the money and the girl went off on her pilgrimage. She later made a good recovery.[41]

Other admirable efforts undertaken are now mostly forgotten. One annual event, run by the Dublin Henry Street store for more than twenty-five years, was never intended to gain publicity. It was an exclusive Christmas shopping night for members of the Irish Wheelchair Association, which was organized by this outlet's management and staff. On the evening it was held, arrangements would be made with the Garda Síochána to block all traffic from Henry Street and Moore Street to allow for ambulance access and parking. Some came from as far away as Kildare, Wicklow, Louth and Meath. Each guest was wheeled around the store for the evening by a volunteer staff member. Everyone involved believed in the traditional Woolworth ethos which dictated that this type of gesture should not be cheapened by commercial gain. Dublin newspapers were asked to avoid publicizing this event and the request was always respected. These special shoppers were given undisturbed privacy and the Dublin photo-journalists never intruded. When the shopping was finished, all the guests were brought up to the store's cafeteria, where a Christmas party awaited them. Later in the evening, further entertainment was put on by artistes from the current shows playing in Dublin's theatre-land. 'We never had a refusal from any of the shows,' one former manager recalls. 'Every big star in town came to do a turn free gratis and for nothing. But we always insisted on no publicity.'[42] The company's marketing gurus might have had a different view.

Smaller acts of kindness are also remembered. When the Furey brothers were very young, their parents spent Saturdays out on the street entertaining passers-by and their mother used to leave her children for hours in the café of the Henry Street store under the watchful care of the girls who worked up there. The staff kept an eye on the youngsters, fed them on the quiet and organized ploys to hide them when the manager made his rounds. In all probability he knew they were there, but chose not to see what was going on.[43]

Figure 62. Presentations for 21 Years of Service always gave the excuse for a party.

Courtesy 3^D and 6^D Pictures Ltd.

Just as charity fundraising was always encouraged, so the company also liked their people to engage in every kind of group activity. Presentations for staff when they reached twenty-one years of service were always an excuse for a party. Annual Christmas dinners or dances, retirement parties and staff outings were all part of traditions that had been established in the earlier decades. A summer day trip as a group was usually arranged. In the late 1950s staff from the Galway store went on boat trips to the Aran Islands and made an annual pilgrimage to the Marian shrine at Knock.[44] When the Clonmel branch went on an outing in 1958, something of the unsophistication of those times is captured by their excitement at being allowed to take a tour around Shannon Airport. Air travel was seen then as glamorous and something reserved for the rich and famous. A report of this trip in the company's house journal *New Bond* describes how 'They were conducted around the airport, visited the Control Tower and airport shops and, after coffee, viewed the airport's floodlit buildings and runways'.[45]

For the branches in the United Kingdom, there was a long-established tradition which encouraged organized field sports, keep-fit classes and rambling, cycling, tennis, swimming and ladies' football. Sporting events provided a means to introduce staff from different branches to each other and so built up the concept of company team spirit. For the Irish stores it was an advantage to have only a small number of branches. Staff members of many outlets often already enjoyed pre-existing social and sporting connections. For example, the ladies' football team from the Woolworth branch in Armagh – who were considered one of the most formidable Irish teams – had members who also played camogie at county level. Fixtures were organized between stores north and south of the border and there were many occasions when the girls had to travel quite some distance. When Cork and Derry met, for example, private bus transport was always laid on after the match. Each team had to be back to work in their own store the following morning.

At management level, the golf course reigned supreme. Since 1954, all the Irish store managers and superintendents, north and south, competed annually for their Perpetual Friendship Cup. The competition was held in Dundalk. In 1976 a second trophy was introduced by the Liverpool Regional Office, which was played for in Royal Birkdale, near Liverpool, at Whitsun. It was called the Woolnordo Golfing Society's President's Cup. The final outing took place in 1982, and the winner was presented with the trophy during the annual dinner and party for retiring colleagues.[46]

Visual Impact? Merging Shopfronts and Streetscapes

During the Woolworth Company's first decade in these islands the instinctive flair demonstrated by the young American expert on real estate and shop fixtures, Louis Denempont, had been highly influential in making decisions over the location and design style of every new store. By the late 1930s the company had appointed him to the board as its managing director, but it would not be too speculative to assume that he probably still kept a very keen eye on the style and location of all new acquisitions.

In Denempont's day, the Woolworth architectural and construction teams between them created two basic templates to be used for almost all building work carried out in England, Scotland, Wales and Ireland during the inter-war years. These plans were conceived and designed by the company's architect, William Priddle, and his colleague, construction manager B.C. Donaldson. The two distinctive styles were known as 'Cinema Front' and 'High Street'. They usually had either an L-shaped or T-shaped floor plan. Examples of the upper storeys of these original façades may still be found everywhere and are instantly recognizable. Old photographs recording some of the complete ground-up rebuilds in the late 1920s and 1930s (such as Waterford, Sligo and Armagh, for example) reveal almost identical features that remained unchanged until the mid twentieth century. This ensured that every new Woolworth store throughout the United Kingdom and Ireland presented itself to shoppers as being as comfortably familiar and unchanged as it had been in their childhood.

Not every new Woolworth store required a complete ground-up build. In the 1950s many of the new outlets in the Republic retained their original late eighteenth-century or early nineteenth-century upper storeys. This strategy allowed the whole building to merge more happily into the existing Irish market town streetscape. Over the decades, the Woolworth company's construction team had acquired a mixed reputation for displaying sensitivity in this regard. Much depended on how vocal a town's conservationists had been when plans were submitted to local authorities.

With the arrival of more stringent planning and conservation laws in the post-war era, concern for the visual impact of a new building in a town's main shopping street dictated that more meticulous care had to be taken. Precedents existed. For instance, in 1924 all the upper storeys of a large sixteenth-century timbered building in Chester were retained,[47] and if earlier aberrations were spotted, then these had to be redressed if permission for further work was to be obtained. For example, the demolition of ancient timbered houses in Faversham's Market Street in the 1920s had been replaced by a single-storey building. When the firm sought permission to expand the size of this store in the 1970s, the planning authorities insisted that a dummy façade be

Figure 63. The Woolworth store in Tralee (4th on left) merged unobtrusively into a typical 1950s Irish rural town streetscape.

Courtesy Gordon Revington.

constructed on the first floor to fill the gap in the streetscape caused fifty years earlier.[48] Likewise, in Guildford, Surrey, a carved stone lion which had once decorated the parapet of the former Lion Hotel on the site for a new store, had to be incorporated into a special niche over one of the new entrances to comply with the requirements of planning permission.[49]

But if they could by any means avoid directives like these, it has to be said that the construction department was always ready to duck swiftly. As a consequence, Woolworth did not acquire a high reputation among serious conservationists. In Ireland, one case in the 1930s whereby they overcame local concern over the historic nature of a building was still remembered decades later. In Kilkenny's High Street today, three small limestone plaques and a few carved stone florets remain set into the upper façade of the building that now houses the former Woolworth premises. This is all that is left to remind passers-by that the building was once the residence of one of the most famous and powerful mayors of Kilkenny, Henry Shee, who lived there in 1610 with his wife Frances Crisp. When Woolworth moved into the original sixteenth-century house that once stood here, the interior had rooms that

Figure 64. A bland and basic design was used in Ferrygate Street, Derry, following modernization of the store in 1966.

Courtesy 3ᴰ and 6ᴰ Pictures Ltd.

were 'still richly panelled' and 'the fine cut-stone chimney pieces were in place. There was also a rather interesting two-windowed southern gable'.[50] The late Hubert Butler, writing later about what he held to be 'an outrage', recalled that the Woolworth construction team was 'faithful to their pledge [to keep] that unique gable for several years. Then one day, when everyone had forgotten, they blocked up both the windows and plastered over the gable'.[51]

Terms of Employment:
The British Unfair Contract Terms Act, 1977

In the mid 1970s a new concern had drawn the attention of the men who occupied the boardroom in Woolworth Executive Office. A new British government act would shortly come into force for their employees in England, Scotland, Wales and Northern Ireland, but before this took place, the F.W. Woolworth & Co. Ltd legal team needed to take a fresh look at their store managers' contracts.[52]

In broad terms, under the system set up by the founder in 1909, a store manager's contract ensured he was in control of his earnings capacity (see chapter 2). As has been outlined earlier, he could draw a fixed sum each week in cash from his store's takings. This was, in effect, an advance on his salary. At the end of each year's trading he would be paid a bonus, which was a percentage of the net profit he had made over the twelve months minus his shrinkage.

Efforts had been made from time to time to improve on this system. By the 1970s, for example, a man going in to manage a new store would remain on a fixed salary until the potential for that store had been established. Steady business had to get underway before the outlet's sales and net profit figures settled into a pattern that could be assessed to calculate what percentage he received. With inflation, stock values often rose, and instead of returning an annual shrinkage figure, stores more often showed an 'overage'. Moreover, during the Troubles in Northern Ireland, a manager's ability to keep strict control over inventory records was particular difficult. Stock had to be moved around from store to store frequently and at short notice, when branches suffered damage.[53]

The 1970s also brought in many more difficulties in the practice of moving men up-rank by relocating them to larger stores with potential for higher earnings. A number of allowances were given to assist with the expense of moving home and family, and other benefits had been gradually introduced such as improved holiday entitlements. All in all, many systems had undergone radical revision since mid-century.

But traditions died hard within the Woolworth Company. For decades, the directors had aimed to keep a kindly, if paternalistic eye on the earning capacity of their managers, just as it had been done in Stephenson's day. But times had changed, and so had commercial life. When the chairman observed (in 1971) that the company was now being driven by 'the market', he had articulated a growing awareness within Woolworth that a new-style commercial world was about to engulf them.

It was now a matter of some urgency to bring store managers' contracts up to date, and there was one clause in the existing contracts that the board was strongly advised to refine in the light of impending legislation. To put it simply, this was the clause that governed the right of the company to relocate their managers to other stores or new positions whenever they deemed it necessary. As a rule, managers usually welcomed a move because it brought promotion and an increase in salary. However, the wording in the old-style contracts still acknowledged that the relocation of a man could only be undertaken if accepted by 'mutual consent' between the company and the employee. In other words, if a manager did not wish to be moved for whatever reason, he had the option to refuse and his job would remain secure. He could not be dismissed. For a man to display such lack of ambition did not go down well with his superiors. The outcome was stark. Recalcitrant managers received no further offers or promotion (see chapter 2).

There were a number of reasons why a man might want to turn away from the nomadic existence that serviced the Woolworth management system for decades. Not everyone desired to be a high-flyer. Some were happy to be settled in a successful store that provided them with an adequate salary and pension. There might be a refusal for health reasons or an over-ruling family commitment. By the 1970s the offer of a relocation came around about every five years or so (in the pre-war era, they averaged every two to three years). In the post-war years a trend had developed whereby to own, rather than rent, a property was favoured, and managers were experiencing greater difficulties in finding housing and negotiating mortgages. Moreover, there was far more cognizance of the rights of wives, especially in England where women were more likely to continue working after marriage. More assertiveness was being shown by managers over the disruptive effects of a relocation on their children's education. In the old days, few men ever refused a move. This was increasingly not the case.

In anticipation of the forthcoming Unfair Contract Terms Act in Britain in 1977 and the similar legislation that was about to be introduced in Ireland, the company now proposed changing this relevant clause in the contracts. The term 'by mutual agreement' was to be scrapped. Instead, the new contracts would ensure that the relocation of a manager was complied with if the move was one the company felt was a 'reasonable request'. If a manager refused to accept, he would be in breach of contract and the Woolworth Company was entitled to dismiss him.

By 1976 many of the stores in the Republic were being managed by men who had been very happy when the company repatriated them back to Ireland. All would have spent several years away from home working in branches in the north of England or Scotland, and this new change to their contracts was not welcome. Meetings were held. Discussions thrashed out the realities and pitfalls, and a few tried to stand firm against signing up to these less favourable terms of employment. But in the end, the majority of the managers realized there was no option left to them but to accept the new wording. Opposition fizzled out.[54]

The British Unfair Contract Terms Act came into force in 1977. It was later subject to a number of amendments. How effective the new contract would be in Ireland was soon to be tested. The following year, the Woolworth store in Main Street, Tipperary Town closed. Its demise makes an interesting case history.

A Tale from Tipperary Town

The Woolworth store at 5–6 Main Street, Tipperary Town was opened on 8 April 1954. It bore the revised number of a bombed-out London store, 337. A house-furnishing and builder's ironmongery business called Duggan had traded here in 1863 and the building was a typical example of an Irish market town's main street shop premises which had been in continuous use as a retail outlet for almost a hundred years. When Woolworth took possession of the building, they installed a standard post-war Woolworth shopfront at street level and the two upper storeys and roof pitch were left undisturbed. The branch thus merged neatly into the vista of the existing streetscape.

In the early 1970s the ground floor shop floor was given a complete upgrade when the store was converted to a self-service outlet. The old-style front windows were replaced by the company's new see-through versions, and, as was normal practice, the building work was contracted out to a number of Irish firms, who worked under the supervision of the Woolworth construction department. Prior to carrying out the refurbishment, a survey may have been carried out, but no structural repairs were made to the upper floors. It seemed sturdy enough, yet a few years later the front wall of the building began to show signs of distress. Cracks appeared in the façade and gaps had opened up around the new plate-glass windows. Something was out of kilter and it was clear that some serious repair work was needed.

The problem was reported by the manager. Time passed. In the meantime, the deterioration continued, and by 1977 it had become a matter of some urgency. Finally, word came that the foreman of the local firm who had carried out the refurbishment would be asked what could be done. The solution was simple. His advice was to rebuild the façade and make good the roof, back and side walls.

The year 1977 was a difficult one for the company. There were escalating marketing costs for advertising campaigns, brand design and development projects. Stiff competition was eating into profits, while money continued to be poured into several new concepts. In August a business column in the press announced 'Interim profits slip by £1.2m at Woolworth'.[55] By the end of the year the same financial commentators were reporting that 'There was nothing wonderful in the set of figures produced yesterday by F.W.Woolworth ... Lack of money in the housewife's purse was blamed for the poor results'.[56]

At some stage before the New Year, a meeting of executives would have taken a look at the cost of rebuilding the façade of the Tipperary store. It is not beyond the realms of speculation to assume a swift decision was made. The branch was a typical small market town outlet with a steady turnover that ticked along without any problems, but it was a mere minnow in a chain of well over a thousand branches. Expending money to restore the upper floors of a crumbling shop premises in this Irish backwater was not a viable proposition. Yet some justification for its abandonment had to be found. If it became known that they had refused to undertake urgent structural repairs to a thriving little Irish store, the news would not go down well. Some prudence was required. Irish store managers had already gained an uncomfortable reputation for closing ranks in solidarity when faced with situations not to their liking. The only acceptable excuse for the closing-down of a store was to claim the volume of trade was not sufficient to keep it going. In this case, this was not strictly true. The previous twelve months' returns for the Tipperary outlet had shown a marked improvement. But it was the best line to take.

The manager was summoned to Dublin Office on the second week in January.[57] He was expecting to be congratulated. Sales were up. His bonus had been good and the store was beginning to buzz. He could not believe what he was hearing when he was told the branch was to be shut in three weeks' time. His staff were being served notice straight away and he was to go back and arrange for all the stock to be sent up to Dublin. Fixtures and fittings had to be dismantled and despatched to Waterford, where a refurbishment was taking place. His own position was secure, of course. Under the terms of his contract, he would be transferred to manage a similar grade of store. There was a vacancy in England, not far from Manchester.

Meanwhile, his cashier, who had been left in charge during his absence, was receiving this news via a phone call from the staff relations department. Thirty years later, she clearly remembers taking the call. 'It was a Friday the thirteenth. I got such a shock. I can still get the shivers whenever that date comes around.'[58]

Under the terms of the recently signed new contracts, the young manager had to accept that being moved back to England was a 'reasonable' request.

The former concept of 'mutual agreement' within contracts, which allowed managers to decline a move, no longer existed. If he did not comply, the company could rule that he was in breach of contract, as was their right. It was not good news. He had already spent about ten years away working in English stores and had enjoyed being settled back in Ireland with family and friends. The idea of being sent away again appalled him, but if he refused to go he would be instantly dismissed, and that was the end of it. He was young and ambitious and he enjoyed his work. But this was the end of the road. The offer of relocation was refused. At that time he had no idea a happy outcome lay ahead.

As soon as the store closed, the local builder whom Woolworth had consulted over the cost of rebuilding the store façade went to have a quiet chat with the owner of the adjoining licensed premises. A discussion took place. When the 'For Sale' sign went up, the next-door publican made a successful bid for the outlet. He immediately sought out the former store manager, who had already found himself another job not far away, and offered to reinstall him with a rise in salary if he was prepared to carry on with as many of his old staff as he could find to re-employ. The interior was refitted, the repairs were tackled and business got going again. The new management partnership cheekily renamed the store Wellworths – which the Northern Ireland Moore brothers tried to block but could not legally challenge.

The venture became a success under the new ownership. Its well-trained manager and his long-service staff ensured that many of the traditional Woolworth core values held good. Business thrived and the patronage of local shoppers continued.

Looking Back on the 1970s

By the end of 1979 there were thirty-seven Woolworth branches operating in Ireland. There were nineteen outlets in the Republic and seventeen in Northern Ireland, and although trading in each region of Ireland now carried a focus on brands and ranges of goods that often differed, the excellent cross-border rapport that had always marked the networking ability of Irish stores and Irish store managers remained intact.

When reviewed in hindsight, the overall performance of F.W. Woolworth & Co. Ltd throughout the 1970s has been neatly summed up by Seaton as having been more concentrated on 'exploring alternatives rather than nurturing their core business'.[59] As the decade drew to its close, Woolworth

Figure 65. The former Woolworth branch in Main Street,
Tipperary changed in nothing but name.

Courtesy 3ᴰ and 6ᴰ Pictures Ltd; photograph: Barbara Walsh.

capital expenditure continued to run high, stoked up by the demands being made not only by the Woolco division, but also from the cost of the continuing store modernization programme and several other innovative diversifications. All needed a lot of money. And times were about to get harder.

Warning Bells Ring

As the final year of the decade began to unroll, the American parent company in New York had been busy preparing a big fanfare celebration of their centenary, which was due to take place in June. Behind the scenes, the enemy was at the gate. On 10 April 1979, leading newspapers' financial columns announced a £500 million takeover bid had been made for the Woolworth Company by a Canadian holding company, Brascan Limited. Brascan had 'investments and management agreements with electric utilities, natural resources and consumer products firms and companies engaged in financial services in Canada and Brazil'.[60]

On both sides of the Atlantic, the shock of this news pulled everyone up very sharply indeed. For the managers of the Irish stores, it was little consolation to be reminded that the British Woolworth operation was but a small segment of the global Woolworth operation. Financial columns in the press reported that the American company 'runs over 5,000 stores and leased departments in the United States and abroad, including Britain. Its latest figures showed sales of £2,250 million and profits of £135 million'.[61]

To everyone's relief, the Brascan bid was unsuccessful. However, there were other threatening storm clouds gathering on the horizon. As Seaton explains, 'Directors assured investors that the [Brascan] bid undervalued the business, which was on track for good returns in the 1980s. But a number of long-term loans from the 1950s expansion were almost due for settlement, while reserves were limited.'[62]

To understand what was happening at this time, is it necessary to refer back to the 1950s, when the American Woolworth Company was engaged in expansion and diversification. As has been already described, they were urging their British subsidiary to follow their example by changing their image and methods of retailing. The American board had no compunction to fund projected growth by taking on a number of long-term loans. Borrowing long for capital expansion was considered a sound business strategy. Nevertheless – as a result – the American company did not own the majority of their sales outlets, shopping malls and Woolco complexes.

By contrast, the British company had spent their profits on acquiring freehold premises or long leaseholds for their stores whenever possible. The British arm owned prime retail sites in every city and town of substance across the whole of the United Kingdom and Ireland. It was an asset-rich property portfolio to die for; a veritable goldmine.

By 1979, conscious there was one possible way to ease the company out of its current difficulties, the eyes of the directors in New York looked across the Atlantic and came to rest on the potential offered by their wealthy, well-capitalized British subsidiary. The American company's ownership of 52.7 per cent of the British F.W. Woolworth & Co. Ltd shareholding offered a lifeline to recovery. Momentous decisions would have to be made.

Chapter 8

Sea Change in Ireland

1980–2008

The 1980s were to be a momentous decade for the Woolworth Company in Ireland. The geographical pattern of its outlets north and south, which had undergone only minor adjustments since the end of the 1960s, had remained virtually unchanged for over two decades (see Appendix II and map Appendix IV). Branches in the Republic were widely dispersed, rarely less than fifty miles of each other – and often considerably more. The area around Dublin was the only exception. It had four stores within a radius of ten miles. By contrast, the Ulster stores were packed tightly together within the six counties, in much the same fashion as many urban areas in England. Nonetheless, each region still retained approximately the same number of stores. By mid-decade the scene would be transformed.

At the start of the 1980s it was business as usual for the Irish stores. Several modernization projects were in the pipeline. The outlet in Newry was due an extension in April and the manager in Sligo had been told to expect a big refurbishment in about eighteen months' time. The budget for the latter was £50,000 sterling. Despite a gathering economic depression and a downturn in trade that brought about job losses within many other sectors of commercial life, the nineteen Woolworth outlets in the Republic were still thriving. It may have been to their advantage that they carried a less complicated range of goods than stores in either Northern Ireland or the United Kingdom. There were no large frozen food and grocery departments; no large drapery or shoe sections; no sales of furniture or carpets. Instead, their confectionery, music, cosmetics and toys were pitched perfectly at Ireland's young population, almost half of whom were under 25 years of age. Moreover, a steady stream of visitors to Ireland was still keeping the tills ringing.

The fortunes of the Irish tourist industry had fluctuated during the early and mid 1970s, but it had regained its former peak by 1977 and was once more displaying steady growth. As the 1980s approached, 14 per cent of visitors now came from Europe.[1] In the early years of the new decade, 85,000 John Hinde picture postcards would be sold from just one of the company's Dublin stores, and, likewise, large volumes of other souvenir lines such as handkerchiefs, scarves, tea-towels, ornaments and Irish-themed costume jewellery were keeping business brisk across the Republic.[2] For their colleagues in Ulster, however, it was deeply disappointing that, despite all the best efforts of the NITB (Northern Ireland Tourist Board), the bulk of tourist traffic was still mostly headed towards destinations in the south of the country. As one frustrated former manager later remarked, 'Despite the Giant's Causeway being one of the top three tourist attractions in Ireland, we were unable to tap into this goldmine. The number of visitors coming to Northern Ireland was very poor.'[3] It was a curious situation, there had been several wide-ranging surveys commissioned with the aid of research material obtained from Bord Fáilte and BHTA (the British Travel and Holiday Association), innovative and cooperative initiatives between Bord Fáilte and the NITB, and serious attempts to set targets in the past decade.[4] Nonetheless, as has been pointed out, 'certain problems persisted' in negating these efforts, and the Province continued to receive 'extremely bad publicity abroad as a result of civil distur-bances, often exaggerated by foreign news media'.[5]

Meanwhile, souvenir lines apart, many other Irish-made goods filled the counters of the stores in the Republic. It was reckoned that 81 per cent of stock sold from these branches in the early 1980s was of local manufacture.[6] Even so, the convoluted practice of buying for these outlets through an agent still persisted. Dublin Office could not buy direct from British manufacturers and the practice of concessions to those Irish manufacturers who were export-only firms continued. For example, ladies' hair rollers made in Kerry had to be sent to a warehouse in the United Kingdom and invoiced to London before being re-imported to Irish stores.[7] To make things even more complicated, the Woolworth accounting system was centralized in Castleton, near Rochdale in Lancashire. It was here that 'a whole department was required to look after the Republic stores because of the different tax regimes and currency questions'. It was thought at the time that 'this team considered themselves to be an elite and always created a lot of mystique about what exactly they did'.[8]

Republic's Stores Carry 81 per cent Irish-made Merchandise

By the 1980s the increasing difficulty of sourcing reliable Irish merchandise. had become irksome. Dublin buying office was finding that 'a lot of the items we were offered were shoddily made … badly finished. They didn't match Woolworth standards.'[9] Likewise, there was frustration and disputes created in store stockrooms over unreliable deliveries. Consignments of stock were often short. 'We would order up both English and Irish Christmas Cards. The six-dozen packs of Irish-made cards were often half a dozen short when delivered … you couldn't rely on them.'[10]

It was clear to many that the old-style tradition of quality to which the Dublin buying office had always aspired was being undermined by new policies that attempted to replace old favourites with cheaper ranges. The emphasis had shifted from the technique of good buying to the skills of marketing. The complaints of store managers were largely ignored. As one remembers:

> In the late 1970s and 1980s a great deal of the stock became unreliable. We might get a batch of hammers with handles that fell off as soon as they were used and we would have to replace them when shoppers returned with complaints. The choice of goods had also become too large and unwieldy, there were too many different choices of colours in things like combs and zips. Good lines were withdrawn. We had some pairs of really excellent binoculars which were selling very well for £5. Then someone decided this was too high a quality and too high a price for Woolworth to carry – and they were all withdrawn.[11]

In Dublin's largest store, Henry Street, the original six soft ice cream machines remained a great draw in the early 1980s. They had acquired a legendary reputation. The special recipe mix for Woolworth which H.B. delivered in one-gallon containers continued to be used, and the same six machines sold unbelievable quantities of ice cream cones all day, six days a week from 9 a.m. in the morning until closing time, generating £47,000 annual sales. By the 1980s, fears for the health and well-being of these aging machines saw Hughes Brothers paying for an engineer to be in attendance every Saturday. His sole job was to wait in the stockroom all day in case any machine gave trouble and needed fixing.[12]

The confectionery department in the Woolworth Henry Street store also continued to produce a higher volume of sales than any other branch in the whole Woolworth chain of one thousand outlets. Since the mid 1970s an increasing number of long-established Irish suppliers to this department had changed hands or gone out of business. The Gallagher's Urney Chocolate manufacturing plant, established in 1924, had been bought out in 1963, sold on to Unilever in 1970 and closed in 1980. Old favourites like Lemons Sweets, a fully owned subsidiary of Barker & Dobson in Liverpool, which had manufactured sweets in Dublin for 135 years, struggled with financial problems for several years before finally going into receivership in 1983.[13] Both of these firms had been doing business with Woolworth Irish stores for decades. In the early 1980s, nonetheless, the store in Henry Street still liked to claim the distinction of carrying the largest pick 'n' mix sweet counter in the world.[14] By that time, the sweets sold from this display originated in South Africa and were distributed by a British supplier. This English firm received an order for the Henry Street store every month for one ton of sweets, calculated in different hundredweight amounts according to their popularity with customers.[15] The confectionery department also retained some of the old traditions, such as sales of all the misshaped or damaged chocolates and chocolate bars produced by the Cadbury's factory in Dublin. These chocolate pieces were dispatched in bulk to Henry Street, where two girls were employed all day, six days a week, doing nothing but pre-weighing this mixture into half-pound bags – to be sold cheap as broken chocolate.[16]

Jacob's biscuits continued to be sold loose by Woolworth long after the introduction of their more expensive prepackaged varieties were stocked by the supermarkets. This Dublin biscuit-making firm delivered each variety in large old-style tins. All that had to be done to create an instant display was to place a hinged glass cover over the contents. The tallest girls employed in a store were usually chosen to be counter assistants in this department, so that they could serve from these higher than normal counters.[17] This firm also delivered tins of unsorted broken biscuits from their factory, and these remained popular with shoppers who were on a tight budget. If supplies ever ran short, the standing joke for disappointed customers was to tell them, 'The girl who breaks the biscuits is on holiday today'. Sometimes people believed it.

By this time, too, the top-selling range of cosmetics in all the Irish stores was made by Rimmel. Their London agent liked to claim that the largest single retail outlet for the sale of their products in Europe was the Woolworth store in Henry Street.[18]

Figure 66. Loose biscuits were always popular with shoppers.

Courtesy 3ᴰ and 6ᴰ Pictures Ltd.

Reviewed in hindsight, earlier decisions to withdraw from direct competition with the food-focused supermarkets and the larger drapery and footwear retailers had proved the right strategy for the stores in the Republic. The Irish Woolworth customer base was still family-centred and conservative in attitude. Although shopping habits were catching up with trends in the United Kingdom, some opportunities to profit from drapery may have been missed. For example, since the late 1960s the Dublin Henry Street thoroughfare had held the reputation as being Europe's busiest shopping street for children's clothing. But efforts to turn the basement of the Woolworth branch in this street into a dedicated kiddies clothing department were frustrated when the idea was blocked by higher authorities in London's Executive Office.[19] Thousands of pounds worth of potential sales were probably lost. The Republic's merchandiser in Dublin Office had argued for it in vain and the store manager's pleas were ignored. At the time, the men on the ground attributed this to London's lack of understanding of the Irish market.

Under Fire from Critics Again

Since the American company's difficulties in 1979, the financial press in London had been casting an anxious eye over the British subsidiary's performance. Profits had recovered in the late 1970s, but their most recent United Kingdom advertising campaigns, which ran with the slogans 'The Wonder of Woolworths' and 'You'll Love to Change', were the target of some sharp criticism. In February 1980 one market analyst opined that 'For a lot of people the real "Wonder of Woolworths" is that for the past few years they have managed to go on making any profit at all … investors are concerned'.[20] Within six months some startling news was to break. August was to live up to its reputation as a wicked month.

One week before their half-year returns were published, news broke that Woolworth had bought the 33-store-strong DIY chain, B&Q, reportedly for just under £17 million.[21] In a statement to accompany this announcement, the board let it be known that

> DIY already represents a substantial and profitable part of Woolworth's business … the B&Q acquisition will involve a move into new types of stores which it is hoped will prove to be a valuable addition to existing activities in this area. It will be maintained as a separate business with its existing management and employees.[22]

It was the very first time the Woolworth British company had ventured into acquisition of another firm's ready-made business. This was new territory. The cost was covered by closing down and selling off 'six large freehold Woolworths properties in London'.[23] To the outside observer, the move to buy B&Q made sense. Woolworth already had very small but thriving DIY and horticulture departments in most branches. Shoppers were increasingly keen on any products that aided home improvements and gardening. There was money to be made. Was this huge investment justified? There were mixed opinions.

Bleak news soon followed, however. Just over a week later, F. W. Woolworth & Co. Ltd published its results. 'It's a disaster,' wrote one correspondent, describing their performance as 'crashing to losses of £2.57m in the second three months of the year against a pre-tax profit of £8.75m last time'. Yet, the chairman of Woolworth remained calm. He was determined to reject gloomy forecasts. 'The problems are entirely due to the lack of spending power in peoples' pockets,' he said. 'The present position is grim, but I have no worries about the future. Over 60 per cent of our profits come in the last quarter, the Christmas period.' Market watchers did not share his optimism. By then Woolworth shares had fallen to their lowest level since 1977.[24]

That summer, in what seemed to have been a move to support increasing sales of adult drapery items in the British stores, Executive Office had put wheels in motion to accelerate the purchase and sales of clothing from Ireland. On 1 August 1980 an advertisement appeared in a Dublin newspaper for an 'Area Clothing Supervisor'. The Woolworth Company was seeking 'candidates with knowledge of Ladies' Fashions, Menswear or Children's Wear … due to the success and expansion of our textile division'.[25] Applicants were expected to have 'previously held a managerial position with a major department store, fashion multiple or chain store group', and the notice added that the vacancy was based in Dublin, a company car was supplied and there was no Saturday work. By December that same year, another advertisement for an 'Export Accounts Administrator' announced that this post would be attached to 'a new dynamic company based in Dublin'.[26] The successful candidate for this post was to have 'knowledge of export/import procedures and documentation, the ability to understand and reconcile accounts and deal with telephone queries and correspondence'. The Dublin Import and Export Office people, it would seem, were not being directly involved in this new venture. It was something being set up by London, but no one was told. Subtle cracks were already beginning to appear in the hitherto close communications system that linked Liverpool, London and Dublin.

September saw another issue affecting the return on investment when the London board announced they were to close their chain of eight Espana shops in Spain. The winding up of the Spanish operation would entail 585 job losses and would be completed by Christmas. Having been set up in 1965, it had sustained losses in each of the previous four years.[27]

By March 1981 expectations for the Woolworth Company's 1980/1 results were not high. To offset the impending bad news, a campaign to chop the prices of 800 fast-selling items in all Woolworth and Woolco stores had been launched in February 1981. Called 'Operation Crackdown', this campaign was to run to the end of the year.[28]

In the meantime, another tack was being investigated which specifically involved Irish suppliers. In April 1981 a routine press release from the Irish Consumer Products department of CTT (Córus Trácthála Teo), an Irish semi-state body dedicated to assisting exports, announced three days of meetings between Woolworth senior executives and 120 Irish companies with the intention of 'increasing the number of Irish suppliers to the 1,000 Woolworths outlets throughout Britain and Ireland'. It was reported that 'Woolworths were currently buying £2.5m worth of Irish goods and it was planned to increase this to £7m over the next year and to £15m per annum over the next five years'.[29] The prognosis looked good. The CTT staff enjoyed a high reputation for advising and smoothing the way for aspiring Irish manufacturers who sought to win orders from retailers such as Woolworth, and many successes were chalked up as a result of their efforts.[30]

By the end of the year the signs were that Woolworth plc was being distracted by another big purchase, which had the potential to allow further expansion and diversification in the United Kingdom. On 20 November the financial columns were reporting that a £20.1 million cash takeover of the Dodge City chain of thirty-two DIY centres 'was to go ahead despite an Office of the Fair Trading recommendation that the takeover should be referred to the Monopolies Commission'.[31]

New York Sells their Share of the British Company

By 1981 the American parent company's financial problems had risen to an even more dangerous level. The New York board was in deep trouble. They needed capital to pay the long-standing debts incurred by the 1950s expansion programme, which were falling due for repayment. Sales of assets such as their F. W. Woolworth & Co. Ltd shareholding could not be put off any longer, and the board in London was put under pressure. The British directors were cautious. A management buy-in was being suggested. As the rumours grew, the two serving board members who represented the interests of the American parent company pushed for urgent action. These men held senior positions on the New York board and knew the seriousness of the situation there. Talks were held with a London consortium of venture capitalists and merchant bankers, Paternoster Stores plc, led by a former chairman of British Sugar. They developed a proposal that persuaded the British board that it was possible for F. W. Woolworth & Co. Ltd to detach themselves from the American parent company and go it alone as part of their group. No British equity need change hands.[32]

In September 1982 the news broke that the Woolworth chain might become a wholly British-owned firm. In mid November an extraordinary meeting of the shareholders voted in favour of 'a capital reorganization which could save Paternoster up to £6m in stamp duty'.[33] Full board agreement to this transaction was required and prior to the shareholders' meeting, commentators in the financial press hinted at the unease among some 'Independent Woolworth Directors [who said] they were "still seeking further information on many points" of the offer and will give shareholders advice as soon as possible'.[34] But, as this report confirmed, the offer had already been accepted by the company's American parent. Soon afterwards, Paternoster Stores plc was renamed Woolworth Holdings plc. As Seaton observes, 'Within weeks there was a new team at the helm. All but one of the old Board had been sent packing'.[35] He also notes that this surviving board member was now the only director with any previous experience of retailing.

The first results for the new group was described by a financial correspondent in an Irish broadsheet as the outcome of a difficult year. The increased profits were attributable to the thriving DIY outlets run by B&Q and it was noted that 'The Woolworths store chain itself lost money'.[36] This was disappointing news. The Woolworth Holdings annual report for 1983 showed a surplus of £36 million on property disposals. This surplus had been achieved by closing down the company's forty-five Shoppers' World catalogue stores, in addition to selling off seventeen Woolworth outlets in other prime locations. The most significant branch to go was the first ever store to open in the United Kingdom company's chain, in Liverpool's Church Street. It had been selected by Frank Woolworth as the base for his empire in the British Isles. Opened on 5 November 1909, this outlet closed for good on 4 June 1983. The following year, the Liverpool Regional Office was gone too, having been transferred from the building in Water Street, its home since 1936, to the company's Castleton Complex. For many of the old-timers, 'the leaving of Liverpool' augured frighteningly uncertain times ahead.

A few months later plans were being laid for another swathe of store closures in the United Kingdom. By April 1984 the press had been alerted 'by leaders of the shop staff USDAW [the Union of Shop, Distributive and Allied Workers] that Woolworth is seeking buyers for 34 of its British high street chain stores'.[37] By this time the Woolworth portfolio of prime sites was already depleted, but there was plenty left to feast on and property investors were still hungry. The thirty-eight prime retail outlets across the water in Ireland looked attractive.

Figure 67. Shock headline on 5 April 1984.

Main image: © RTÉ Stills Library.

Close-downs in the Republic, 1984

Many former Woolworth people now recall 1984 as a 'very sad and unhappy time'. Apart from one or two outlets that were struggling to meet their targets, the majority of the Irish end-of-year results were good; several branches had even achieved profits that were better than ever. These mixed results made no difference. A decision had been made in London to exit Ireland.

What few ever knew until much later was that, at the onset, the board had debated whether or not a few of the highly profitable Irish stores might be retained. Several outlets north and south were high-earners and Dublin's Henry Street store, in particular, was one branch the company was loath to sacrifice.[38] In practical terms, however, such an arrangement would not make for easy administration. Relationships with the unions could be difficult. Each jurisdiction had its own statutory laws governing many aspects of the retail trade. There were different levels of VAT and currency exchange problems.

Taking everything into consideration, it seemed a far more reasonable proposal to pull the whole store chain out of the north and south of Ireland at once. Woolworth plc wanted a clean break.

The plans were kept quiet. The opinion of a superintendent working in Northern Ireland had been sought in confidence, but no one in the Republic was consulted.[39] The board's final decision was still unresolved when another aspect arose. An important political agenda was attached to the company's presence in Ulster, and on getting wind of their proposed exit plans, swift moves were made by the Northern Ireland Office to ensure no store in the Province was to be axed.[40] People in higher places were consulted. Concerns were voiced. In diplomatic circles, it was felt the role played by Woolworth in this divided community was too useful a vehicle for positive PR to be let slip away. In both loyalist and nationalist areas there was a high level of support and affection for the store chain and it had been long recognized that the Woolworth workplace ethic nurtured a friendly 'family spirit' to encourage colleagues to work and socialize together, irrespective of their different backgrounds and affiliations.[41] This was something to be cherished. The board was approached. It was agreed that all the Woolworth outlets in the north of Ireland would stay in business.[42]

With the go-ahead given, the behind-the-scenes agreements that had been already negotiated for the disposal of nineteen properties in the Republic were swiftly concluded. The sale of this portfolio of prime locations was later estimated to have raised £9 million. Was it seen as appropriate that the company's first branch in Ireland, in Dublin's Grafton Street, should be the first to leave the scene? Probably not. It was more likely merely a coincidence. The sale of the Woolworth building in Grafton Street for an estimated £4.75 million was announced in a press release published on 5 April 1984. The purchasers of the outlet were given as 'three financial institutions acting in unison: the Guinness Ireland Pension Fund, Life Association Ireland Ltd, and an investment vehicle within the Investment Bank of Ireland Ltd'.[43]

For Dubliners, the closure of this piece of retail heritage was an unwelcome sign of increasingly depressed times; the Grafton Street Woolworth branch had been an icon for seventy years. Its disappearance from the streetscape was almost unthinkable. But there was little time for any demonstrations of nostalgia, for the speed with which the closure was implemented took everyone by surprise. The manager was transferred to Northern Ireland to run the branch in Derry, and the company had a redundancy package swiftly prepared for the thirty staff members. Full settlements were made without delay. It was a smooth, clinical operation. The tactic had worked. Not a hint was leaked that more closures were to follow.

A week later, financial columns in London were distracting attention away from Ireland with the news of another substantial new acquisition for Woolworth. The group had bought an electrical goods discount chain called Comet at a cost of £177 million.[44] By 3 May it was announced that Woolworth would be raising £70 million by selling off thirty-four of its stores in the United Kingdom, including the most famous Oxford Street branch. A further six outlets were to be sold in a few months' time.[45] In Dublin rumours were rife. Would there be other Woolworth branches closed in Ireland? By June *Irish Times* reporters were pressing Woolworth for a statement on their plans for their other Irish branches, later reporting that on at least two occasions the company had 'issued categorical denials that it was contemplating either the closure or the sale of any of their outlets in the Republic'.[46] No one suspected that a storm was about to break.

On the morning of Wednesday, 25 July eighteen store managers gathered to attend a meeting in Dublin. They had been summoned at short notice. No one was forewarned of the news they were about to hear. The Woolworth regional manager, sent across by the directors in London, had a prepared statement for the press and media. This was the message the public would soon be hearing and reading:

> Trading from the stores in the Republic had failed to provide an adequate return for investment for some time. Sales were clearly being affected by the depressed economy and the high level of VAT at 23 and 35 per cent.[47] As a consequence, every store in the Republic had been sold and they would be all closed in two months' time, on 6 October.[48]

He went on to tell them that Woolworth had disposed of twelve premises to House & Land Ltd, a wholly owned subsidiary of the British-based MEPC organization, MEPC (Ireland) Ltd. One store had been bought by the Royal Life Insurance Company and the remaining five had gone to Primark, a drapery chain that traded in Ireland as Penneys.[49] The whole statement was going to be issued to RTÉ for that evening's TV and radio channels. The assembled managers were instructed to return immediately to their stores to convey the news to staff before it was broadcast that evening. The press would have it in time for the morning's papers.

The occupants of the room were shocked to the core. The managers of branches that had the highest returns knew the Woolworth blanket claim of 'unprofitable trading' for the entire chain was not entirely credible. Many felt the true core issue was that wages in the Republic were 25 per cent higher than the rates in Northern Ireland. Others saw the closures as part of a wider picture. Woolworth was selling off its real estate to raise funds for the group's new ventures.

The mood was clear. Putting this PR spin on the reason of the closures was not going to work. But there was little time for the managers to linger for discussion or clarification. For the men who had travelled up from Killarney, Ballina, Sligo or Cork, a marathon return journey lay ahead. They had to get back to their stores before closing time that evening so that they could tell their staff.[50]

The Irish business world is small and it recognized the value of the contribution made by Woolworth branches in towns and cities to the economy. It did not go unheeded that the announcement of these eighteen store closures and over three hundred job losses had been delayed until the Dáil had gone into its summer recess. By the time the Deputies returned to the House the closures would be completed. However, silencing the press was not possible. Media support against the closures was rallied and front-page headlines everywhere featured the plight of the Woolworth workers.

The *Cork Examiner* reported: 'news of the closure was received yesterday with "total shock". There had been no indication that the store was under threat.' This paper's correspondent also noted that 'The purchasing companies cannot ensure the continued employment of Woolworth employees'.[51] Up and down the country spokesmen from Irish Chambers of Commerce also published protests. The chief of the Limerick Chamber of Commerce announced he was 'making representations to the Woolworth hierarchy in a bid to postpone the closure and if possible to make them look on Limerick in a different light'. He was too late, of course. The stores were sold. Not one would continue to be run as a going concern with its existing staff retained.

Noting that the branch in Galway had been refurbished at a cost of £150,000 only two years earlier, one newspaper correspondent tried to balance the negative aspects of the story by writing that 'A specialized personnel team from the company's head office in London will visit all of its stores in an effort to help employees find alternative employment in the retail business. The company has also undertaken to prepare Curriculum Vitae for all its employees.'[52] In one ex-employee's view, such offers were merely 'a

Figure 68. Press stories followed the escalating dispute: July–September 1984

smokescreen'.[53] Although promised at the time of the sales, only a handful of the Woolworth counter assistants were re-employed by the new retail outlets that replaced their former workplaces. No manager was offered a position. When the *Connact Sentinal* revisited this topic in September, it cited the opinion of a representative from IDATU (the Irish Distributive Workers and Administrative Trade Union), who argued that 'no attempt had been made to dispose of the shops as a going concern to protect staff jobs'.[54] Shock and dismay had soon turned to anger.

In August the mood of the headlines had changed to 'Woolworths Row Flares Up Again', as severance pay proposals for staff began to be rejected in a number of branches. Many of the older counter assistants had served the company for more than thirty years. It was unlikely many of these would find new jobs, and by September the trouble had escalated. Sit-ins were organized in fifteen of the stores. The news 'Woolworths closed down by dispute' was featured on the front page of a Galway broadsheet, which added that it was the outlet's 'first trade dispute in its history'.[55] The same could be said of a great number of the other stores. Moreover, in the majority of the branches, the managers supported the claims of their staff. The legacy of mutual loyalty had stood firm. As one former boss recalls:

> My staff were great people. I'd the reputation for being a tough manager, but a fair one. Their union man would come in to me and we'd go for a cup of coffee and if there was a problem I'd say 'Let's see what we can work out together.' It was barter. We each had our own positions but we always sorted things out between us. He knew my staff were very loyal to me.[56]

Several other branches underwent more dramatic reactions, which gave provincial papers plenty of stories to follow up. In Tralee, one headline read: 'Woolworths staff lock out store manager' and pointed out that 'One of the staff members had worked here for 32 years'.[57] Elsewhere, there were even longer serving employees. Two of the 'girls' in Dublin's Henry Street had each worked forty-seven years behind a counter, while one of their colleagues, a staff supervisor, had spent forty years with the company.[58] In Wexford, the claim of support from a local 'Women's Group' appears to have been exaggerated, although a piece reporting on the staff's 'determination to sit it out' was entirely correct. That same week, a meeting of Wexford Council of Trade Unions passed a unanimous vote of solidarity with the Woolworth workers in their action.[59]

The dispute lasted for three weeks and press coverage for the sit-ins was hugely sympathetic. The *Sligo Champion* was forced to duck out of trouble by publishing an apologetic recant for misinterpreting a Woolworth statement, which stated that sales projections in June had projected a decline in profits. Having written that 'Woolworth sales projections had pointed to losses in the second half of the year in Sligo', they had to admit being mistaken in their interpretation of profit and loss. 'We have now been assured that this [loss] was not the case, and that a substantial profit and not a loss was anticipated in respect of the Sligo store … no implication about the ability of [the manager] was intended. We regret any inconvenience or distress which may have been caused unintentionally and we offer apologies'.[60]

Faced by sit-ins and increased union pressure over the rates of redundancy, Woolworth obtained court orders to remove staff from store premises and the matter was referred to the Labour Court.[61] In the negotiaions that followed the company upped their initial offer of two weeks' pay per year of service with a ceiling of £17,000, to five weeks' pay per year of service in addition to statutory redundancy terms up to a maximum of £20,000, and a minimum of ten weeks pay.[62] A national ballot of IDATU members was taken. The staff agreed to accept the offer. Their dispute was over.

Notably, the union's efforts to negotiate better terms for the managers' severance package did not fare so well. Some twelve months earlier, aware that one or two of the less profitable Irish stores might be threatened with closure under the new regime, the more wary of the managers had begun to consider if it might not be wise to join a union to protect their interests. It could be argued that under Irish Constitutional Law they had a right to do so, and discussions were held over a document that had been seen. It was described as a 'Security of Employment Policy'. As one senior manager now recalls, 'it was realized this document was a redundancy package'.[63] Behind the scenes, battle lines had been drawn up. It was an unheard-of situation. That managers should consider joining a union constituted a serious stepping out of line. Nonetheless, all the Irish managers agreed to take this step.

The case for an increase in the rate of redundancy for management came before the Labour Court shortly before the stores all closed for good. On this occasion however, the company would not budge from their original offer of two weeks' pay per year of service. This was because the severance package for managers had been generous. Not only were their pensions to be enhanced by 50 per cent, they also had the option of taking a reduced pension at the age of 50. It is not altogether surprising that their appeal to the Labour Court failed.[64]

By Monday, 8 October the remaining eighteen Woolworth branches had closed their doors for the last time. Their departure from main shopping areas throughout the south of the country prompted a spate of reflective journalism. In Galway, under the headline 'Nothing could replace Galway's "Woolies"', a piece begins 'The unthinkable has happened' and goes on to reflect that 'Going to Woolworths was like going to Mass. It was a must for everybody coming into town, a Mecca where everybody met ... There will be no replacing "Woolies"'.[65]

In Limerick, another newspaper correspondent recalled how the city's store had survived through some traumatic historical times and reflected that the closing down of their Woolworth store 'brought to an end an era spanning 63 years – a whole lifetime for many'; the headline read 'Woolworths: the end of a legend in Limerick – and an era in Ireland'.[66]

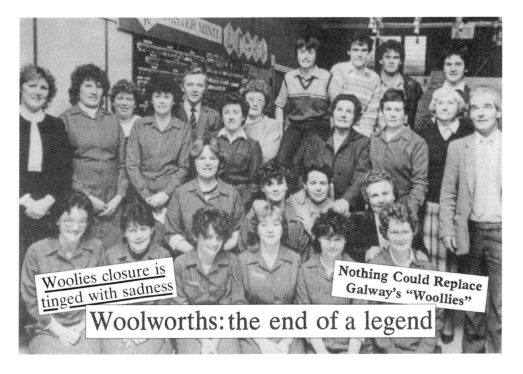

Figure 69. Drogheda staff gathered on their last day, 8 October 1984:
elsewhere, press headlines were equally nostalgic.

Main image courtesy *Drogheda Independent*.

In Dublin, Elgy Gillespie wrote a piece for the *Irish Times* and quoted the views of departing workers from Dublin's Henry Street branch, noting that 'The staff were very slow to condemn their head office'.[67] One long-serving counter assistant was nostalgic. She told the journalist how 'the best times were during the 1960s when everyone felt as though things were looking up'. She remembered that their large staff held annual dress dances in the Metropole Ballroom, just around the corner in O'Connell Street, and how former sales girls kept in touch with their old workmates: 'They came in regularly for cups of tea in the canteen'.[68] Since the introduction a decade earlier of legislation for workers' rights and conditions of employment, the benefits Woolworth offered their staff members were no longer the novelty they had been for workers in the 1920s and 1930s. Nonetheless, the older girls had remained appreciative of gestures like 'three course lunches for 65 pence' and good sick pay, 'a week for every year's service'.[69]

With the close-downs completed, each Irish manager was left to negotiate his own future with the company. (It is interesting to note that British stores had not experienced similar sit-ins or contentious negotiations when a large number of their branches were also closed down around the same time.) For these employees the settlements were generous. As explained above, the company's relationship with the British union USDAW had grown benign since 1982. While 'only about 5 per cent' of their employees had joined it, the union was still officially recognized by the company. 'Union contributions were collected from payslips automatically and forwarded to the union unless people opted out.'[70]

Following the Irish branch closures, only two or three men accepted the offer of relocation to a store in England or Scotland. The majority of managers were well settled back home with their families in Ireland. They had integrated well into the commercial life of their communities; they had friends, interests in sports and hobbies. A number had children poised for entrance into Irish universities or about to take leaving certificate examinations. Only one, who was close to the age of 60, settled for early retirement.

For most, their expertise and experience were put to good use. A number of ex-managers opened up shops or similar retail business on their own account, or re-engaged in family businesses. Several re-employed former staff members in their own businesses. A few others were offered senior positions in Irish wholesale firms supplying the grocery trade, or in one or other of the leading supermarket chains. At least one ex-employee was later approached by his local authority for his organizational skills and experience of team building. Interesting careers lay ahead. These men had much to offer the Irish business world. It may be recognized, moreover, that it was not unknown for former Woolworth managers to enter the portals of the company's competitors. Firms such as Dunnes Stores, Quinnsworth, Marks & Spencer, Chadwicks, Wellworths and Tesco had all benefited in the past from employing ex-Woolworth men at one time or another.

Nonetheless, in the wake of the Woolworth close-downs in the Republic, for those who found themselves suddenly unemployed for the first time in their long and successful careers, the readjustment was difficult. A great deal of disappointment was suffered, especially over the circumstances that brought about disputes between colleagues. For men of this calibre, the experience was shattering. When asked to recollect those traumatic days, responses are similar: 'The way it was done was awful.' 'Divisions were caused. In most big organizations a man will form friendships – everyone has their comrades – but all that was destroyed.' 'Signing on the dole for the first time in my life was dreadful. My neighbours felt so sorry for me ...'

It was little consolation to know one was not alone. As the 1980s recession deepened in the Republic, other firms shut or pulled out of the country. Cork lost Ford and Dunlops and many other large industries closed down. At every turn there were senior management people being let go. The Department of Social Welfare set up a series of structured courses, seminars and temporary work experience for redundant managers. Run by AnCO in conjunction with the National Manpower Service (the forerunner of FAS), new careers and new businesses were born.

It should not be forgotten that several Irish suppliers of goods to Woolworths were also hit by the closure of the nineteen stores. One producer recalls the efficiency of the system: 'Woolworth had these yellow validated order slips. They would arrive in the post every Tuesday morning and the goods would have to be despatched within a week. It worked like clockwork. Payment was received in thirty days without fail. We lost all that regular business when they closed down nineteen Irish branches.'[71]

There are two ways of assessing the departure of Woolworth stores from the Republic of Ireland in 1984. On the one hand, there is the human aspect, which reacts sympathetically to the job losses, the downturn suffered by local suppliers and the genuine regrets of customers who regarded shopping in their local branches as a leisure pursuit. On the other hand, there is the corporate view. Clearly, the break with the American parent company in 1982 and purchase by the Paternoster Group had indeed marked the onset of the terminal illness of a company founded some seventy years earlier as F.W. Woolworth & Co. Ltd. The closure of nineteen outlets in southern Ireland encapsulated the new thinking at board level, and it should be recognized that the position of the Woolworth directors was dictated by an agenda. Tough decisions had to be made. There were to be more closures to come, and the board had to be careful not to set new precedents by agreeing to significant increases in the redundancy rates for staff in the Irish stores. Investment in a diversity of other ventures was planned. Cash was needed, and in order to raise it 117 more stores were to be sold off across the United Kingdom between 1986 and 1998.[72] The past generation of Woolworth directors had locked away profits in prime real estate to provide the company with a safe and secure financial foundation. It had been a wise policy at the time, but by the mid 1980s the corporate world had changed. The firm that had been founded in 1909 to run a chain of successful retail shops as the F.W.

Woolworth & Co. Ltd now functioned as one of several other components of a large group called Woolworth plc.

The Spotlight Falls on Northern Ireland

The removal of Woolworth stores from the Republic in 1984 created an extra bonanza for the company's thriving stores in Ulster. For at least two years prior to this, many branches on the northern side of the border had been experiencing huge boosts to their turnovers because the imposition of higher rates of VAT had pushed up prices in the Republic. Shoppers from the south had been travelling to Ulster in increasing numbers, and the amount of retail business conducted in December 1982 had broken all records in Newry. Stocks of Christmas decorations were sold out a week before Christmas Eve. As one spokesman put it, 'the toys were leaping into trolleys'.[73] People from Cork were arriving at 9.30 in the morning, having left their homes at 2 a.m. Special private charter buses from the Republic rolled into border towns. As many as fifty buses were counted in Newry on one of the Saturdays in early December.[74]

The following year, 1983, saw further currency fluctuations affecting both excise duties and VAT. Christmas shoppers from the Republic began arriving into Northern border towns as early as October. Claiming that 'Newry traders welcome Southern VAT refugees', one correspondent reported how one shopkeeper had told him:

> Saturday was just unbelievable, it broke all sales records. There were 109 coach loads of Southern shoppers … about 30 of them from Dublin or further south. Essential toiletries, VAT-free in the North but taxed as luxuries in the South, are bought in bulk. As for washing powder the bigger the packet, the quicker they will buy them. One store began stocking extra large tubs because shoppers from the 26 counties were buying the normal sized packets by the case, and the large tubs now sell 'as though they were going out of fashion'.[75]

Not only was the rate of exchange beneficial, the price differential was highest on toys, toiletries, records and electrical goods. The Woolworth store in Newry became a top earner. In the wake of branch closures in the south, Christmas 1984 was to bring many more extra customers over the border.

People from Donegal had always patronized the Woolworth branch in Derry's Ferrygate Street, but now Sligo shoppers descended into Enniskillen, and the Armagh branch also gained customers from all the border areas.[76]

Corporate Events within Woolworth Plc

Although shoppers would have been largely unaware of the changes that were taking place at the top of the Woolworth management structure, the next two years, from 1985 to 1987, were marked by some noteworthy events that affected the future of the Northern Ireland branches. In what Seaton has described as a 'shake-up', a new strategy called 'Focus' was introduced into stores in 1985.[77] It aimed to pare back the range of merchandise to a few basic lines, not unlike the limited stock that the now defunct stores in the Republic had found to be so reliable in the past. These were toys, gifts, confectionery, records and cassettes, kitchen, home and garden accessories, children's clothes and cosmetics. Two departments were abandoned – food and adult clothing – even though they contributed 30 per cent of stores' overall sales.[78]

In London, Woolworth plc was still selling off assets, and in 1985 one of the company's overseas subsidiaries, a store in Cyprus, was shut down and sold. Opened in 1974, it had lasted just over a decade. Further closures of subsidiaries in the West Indies and Africa were to follow over the next few years. Meanwhile, at home in the United Kingdom, by the following spring, in March 1986, in what might be seen as a more significant move, the F.W. Woolworth & Co. Ltd trading name was changed to 'Woolworths'. Any remaining store still displaying an old façade depicting the gold-lettered F.W. Woolworth & Co. Ltd had this final link to the old company removed. The same month, March, saw the first of the rumours – denied at first – that a hostile £1.75 billion takeover bid for Woolworth was being mounted by the Dixons Group plc (now Currys), the big United Kingdom electrical goods chain. The opening shots were fired in early April and pressure continued throughout May. On 7 June, Woolworth plc forecast a 30 per cent rise in profits to £105.5m for 1985/6.[79] By 12 June, Dixons had increased their offer – but just under a month later, on 3 July, the battle was over. 'Woolworth fends off Dixon's bid' the headlines declared and revealed that the deal had been called off by lunchtime the previous day.[80]

Midsummer 1986 also witnessed the demise of all the Woolco outlets. These were sold to the Dee Corporation plc for £26 million. In Newtownards, the much trumpeted Woolco Hypermarket was replaced by their old adversary,

Wellworths, which was now owned by the Dee Corporation. The Moore brothers had sold off their flourishing Northern Ireland chain to them about twelve months earlier, and as a result competition from this quarter had heightened considerably.[81] Dee had put underway a programme of improvements for this chain of stores. The existing Wellworths in Bangor and Strabane were to soon undergo extensions and refits; new outlets were to open in Armagh and Comber, and new premises in Limavady, Ballyclare, Downpatrick and Coleraine were already under construction. A distribution warehouse in Antrim was to be in operation after Christmas.[82] The rival was also planning a further three stores for openings in 1988.[83] Woolworth managers, faced with this heightened level of competition, were going to find the going tough from here on.

Irish Managers in Northern Ireland keep up Traditions

Hard times did not mean abandonment of all former traditions. Each store still fostered its own fund-raising events for charity and staff events. Many were arranged quietly while others assisted campaigns for which publicity would be of benefit, and, on occasions, the Irish stores were joined by colleagues from all other parts of the United Kingdom.

One such event was the firm's participation in the 1986 Sport Aid Marathon, which united 20 million people across the globe to raise funds to fight famine in Africa. Held simultaneously in five continents, the Woolworth contingent ran their 10 km marathon in Birmingham. Their involvement in the cause was organized by the manager of the branch in Newry, Northern Ireland. Colleagues from many parts of the United Kingdom took part, in addition to representatives from Executive Office and the Castleton complex.

Woolworth branches in Northern Ireland have always provided input to town festivals and special event weeks. Among more recent projects supported by staff from the Province was a £37,000 donation towards the purchase of a specially equipped van for children with disabilities and special needs.

The Increasing Importance of Music Departments

During the mid 1980s the emphasis in Woolworth stores was shifting even more heavily towards sales of music and other media products. In 1986 Woolworth plc had acquired a firm called Record Merchandisers, which the company would rename as Entertainment UK. It distributed music CDs,

Figure 70. Sport Aid – the Race Against Time, 25 May 1986: the participation of Woolworth colleagues from across the UK was organized by the store manager of Newry, County Down.

Courtesy Pat Kelly.

videos and computer software. As a result, all the stores in Northern Ireland revamped their music departments and sales of tapes and CDs became hugely important in the Province.

There is a rich heritage of traditional music throughout the whole of Ireland, and every community in the Northern Province has nurtured melodies and songs for generations. For decades, the music departments in all the Irish stores, north and south of the border, had taken the initiative to cater for this interest by placing orders through an independent agent who specialized in the distribution of Irish labels. Entertainment UK was able to boost these Ulster branches' well-established base for growth, and the selection of records, tapes and CDs steadily improved throughout the 1990s. By the time the millennium was on the horizon, sales of music would account for more than 30 per cent of most Ulster stores' total takings.[84] Notably, the most popular outlet was Belfast's High Street store, which enjoyed a phenomenal reputation for having the best music department in the whole of Northern

Figure 71. The Ulster Youth Orchestra performs
for customers during Armagh Festival Week, 1987.

Courtesy Pat Kelly.

Ireland. All the well-known musical celebrities of local and international fame
who came to Belfast would take time out to make a visit to this branch, much
the delight of hundreds of music-loving customers.[85]

Further Corporate Changes coming down the Track

By March 1987 the London executives in Woolworth plc were veering off in
yet another direction by buying out a substantial chain of chemists, Superdrug,
to which they added a smaller chain, Tip Top Drugstores, in mid February
1988. The following year, on 17 March 1989, Woolworth plc announced that,
henceforth, the group was to be called Kingfisher plc. The link with the
founding firm was retained and what remained of the retail store chain they
had re-branded as 'Woolworths' soldiered on. By now, the Liverpool regional
office was no more. Its responsibilities had been subsumed into a new set of
administrative divisions, which categorized stores into types and sizes.

Since the demise of the Woolco Hypermarket in Newtownards, there had been no further major changes for Woolworth in Northern Ireland apart from the closure of the store in Larne on 29 September 1990. As the millennium approached, however, moves were afoot to revitalize the commercial life of Belfast, and on 21 June 1999 a Woolworth outlet in the new East City Shopping Centre at Connswater got off to a good start. Business formerly conducted in the company's large building in High Street was transferred there and a programme of extensive restoration to the structure of the old premises commenced. Since its opening in 1915 as the second Woolworth store in Ireland, the premises in High Street had been massively extended far beyond the original site. It had been damaged by air raids during World War Two and the fabric of the building had deteriorated during the more recent Troubles. By mid August 2001, however, financial columns were announcing that Kingfisher was to sell off this former flagship store as part of a property deal that would see a further 182 stores across the United Kingdom being disposed of in a package worth some £614 million.[86]

Within two weeks a more dramatic event was to introduce a radical change. Following a realignment of finances by Kingfisher plc, the Woolworth chain of stores, warehouses and distribution centres was about to be demerged from the Kingfisher plc Group and launched as an independent company. The new group, to be called Woolworths plc, would no longer have the security of a valuable property portfolio, however. Apart from five shops, which remained in their ownership, all the retail outlets had been sold off by Kingfisher to fund other investments, and the business was now being operated out of leased premises. In addition, the group was to take on responsibility for an overdraft of £200 million. To quote Seaton, 'Freedom, it seemed, had a high price'.[87]

The demerger took place on 28 August 2001.[88] With new directors at the helm, store managers in Northern Ireland anticipated a shake-up. Was this to be the much needed renaissance? When plans for the Province were unrolled exciting suggestions were mooted, and it was not long before the first of several new outlets opened. On 2 November a very different style of store, called Big W, opened with a flourish in Belfast's Yorkgate Shopping Centre. The Big W store concept was a recent innovation which had been very successful in Newcastle in the north-east of England. Big W were large, warehouse-like buildings that carried large stocks of merchandise bought in bulk. They also sold furniture and adult and children's clothing. As one former Northern Ireland store manager explains, 'Where a normal store might have a budget of £8 million, these outlets would have double that, perhaps £16 million or so.'[89] The Belfast Big W was to be the first one in Ireland. As Seaton has put it, the idea was to 'showcase Kingfisher's retail brands, with Woolworths, Superdrug, B&Q, Comet and music specialists MVC in a single Walmart-like out-of-town store'.[90]

Press coverage for the new store's opening was enthusiastic. Commentary described the outlet as a superstore and senior politicians were interviewed. It was like the old times again, when the coming of a Woolworth outlet augured good times ahead. Praise was lavish. As one correspondent observed, 'The Northern Minister of Employment and Learning said the creation of 250 jobs was a welcome boost to the economy and welcomed the [Woolworths] group's commitment to recruit locally and to interview unemployed people for vacancies.'[91]

Yet, the Big W concept turned out to be as short-lived as a number of other initiatives entered into after the demerger.[92] By the end of 2003, Seaton points out that all the Big W stores 'had either been sold or … were converted to large out-of-town Woolworths'.[93] By the summer of 2003 most of the stores had already replaced their large Big W signs with a smaller fascia sign that read: Woolworths. From then on, 'the Big W name just faded away between Spring 2004 and Christmas 2006'.[94]

One former manager from Northern Ireland has described the change-over: 'During the final decline of Big W, when we were unable to source bulk purchasing to fill these vast sites, we commenced a cut down or a simple boarding up operation to reduce the size to a more manageable Woolworths store. This was completed very quickly and the areas vacated were simply left empty'.[95]

Despite the disappointing fate of their Big W store, by January 2008 the Woolworths group renaissance in Northern Ireland appeared to be in full swing. On the ground the verdict was positive. It was good to see things moving at speed. One of the people involved still enthuses over the excitement that was generated:

> It was a fabulous initiative to get for Northern Ireland. Between March and June 2008 we opened three new outlets all within about six weeks of each other. Ballymena had been already relocated into the tower centre and its old site sold. We were recruiting, training, merchandising and getting everything ready for the new store openings.[96]

A branch in Antrim opened on 13 March 2008; the next outlet commenced trading in Magherafelt on 17 April and the new store in Park Centre in West Belfast opened on 19 June. Optimism was riding high.

Figure 72. A new store for Antrim in 2008.

Courtesy 3ᴰ and 6ᴰ Pictures Ltd.

For the past three years or so, the performance of the stores in Northern Ireland had retained an enviable position as the second highest-earning district in the Woolworths Northern Region; volume of sales and profits were only surpassed by the returns made by Scotland. Both areas were well ahead of the results brought in by the other regional offices.[97] Yet, within weeks of the celebration marking the start-up in Belfast's Park Centre, seriously disturbing rumours were filtering out from London. All was not well with the company. The news darkened. Financial columnists fretted. Markets were gripped by heightening speculation. The group had debts amounting to £385 million. Could a rescue be mounted? Hopes were raised, only to be dashed. Rumour became fact. The group was in trouble. Then, on 26 November 2008 trading in Woolworths Group plc shares was suspended.[98] Administrators were appointed and shortly afterwards it was announced that the chain would close

Figure 73. A fine premises in Banbridge seeks a new retailer, 2009.

Photograph: Barbara Walsh.

all its branches within weeks. This meant that 27,000 United Kingdom employees would lose their jobs.

At local level, the shock wave caused by this news across the Province might be compared to the sudden announcement of close-downs in the Republic almost twenty-five years earlier. The end was equally as swift and clinical in its operation. When a former manager in Northern Ireland was asked by the BBC in Belfast to give his views on the local reaction, his response was simple. 'Everybody is very, very upset about the situation,' he said, 'The Northern Ireland outlets formed one of the company's top regions ... the stores were always the top in performance, both in sales and profit'.[99]

Christmas brought closing-down sales of stock. The liquidators also stripped every branch of its fixtures and fittings and sold the lot. By 7 January 2009 the United Kingdom chain of 807 retail outlets was gone. In Northern Ireland, the last two of nineteen stores closed their doors on 3 January. These were Belfast's former Big W store at City Side Retail Park and the Woolworths branch in Coleraine. For some, it was the end of the story, but Frank Woolworth's concept of an 'everyday store for everyone' had always retained the ability to regenerate itself when challenged. There would be new chapters and new stories ahead.

Appendix I

Table 1. *The Store Chain in Ireland, 1914–18*

Store No.	Store location and address	Opened	Approx. population of city/town
31	DUBLIN, Grafton Street	23 Apr. 1914	307,200
59	BELFAST, High Street	6 Nov. 1915	393,700
76	DUBLIN, Henry Street	17 Aug. 1918	n/a

Approximate population figures are averaged out and rounded-up to nearest 100.

Table 2. *Additions to the Store Chain in Ireland, 1919–26*

Store No.	Store location and address	Opened	Approx. population of city/town
83	CORK, Patrick Street	6 Feb. 1920	77,800
85	LONDONDERRY, Ferryquay Street	27 Feb. 1920	43,400
90	DUN LAOGHAIRE, Upper Georges Street. (Moved to Lower Georges Street in 1927)	Sept. 1920	Urban D.C. 18,300
93	PORTADOWN, High Street	19 Feb. 1921	11,900
97	LIMERICK, O'Connell Street	7 May 1921	39,100
99	BELFAST, North Street	18 June 1921	403,800
212	BALLYMENA, Bridge Street	19 Feb. 1926	11,900

Table 3. *Additions to the Store Chain in Ireland, 1927–39*

Store No.	Store location and address	Opened	Approx. population of city/town
331	DUNDALK, Clanbrassil Street	21 July 1928	14,100
343	LISBURN, Bow Street	30 Nov. 1928	12,500
380	BANGOR, Main Street	25 Jan. 1930	10,900
407	KILKENNY, High Street	18 July 1930	10,100
414	SLIGO, O'Connell Street	31 Oct. 1930	11,900
418	WATERFORD, Barronstrand Street	31 Oct. 1930	27,200
415	COLERAINE, Church Street	13 Feb. 1931	8,600
446	CLONMEL, O'Connell Street	19 June 1931	9,200
595	LURGAN, Market Street	9 Nov. 1934	14,200
611	ARMAGH, Upper English Street	17 May 1935	10,200

Table 4. *Additions to the Store Chain in Ireland, 1940–55*

Store No.	Store location and address	Opened	Approx. population of city/town
769	NEWRY, Marcus Street	26 July 1946	13,100
770	DROGHEDA, West Street	20 Jan. 1950	15,400
773	WEXFORD, Main Street South	4 April 1952	11,800
775	TRALEE, The Mall	20 June 1952	11,000
801	BRAY, Main Street	18 June 1953	11,800
808	GALWAY, Eyre Square	10 July 1953	21,300
809	MULLINGAR, Oliver Plunkett Street	6 Aug. 1953	5,700
821	THURLES, Liberty Square	26 Nov. 1953	6,300
823	BALLINA, Arran Street,	27 Nov. 1953	6,300
833	OMAGH, Market Square	21 Jan. 1954	7,500
337	TIPPERARY, Main Street	8 April 1954	4,900
839	DUBLIN 8, Thomas Street	27 May 1954	532,600
852	KILLARNEY, New Street	13 Aug. 1954	6,400
856	STRABANE, Castle Street	1 Oct. 1954	7,000
885	CAVAN. Main Street	27 May 1955	3,500
896	LARNE, Main Street	27 July 1955	14,000

Table 5. *Additions to the Store Chain in Ireland, 1956–69*

Store No.	Store location and address	Opened	Approx. population of city/town
1023	NEWTOWNARDS, Conway Square	28 Aug. 1959	12,900
1068	DUNGANNON, Scotch Street	8 Nov. 1962	6,700
1107	BANBRIDGE, Newry Street	30 July 1965	6,500
1128	CARLOW, Tullow Street	27 Oct. 1967	9,400
1126	ENNISKILLEN, High Street	26 Oct. 1967	7,500

Table 6. *Additions to the Store Chain in Northern Ireland, 1970–2008*

Store No.	Store location and address	Opened	Approx. population of city/town
2014	WOOLCO, Ards Shpping Centre	15 June 1979	315,000 (catchment area)
1221	EAST BELFAST, Connswater	21 June 1999	277,800
1248	BELFAST, Big W, Yorkgate	2 Nov. 2001	277,800
1268	ANTRIM, Castle Mall	13 Mar. 2008	20,000
1273	MAGHERAFELT, Meadow Lane	17 Apr. 2008	8,400
1274	WEST BELFAST, Park Centre	19 June 2008	277,400

Table 7. *The Number of Woolworth Stores Opened and Closed in Ireland in each Decade from 1910 to 2010*

	1910 –1919	1920 –1929	1930 –1939	1940 –1949	1950 –1959	1960 –1969	1970 –1979	1980 –1989	1990 –1999	2000 –2009
Start	0	3	12	20	21	37	41	36	16	16
Opened	3	9	8	1	16	4	1		1	4
Closed	0						6	20	1	20★
End	3	12	20	21	37	41	36	16	16	0

★Store No. 59, Belfast High Street, was sold in 2001, leaving 19 stores in all to be closed on the final day.

Table 8. *Street address for 41 Irish stores in 1972*

Store	Address
31	DUBLIN, 65–8 Grafton Street
59	BELFAST, 11–15 High Street
76	DUBLIN, 18–20 Henry Street
83	CORK, 39–41 Patrick Street
85	LONDONDERRY, 28–32 Ferryquay Street
90	DUN LAOGHAIRE, 89 Lower Georges Street
93	PORTADOWN, 35–6 High Street
97	LIMERICK, 37–9 O'Connell Street
99	BELFAST, 157–61 North Street
212	BALLYMENA, 12–16 Bridge Street
331	DUNDALK, 91–3 Clanbrassil Street
343	LISBURN, 45–7 Bow Street
380	BANGOR, 22–30 Main Street
407	KILKENNY, 91–2 High Street
414	SLIGO, 34 O'Connell Street
418	WATERFORD, 31–5 Barronstrand Street
415	COLERAINE, 19–23 Church Street
446	CLONMEL, 74 O'Connell Street
595	LURGAN, 48 Market Street
611	ARMAGH, 5 Upper English Street
769	NEWRY, 1–2–2a Marcus Street
770	DROGHEDA, 6–7 West Street
773	WEXFORD, 29 Main street South
775	TRALEE, 23–4 The Mall
801	BRAY, 10–12 Main Street
808	GALWAY, 36 Eyre Square
809	MULLINGAR, 18 Oliver Plunkett Street
821	THURLES, 33–4 Liberty Square
823	BALLINA, Arran Street
833	OMAGH, 10 Market Square
337	TIPPERARY, 5–6 Main Street
839	DUBLIN, 126–8 Thomas Street
852	KILLARNEY, 7 New Street
856	STRABANE, Castle Street
885	CAVAN. 81–2 Main Street
896	LARNE, 34–6 Main Street
1023	NEWTOWNARDS, 8–10a Conway Square
1068	DUNGANNON, 23–5 Scotch Street
1107	BANBRIDGE, 33–9 Newry Street
1128	CARLOW, 24–5 Tullow Street
1126	ENNISKILLEN, 2–6 High Street

Appendix II

Number of Woolworth Stores per Decade, 1920–2000

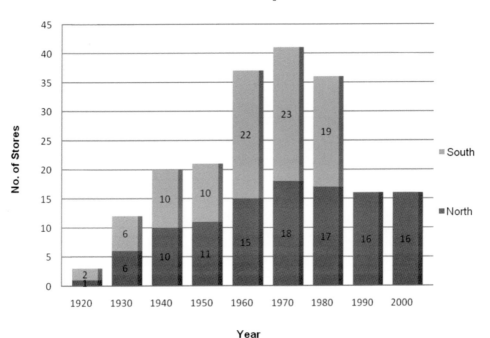

Appendix III

Early Decades: Stock Departments

The Woolworth Company's departmental numbering sequence remained virtually unchanged from 1909 up to the early 1960s. The original 27 departments increased to become 97 when Woolworth expanded into selling furniture, large electrical appliances and many more ranges of food and clothing,

Departments in the 1950

1	Confectionery	14	—	27	—
2A	Café	15	Haberdashery	28	Hardware
2B	Ice Cream	16	Sewing	29	Garlands, Tree Balls, and Xmas Decorations.
2C	Delicatessen and Tea Bar	17	Hosiery		
		18	Drapery and Knitted Goods	30	Toys
3	Food Specialities.			31	—
4	Jewellery and Optical Goods	19	Christmas Cards, Calendars and Seasonable Stationery	32	Horticulture
				33	Tin and Enamelware
5	Biscuits			34	Household Goods
6	—	20	Stationery	35	Crockery and China
7	—	21	Books and Cards	36	Glassware
8	—	22	Toilet Goods	37–39	—
9	Ribbons	23	Fancy Goods	40	Returned Empties
10	—	24	—	50	Store supplies (e.g. staff uniforms, paper bags etc)
11	Boot Goods	25	Paint and Polishes		
12	—	26	Lighting		
13	Handkerchiefs				

Appendix IV

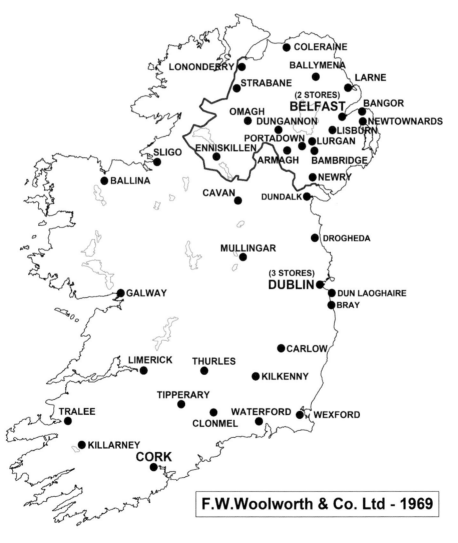

Figure 74. Map showing Woolworth stores in Ireland, January 1969.

Bibliography

Libraries and Archives

Armagh Irish & Local Studies Library
Ballina Library
Ballinahinch Central Library, County Down
Ballymena Library
Carlow Library, Local Studies Department
Cavan, Johnston Central Library
Coleraine Library
Cork County Library, Local Studies Department
Drogheda Library
Dublin City Library and Archive
Dundalk Library
Enniskillen Library, Irish and Local Studies Department
Faversham Library, Kent, England
Foyle Central Library
Galway Library
Irish Architectural Archive, Merrion Square, Dublin
Kilkenny Library, Local Studies Department
Killarney Library, Local Studies Department
Limerick Library, Limerick City Council Local Studies
Mullingar Library
National Library of Ireland
Omagh Library
Sligo Reference and Local History Library

Strabane Library
Thurles Library, Tipperary Studies
Waterford Library
Wexford Library
Wicklow County Council Library Service
Whitstable Library, Kent, England

Newspapers and Journals

The Anglo-Celt
Armagh Guardian
Ballymena Observer
Banbridge Chronicle
Carloviana: Journal of the Old Carlow Society
Coleraine Chronicle
Connacht Sentinal
Connacht Tribune
Cork Examiner
Courier and News
Democrat and People's Journal
Derry Journal
Drogheda Independent
Dublin Evening Mail
Dundalk Examiner and Louth Advertiser
Evening Herald
Faversham and North East Kent News
Fermanagh Herald
Folkestone Express
Freeman's Journal
Galway Advertiser
Impartial Reporter and Farmers' Journal
Irish Independent
Irish Times
The Kerryman
Kilkenny People
Larne Times
Limerick Leader
Lisburn Standard

Londonderry Sentinel
Lurgan Mail
Nationalist and Leinster Times
Nationalist and Munster Advertiser
Nenagh Guardian
Newry Telegraph
Newtownards Chronicle
Northern Constitution
Portadown News
Sinn Féiner (New York 1920–21)
Sligo Champion
Sligo Independent and West of Ireland Telegraph
Strabane Chronicle
Strabane Weekly News
Tipperary Star
Tyrone Constitution
Ulster Herald
Waterford News and Star
Western People
Westmeath Examiner
Wexford Echo
Wexford People
Whitstable Times and Tankerton Press
Wicklow People

Primary sources, F.W. Woolworth & Co. Ltd

A Career in Store for you with Woolworths, 1967

Buyers' Minute Book No. 5, with additional pages (1943–8)

Complete list of stores, November 1972

Directors' Minute Book No. 1 (23 September 190 –April 1915); No. 2 (April 1915–1919); No. 3 (1920–c. 1923)

50th Golden Jubilee Convention, 1909–1959, 2 March 1959, unpublished typescripts

50th Golden Jubilee Convention Programme Jubilee Year, 1959

'First Full Year's Sales of Stores Opened in 1926', notes by Company Chairman William L. Stephenson

General Management Committee Minute Book No. 1 (1936–8); No. 2
(1939–44); No. 3 (1945–8)

J.C.W., 'Woolworth in Britain', in-house information brochure produced
for employees, January 1971

The New Bond Staff Magazine, Vol. 1, No. 8 (August 1936); House journal,
Vol. 7, No. 3 (November 1948); Vol. 9, No. 6 (December 1950); Vol. 17,
No. 3 (June 1953); Vol. 16, No. 6 (December 1957); Vol. 17, No. 5
(October 1958); Vol 18, No 1 (March 1959); Vol. 27, No. 1 (February
1968)

Woolworth's First 75 Years: The story of everybody's story (New York: F.W.
Woolworth, 1954)

Woolworth News, The House Journal of F.W. Woolworth & Co. Ltd., No 35
(July 1976).

Memento, Christmas, 1924.

Twenty Years of Progress, Christmas, 1928.

Twenty-six Years of Progress, Christmas, 1934.

Thirty Years of Progress, Christmas, 1938.

Forty-two Years of Progress, 1909–1950, Christmas 1950.

Fifty Years of Progress, 1909–1959, Christmas, 1959.

Fifty-five Years of Progress, 1909–1964, Christmas, 1964.

Sixty Years of Progress, Christmas, 1969.

A Pictorial Record of Executive and Management Personnel, Christmas, 1974.

A Pictorial Record of Executive and Management Personnel, Christmas, 1979.

Other Primary sources

Census of Population Returns, Saorstát Éireann.
Thom's Directories, 1913–79
United Kingdom Census of Population, Public Records Office, Northern
Ireland.

Secondary sources

Andrew, Christopher, *The Defence of the Realm: The Authorised History of MI5*
(London: Allen Lane, 2009)

Bardwell, Leland, *A Restless Life* (Dublin: Liberties Press, 2008)

Boyce, D.G., 'Nationalism, Unionism and the First World War', in A. Gregory and S. Paseta, *Ireland and the Great War* (Manchester University Press, 2002)

Carlow Chamber of Commerce, *Carlow Chamber of Commerce: Tourism and Industry 50th Anniversary 1947–1997* (Carlow: Chamber of Commerce, 1998)

Carter, R.W.G. and Parker, A.J., *Ireland: A Contemporary Geographical Perspective* (London: Routledge, 1989)

Clear, Caitriona, *Women of the House* (Dublin and Portland, OR: Irish Academic Press, 2000)

Craig, Maurice, *Dublin, 1660–1860* (Dublin: Figgis, 1980)

Daly, Mary E., *Women and Work in Ireland* (Dublin: Economic and Social History Society of Ireland, 1997)

Department of Industry and Commerce, *Official Industrial Directory, 1955* (Dublin: Stationery Office, 1955)

Feeney, Brian, *The Troubles* (Dublin: O'Brien Press, 2004)

Foster, Roy, *Modern Ireland, 1600–1972* (Harmondsworth: Penguin, 1989)

Furlong, Irene, *Tourism in Ireland, 1880–1980* (Dublin and Portland, OR: Irish Academic Press, 2009)

Harrison, Brian, *Seeking a Role: The United Kingdom, 1951–1970* (Oxford: Clarendon Press, 2009)

Henderson, Emmaline, *Thomas Street, Dublin 8* (Dublin: Civic Trust, 2001)

Johnson, David, *The Interwar Economy in Ireland* (Dublin: Economic and Social History Society of Ireland, 1999)

Keogh, Dermot and O'Driscoll, Mervyn (eds), *Ireland in World War Two* (Cork: Mercier Press, 2004)

Killeen, Richard, *A Timeline of Irish History* (Dublin: Gill and Macmillan, 2003)

Lee, J.J., *Ireland 1912–1985: Politics and Society* (Cambridge University Press, 1989)

McDonald, Tommy and Anderson, Robert, *Memories in Focus*, Vol. 1 (Coleraine: Impact Printing of Coleraine Ltd, 1981)

Moriarty, Theresa, 'Work, Warfare and Wages', in Adrian Gregory and Senia Paseta (eds), *Ireland and the Great War* (Manchester University Press, 2002)

O'Donnell, Jim (ed.), *Ireland: The Past Twenty Years. An Illustrated Chronology* (Dublin: Institute of Public Administration, 1986)

O'Halpin, Eunan, *Defending Ireland: The Irish State and its Enemies Since 1922* (Oxford University Press, 2000)

O'Longaigh, Seosamh, 'Emergency Law in Action, 1939–1945', in Keogh and O'Driscoll (eds), *Ireland in World War Two*

Oram, Hugh, *The Advertising Book* (Dublin: MO Books, 1986)

Retail Family Grocers, Purveyors, Dairy Proprietors and Allied Traders [RGDATA], *Talking Shop: 50 Years of the Irish Grocery Trade 1942–1992* (Dublin: RGDATA, 1992)

——*Flying the Flag for Sixty Years: 1941–2002* (Dublin: RGDATA, September 2002)

Seaton, Paul, *A Sixpenny Romance: Celebrating a Century of Value at Woolworths* (London: 3^D and 6^D Pictures Ltd, 2009)

Sligo Family Centre, *Looking back at Sligo's Past* (Sligo: Sligo Family Centre and Sligo Active Retirement Association, 1999)

Snow, Vernon F., *JBS: The Biography of John Ben Snow* (New York, 1974)

Stephens, James, *The Insurrection in Dublin* (Dublin and London: Maunsel & Co., 1916; South Carolina: BiblioLife LLC, 2009)

Vaughan, W.E. and Fitzpatrick, A.J., *Irish Historical Statistics: Population, 1821–1971* (Dublin: Royal Irish Academy, 1987)

Walsh, Barbara, *Roman Catholic Nuns in England and Wales, 1800–1937: A Social History* (Dublin and Portland, OR: Irish Academic Press, 2002)

Winkler, John K., *Five and Ten: The Fabulous Life of F. W. Woolworth*, rev. edn (New York: Bantum Books, 1957 [1940])

Unpublished Theses and Surveys

Charleton, Muireann, 'Cosmopolitanism and nationalism: a cocktail for consumer craving in a rural department store 1878–1930', unpublished thesis, National College of Art and Design, Dublin, 2007

Doyle, Marie, et al., *Thomas St – A Street Study*, complied 1987. Irish Architectural Archive, RPD 196.10

Notes

Introduction

1. Paul Seaton, *A Sixpenny Romance: Celebrating a Century of Value at Woolworths* (London: 3^D and 6^D Pictures Ltd, 2009).
2. John K. Winkler, *Five and Ten: The Fabulous Life of F. W. Woolworth* (New York: Bantum Books, 1957).

Chapter 1

1. This date is sometimes given as 1828.
2. Several years ago, Paul Seaton and I enjoyed exchanging ideas over what this mixture might be. See his comment regarding the link to the American Woolworth stores in *Sixpenny Romance*, p.57.
3. *Nationalist and Leinster Times*, 27 October 1967, p.7.
4. Figures drawn from a typescript of the opening address by chairman R.J. Berridge at the F.W. Woolworth & Co. Ltd, 50th Golden Jubilee Convention, 1909–1959, 2 March 1959, p.7.
5. F.W. Woolworth & Co. Ltd, Directors' Minute Book No. 1 (23 September 1909–April 1915), p.131, 14 November 1913.
6. F.W. Woolworth & Co. Ltd, Directors' Minute Book No. 2 (April 1915–1919), p.25, 26 August 1915.
7. Maurice Craig, *Dublin, 1660–1860* (Dublin: Figgis, 1980), pp.134, 110.
8. *Irish Times*, 27 November 1919, p.10, and 18 December 1919, p.9.
9. *Irish Independent*, 21 and 28 January 1919, p.2; *Irish Times*, 17 November 1921, p.4.
10. See discussion over Irish delegates attending the golden jubilee convention in 1959 in chapter 5 below.
11. Mary E. Daly, *Women and Work in Ireland* (Dublin: Economic and Social History Society of Ireland, 1997), passim. Note pp.3–8 and p.42.

12. *Irish Times,* 29 April 1916, p.3.

13. James Stephens, *The Insurrection in Dublin* (SC: BiblioLife LLC, 2009), pp.34–5.

14. Directors' Minute Book, No. 2, p.91. On 11 April 1917, note of a lease from Bewley Sons & Co. Ltd, 19–20 Henry Street for 50 years, and one for 18–19 Henry Street for 50 years at £1,750 per annum.

15. *Irish Times*, 18 October 1917, p.7.

16. Protectionism in the 1920s and 1930s will be discussed below, in chapters 2 and 3.

17. *Irish Times*, 9 March 1933.

18. *Irish Times*, 16 September 1916.

19. Ibid.

20. *Irish Independent*, 24 February 1921, p.6.

21. *Irish Independent,* 28 November 1928, p.10.

22. David Johnson, *The Interwar Economy in Ireland* (Dublin: Economic and Social History Society of Ireland, 1999), pp.3–4.

23. Ibid.

24. *Irish Times*, 20 February 1915, p.6.

25. *Irish Times*, 28 August 1923, p.7.

26. *Irish Times*, 11 December 1923, p.6.

27. Leland Bardwell, *A Restless Life* (Dublin: Liberties Press, 2008) p.75.

28. He had become a self-made entrepreneur in England as a trader at an early age. Among his earlier colourful attributes, he had been a champion Lancashire 'catch-as catch-can' wrestler. He was 27 when he joined Woolworth, in 1910.

29. Directors' Minute Book No. 1, p.134 cites transfer of preference shares to Charles McCarthy on 12 February 1914. Further share transactions are noted in the Directors' Minute Book No. 2, in 1915, 1916 and in the Directors' Minute Book No. 3 (1920–c.1923) in 1920 and 1921.

30. Interview: 25 November 2009.

31. A retired former Woolworth manager was often entertained by 'Mac's stories in the 1970s.

32. The recent comment of Dr Willie Walsh, the Catholic bishop of Killaloe, speaking to the Association of Journalists, 13 November 2009, cited in Patsy McGarry, 'Analysis', *Irish Times*, 30 December 2009, p.15 and also *Irish Times*, 23 November 2009, p.15. Some of the top schools that educated Woolworth men included the Jesuit-run Clongowes Wood, Kildare, and the Crescent, Limerick; Summerhill Diocesan College, Sligo; the Holy Ghost Fathers in Rockwell College and a number of other well-known religious-run secondary schools.

33. Several successful Irish recruits were the sons of their local city's politically appointed mayors.

34. Indicated by two interviews: 30 June and 29 July 2009.

35. Directors' Minute Book No. 3, 12 May 1923, p.66.

36. D.C. Boyce, 'Nationalism, Unionism and the First World War', in A. Gregory and S. Paseta, *Ireland and the Great War* (Manchester University Press, 2002), p.195.

37. This view was emphasized by a former store manager, interviewed on 30 June 2009.

Chapter 2

1.   *Cork Examiner*, 6 February 1920, p.7.
2.   *Cork Examiner*, 4 February 1920, p.5.
3.   *Cork Examiner*, 6 February 1920.
4.   *Londonderry Sentinel*, 26 February, p.1 and *Derry Journal*, 27 February 1920.
5.   *Derry Journal*, 8 March 1920.
6.   *Evening Herald*, 7 July 1920, p.1. By a resolution adopted by meetings of the Kingstown Urban Council.
7.   *Evening Herald*, 9–21 July, 1920
8.   Suggested by the difficulty in finding any publicity or exact date for the opening. The Dun Laoghaire branch was relocated to larger premises in Lower Georges Street in 1927.
9.   *Irish Independent*, 2 August 1920.
10.   *Irish Independent*, 28 August 1920.
11.   *Irish Times*, 18 December 1920.
12.   There is a little confusion over the actual date of this opening. Company records give the date as 12 February 1921, although an advertisement published in the *Portadown News* states that inspection and business was to commence on the 18/19 February.
13.   *Irish Independent*, 20 June 1921, p.6.
14.   *Ballymena Observer*, 26 February 1926.
15.   Ibid.
16.   Ibid.
17.   Daly, *Women and Work in Ireland*, p.48.
18.   *Irish Times*, 7 September 1918, p.1.
19.   *Irish Independent*, 18 January 1919, p.6.
20.   The remark about having their hair down implied these girls were still not considered fully adult young women. *Irish Times*, 15 April 1922, p.8.
21.   *Irish Independent*, 21 July 1923, p.7.
22.   A point often repeated during interviews with former employees.
23.   An article published in *The Sinn Féiner*, 16 October 1920 (Sinn Féin Publishing Co., New York), states that Sinn Féin had started a boycott of British goods and British-controlled insurance companies about four months earlier.
24.   *Sinn Féiner*, 12 November 1921.
25.   *Sinn Féiner*, 15 October 1921.
26.   *Irish Times*, 25 May 1921, p.3.
27.   Ibid.
28.   *Anglo-Celt*, 2 July 1921, p.6.
29.   *Irish Times*, 18 October 1921, p.7.
30.   Ibid.
31.   *Evening Herald*, 17 October 1921, p.1.
32.   *Evening Herald*, 18 October 1921, p.3.
33.   *Irish Independent*, 20 October 1921.

34. *Dublin Evening Mail*, 19 October 1921, p.3.

35. Greenwood was also the Liberal MP for Sunderland.

36. *Irish Times*, 1 November 1921, p.6.

37. Ibid.

38. *Irish Times*, 6 May 1922, p.7.

39. See also discussion in Chapter 3. Muireann Charleton in 'Cosmopolitanism and nationalism: a cocktail for consumer craving in a rural department store 1878–1930', unpublished thesis, NCAD, Dublin (2007), p.89.

40. Johnson, *Interwar Economy in Ireland*, pp.21–2.

41. Roy Foster, *Modern Ireland, 1600–1972* (Harmondsworth: Penguin, 1989), p.523.

42. Johnson, *Interwar Economy in Ireland*, p.23.

43. Foster, *Modern Ireland*, p.523.

44. *Irish Times,* 15 November 1921, p.5.

45. *Freeman's Journal,* 5 June 1922, p.5.

46. Ibid.

47. *Irish Times*, 26 August 1922, p.8.

48. *Irish Times*, 20 May 1924, p.5.

49. Ibid.

50. *Irish Times*, 24 May 1924, p.7, and 9 August 1924, p.3.

51. *Irish Times*, 14 March 1927, p.12.

52. *New Bond,* Vol. 1 No. 8, August 1936, p.175.

53. Winkler, *Five and Ten,* p.202.

54. F.W. Woolworth & Co. Ltd, *A Career in Store for you with Woolworths*, 1967 recruitment pamphlet for applicants.

55. Ibid.

56. Ibid.

57. Ibid.

58. Interview: 30 June 2009.

59. Interview: 24 June 2009.

60. Interview: 13 June 2009.

61. Interview: 21 August 2008.

62. Ibid.

63. A complicated procedure that involved sending invoices to Head Office and receiving weekly statements, which had to be checked by stores' office staff, became even more convoluted in the post-war era.

64. Interview: 7 September 2009.

65. Opinions voiced in several interviews were inconsistent.

66. Interview: 10 August 2008.

67. Kieran Fagan, *Irish Sunday Independent*, 24 September 2006.

68. Discussed below in chapter 4.

Chapter 3

1.   *Irish Independent*, 25 November 1927, p.7.
2.   *New Bond*, Vol. 18, No. 1, March 1959, p.39.
3.   Seaton, *Sixpenny Romance*, p.67.
4.   Ibid.
5.   Ibid.
6.   Ibid.
7.   Ibid.
8.   Advertisement, *Irish Times*, 11 June 1931, p.14.
9.   *Irish Times*, 12 June 1931, p.7.
10. Ibid.
11. *Irish Independent*, advertisement, 10 May 1927, p.1.
12. *Saturday Herald*, 30 April 1927, advertising announcement to consumers.
13. More fully discussed in Johnson, *Interwar Economy in Ireland,* pp.25–30.
14. Ibid., p.28.
15. *Waterford News and Star*, 2 August 1929, p.3; 23 August 1929, p.7; 22 November 1929, p.5.
16. *Dundalk Examiner and Louth Advertiser,* 21 July 1928, p.5.
17. Ibid., p.4.
18. Similar coverage to the opening was also given in the *Waterford News and Star*, 24 and 31 October 1930.
19. *Nationalist and Munster Advertiser*, 13 June 1931, p.5.
20. Ibid.
21. *Whitstable Times and Tankerton Press*, 25 February 1933, p.12.
22. A lady called Madame Herve Roylance.
23. *Nationalist and Munster Advertiser*, 20 June 1931. For the Preston opening, see Seaton, *Sixpenny Romance*, p.37.
24. *Armagh Guardian*, 24 May 1935, p.2.
25. Ibid.
26. *Portadown News*, 19 February 1921.
27. As discussed by Muireann Charleton in 'Cosmopolitanism and nationalism'.
28. *Nationalist and Munster Advertiser*, 13 June 1931, p.1.
29. *Lisburn Standard*, 30 November 1928, p.4.
30. Ibid.
31. *Lurgan Mail*, 3 November 1934, p.3.
32. Ibid.
33. Advertising for Ulster goods, *Armagh Guardian*, 31 May 1935, p.6.
34. Drawn from the website published history of the Pasold Research Fund. See also Seaton, *Sixpenny Romance,* p.69.
35. *Kilkenny People*, 19 July 1930.
36. *Sligo Champion*, 27 September 1930, p.1.
37. *Kilkenny People*, 10 January 1931.

38. He was made a Papal Count by Pope Pius XI in 1928.
39. *Irish Times*, 18 March 1927, p.7.
40. *Irish Times*, 22 March 1927, p.8.
41. *Irish Times*, 11 November 1929, p.4.
42. As discussed in Muireann Charleton in 'Cosmopolitanism and nationalism'.
43. Notes drawn up by Company Chairman William L. Stephenson, entitled 'First Full Year's Sales of Stores Opened in 1926'.
44. *Sligo Independent and West of Ireland Telegraph*, 1 November 1930, p.5.
45. *Nationalist and Munster Advertiser*, 13 June 1931, p.5.
46. Charleton, 'Cosmopolitanism and nationalism', p.1.
47. Ibid., p.89.
48. *Irish Times,* 22 December 1930, p.7.
49. British Shopping Week featured in the *Folkestone Express*, February–April 1926, and the Faversham & District Chamber of Commerce advertisements in the *Faversham and North East Kent News*, May 1926; likewise, the Whitstable and Tankerton Traders' Association campaign throughout February and March 1933 in the *Whitstable Times and Tankerton Press.*
50. Caitriona Clear, *Women of the House* (Dublin: Irish Academic Press, 2000), pp.13–14.
51. Ibid.
52. Barbara Walsh, *Roman Catholic Nuns in England and Wales, 1800–1937* (Dublin: Irish Academic Press, 2002), chapter 6.
53. *Armagh Guardian*, 17 May 1935, p.2.
54. *Kilkenny People*, 19 July 1930.
55. *Northern Constitution*, 14 February 1931, p.9.
56. *Waterford News and Star*, 7 November 1930, p.1.
57. *Waterford News and Star*, 24 October 1930, p.7.
58. *Waterford News and Star*, 7 November 1930, p.1.
59. J.J. Lee, *Ireland, 1912–1985* (Cambridge University Press, 1989), p.158.
60. *Waterford News and Star*, 4 March 1932, p.7.
61. *Irish Times,* 23 April 1932, p.7.
62. Ibid.
63. Ibid.
64. *Irish Times*, 11 May 1938, p.7.
65. Interview: 21 August 2008.
66. I am grateful to Paul Seaton for this information.
67. Interview: 29 January 2009.
68. Winkler, *Five and Ten,* p.236.
69. I am grateful to Paul Seaton for this information.
70. Vernon F. Snow, *JBS: The Biography of John Ben Snow* (New York, 1974), pp.15–34.
71. Announced in the *Irish Independent* on 17 November 1936. See also *Irish Times*, 22 October 1949, p.8.
72. Interview: 20 August 2009.
73. Ibid.

74.   Lee, *Ireland, 1912–1985*, p.214.
75.   F.W. Woolworth & Co. Ltd, General Management Committee Minute Book No. 1 (1936–8), meeting of 18–19 January 1938, p.188.
76.   Ibid.
77.   It is very possible that Powers had an inherited Irish link within his American family's background.

Chapter 4

1.   Brian Harrison, *Seeking a Role: The United Kingdom, 1951–1970* (Oxford University Press, 2009), p.1.
2.   Lee, *Ireland, 1912–1985*, p.234.
3.   Seosamh O'Longaigh, 'Emergency Law in Action, 1939–1945', in Dermot Keogh and Mervyn O'Driscoll (eds), *Ireland in World War Two* (Cork: Mercier Press, 2004), p.75.
4.   Lee, *Ireland, 1912–1985*, p.234.
5.   Ibid., p.226.
6.   Ibid., p.256.
7.   Seaton, *Sixpenny Romance*, p.83.
8.   Ibid.
9.   Lee, *Ireland, 1912–1985*, p.233.
10.   Ibid.
11.   F.W. Woolworth & Co. Ltd, Buyers' Minute Book No. 5 (1943–8), meeting to review Buyers' Department showings, 26–7 January 1944, p.25.
12.   F.W. Woolworth & Co. Ltd, General Management Committee Minute Book No. 3 (1945–8), 22 January 1945.
13.   Interviews with members of a former senior manager's family.
14.   F.W. Woolworth & Co. Ltd, General Management Committee Minute Book No. 2 (1939–44), January 1939, p.6.
15.   General Management Committee Minute Book No. 3, 5–6 March 1946, p.86.
16.   Ibid.
17.   Ibid., 18 June 1946, p.128.
18.   F.W. Woolworth Co. Ltd, *Woolworth's First 75 Years: The Story of Everybody's Story* (New York, 1954), p.57.
19.   Seaton, *Sixpenny Romance*, p.87.
20.   *Woolworth's First 75 Years*, p.57. See also Seaton, *Sixpenny Romance*, p.91.
21.   Ibid.
22.   General Management Committee Minute Book No. 3, meeting held on 4 September 1945, p.47.
23.   Ibid.
24.   Ibid.
25.   Ibid., meeting held on 31 December 1945, p.76.
26.   Information drawn from www.irish-sugar.ie - accessed 15/08/2008.

27.   *Irish Times,* 23 May 1946, p.8.
28.   General Management Committee Minute Book No. 3, 5–6 March 1946, p.86.
29.   Ibid., annual review meeting, 21–3 January 1948, pp.211–13.
30.   Ibid., p.205.
31.   Ibid.
32.   Ibid.
33.   Ibid., p.299.
34.   General Management Committee Minute Book No. 1, meeting held on 18–19 January 1938, p.187.
35.   Ibid.
36.   Interview: 25 November 2009.
37.   F.W. Woolworth & Co. Ltd, Buyers' Minute Book No. 5 (1943–1948, with additional pages), review meeting, January 1948, p.232.
38.   Ibid., p.69.
39.   Ibid., p.58.
40.   Ibid.
41.   Ibid., p.298.
42.   Ibid.
43.   Ibid.
44.   Interview: 11 July 2008.
45.   Ibid.
46.   General Management Committee Minute Book No. 3, meeting held on 6 November 1945, p.56.
47.   Ibid., meeting held on 27 April 1945.
48.   Ibid., meeting held on 18 March 1947.
49.   Interview: 29 January 2010.
50.   Charleton, 'Cosmopolitanism and nationalism', Appendix A, pp.107–9.
51.   Ibid.
52.   Interview: 31 July 2009.
53.   Interview: 7 September 2009.
54.   Betty Smith, Maura Kennedy and Hugh Gillen, 'Woolies', in *Looking back at Sligo's Past* (Sligo: Sligo Family Centre and Active Retirement Association, 1999), p.18.
55.   Ibid.
56.   Ibid.
57.   *New Bond,* Vol. 7, No. 3, November 1948, p.52.
58.   Interview: 29 November 2009.

Chapter 5

1.   *Irish Times*, 22 October 1949, p.8.
2.   Ibid.
3.   F.W. Woolworth & Co. Ltd, General Management Committee Minute Book No. 2, p.2.

4.   H.C. Dear, Director, typescript of address entitled 'Expansion of Business through Store Modernization' given at the F.W. Woolworth & Co. Ltd 50th Jubilee Convention on 2 March 1959, p.35.

5.   See Irene Furlong, *Tourism in Ireland, 1880–1980* (Dublin and Portland, OR: Irish Academic Press, 2009), chapter 7, pp.159–82.

6.   Ibid., p.214.

7.   Ibid., pp.178–9.

8.   Ibid., p.180.

9.   This is the general consensus of retailers, wholesalers and manufacturers interviewed.

10.   Interview: 21 August 2008.

11.   Seaton, *Sixpenny Romance*, p.97.

12.   Ibid.

13.   Interview with Paul Seaton, 14 February 2010.

14.   Interview: 8 February 2010.

15.   Interview: 7 September 2009.

16.   Ibid.

17.   Interview with the supplier's marketing department.

18.   Interview: 6 February 2010.

19.   Interview: 29 January 2010.

20.   Nicholas Furlong, 'The Friary Tunnel', *Wexford Echo*, 21 October 2009, p.90.

21.   Interview: 31 July 2008.

22.   *Connacht Tribune*, 11 July 1953, p.7.

23.   *Westmeath Examiner*, 1 August 1953.

24.   *Drogheda Independent*, 20 January 1950, p.9.

25.   *Western People*, 21 November 1953, p.4.

26.   Ibid.

27.   *Tipperary Star*, 21 April 1953, p.1.

28.   F.W. Woolworth & Co. Ltd, General Management Committee Minute Book No. 3, 5–6 March 1946, p.86.

29.   Data courtesy Paul Seaton.

30.   Interview: 21 August 2008.

31.   *Westmeath Examiner*, 1 August 1953.

32.   Department of Industry and Commerce, *Official Industrial Directory* (Dublin: Stationery Office, 1955).

33.   Interview with Paul Seaton, 1 December 2009.

34.   *Thomas St – A Street Study*, survey complied by Marie Doyle, Eileen Fox, Isobel McNally, Dymphna McCarthy, Liam Kilbride and Peter McCarney (1987), p.25. National Architectural Archive, Dublin, RPD 196.10.

35.   Interview: 20 August 2009.

36.   Interview: 10 February 2008.

37.   Interview: 29 January 2010.

38.   Interview: 7 September 2009.

39. *New Bond*, Vol. 9, No. 6 (December 1950), p.7.

40. Interview: 21 August 2008.

41. Interview: 25 September 2009.

42. Interview: 1 September 2009.

43. The Rank Organization film *Carve Her Name with Pride* (1957) was directed by Lewis Gilbert. It featured in *New Bond*, Vol. 16, No. 6 (December 1957), p.53.

44. *Irish Times*, 3 August 1931, p.5; 7 November 1934, p.9; and 15 August 1949, p.3.

45. The late Pat Quinn in interview with the author, August 2009.

46. W.J. Turner, Managing Director, typescript of address entitled 'Overseas Development' given at the F.W. Woolworth & Co. Ltd 50th Jubilee Convention on 2 March 1959, p.16.

47. Interview: 21 August 2009.

48. J.L. Farmer, Director and District Manager B.D.O., typescript of address entitled 'The District Angle' given at the F.W. Woolworth & Co. Ltd 50th Jubilee Convention on 2 March 1959, p.20.

49. Ibid., p.21.

50. F.L. Chaplin, Director, typescript of address entitled 'The Buying of Merchandise' given at the F.W. Woolworth & Co. Ltd 50th Jubilee Convention on 2 March 1959, p.22.

51. F.W. Woolworth & Co. Ltd, *Golden Jubilee Year Convention Programme Alphabetical Index*, pp.5–37.

52. General Management Committee Minute Book No. 3, April 1945.

53. *Golden Jubilee Year Convention Programme Alphabetical Index*.

54. Eleven of the retired delegates were former manageresses.

55. E.G. Britten, typescript of his response to Mr Kirkwood's address at the F.W. Woolworth & Co. Ltd 50th Jubilee Convention Dinner on 2 March 1959, p.12.

56. R.C. Kirkwood, President, F.W. Woolworth Co., USA, typescript of address given at the F.W. Woolworth & Co. Ltd 50th Jubilee Convention Dinner on 2 March 1959, p.9.

57. Ibid., p.11.

58. Interview: 30 June 2009.

59. Interview: 24 September 2009.

60. Retail Family Grocers, Purveyors, Dairy Proprietors and Allied Traders, *Talking Shop: 50 Years of the Irish Grocery Trade 1942–1992* (Dublin: RGDATA, 1992), p.25.

61. Brian Harrison, *Seeking a Role: The United Kingdom, 1951–1970* (Oxford: Clarendon Press, 2009), p.335.

62. Data sourced ibid., p.336.

63. J.B. Cottam, Director, typescript of address entitled 'Jubilee Year Advertising, Self-Service, Personnel', given at the F.W. Woolworth & Co. Ltd 50th Jubilee Convention on 2 March 1959, p.45.

64. Data drawn from the Retail Family Grocers, Purveyors, Dairy Proprietors and Allied Traders booklet, *Flying the Flag for Sixty Years: 1941–2002* (Dublin: RGDATA, September 2002), p.9 and p.14.

65. There appears to be no further information available about GMT.

66. *Newtownards Chronicle and County Down Observer*, 21 August 1959, pp.14–15.

67. Interview: 29 July 2009.

Chapter 6

1.   Cottam, 'Jubilee Year Advertising, Self-Service, Personnel', pp.46–7.
2.   Hugh Oram, *The Advertising Book* (Dublin: MO Books, 1986), p.234.
3.   RGDATA, *Flying the Flag for Sixty Years*, p.23.
4.   Ibid., p.24.
5.   R.W.G. Carter and A.J. Parker, *Ireland: A Contemporary Geographical Perspective,* (London: Routledge, 1989), p.249.
6.   *Limerick Leader*, 30 March 1963, p.2.
7.   Ibid.
8.   Ibid., p.3.
9.   See RGDATA, *Flying the Flag for Sixty Years, 1941–2002*, p.20.
10. *Courier and News*, 8 November 1962, pp.4–5.
11. Ibid., p.6.
12. *Banbridge Chronicle*, 6 August, 13 August and 27 August 1965.
13. *Banbridge Chronicle*, 17 September 1965, p.2.
14. Interview: 20 August 2009. This system was called the 'Grantham System', an in-house term first tried out successfully in the town of Grantham in England to see off strong competition.
15. *Banbridge Chronicle*, 24 September 1965, p.8.
16. *Banbridge Chronicle*, 8 October 1965, p.3.
17. *Banbridge Chronicle*, 3 December 1965, p.2.
18. Interviews: 30 June 2009 and 20 August 2009.
19. Seaton, *Sixpenny Romance*, p.109.
20. J.C.W., 'Woolworth in Britain': an in-house F.W. Woolworth brochure produced for employees, January 1971.
21. Ibid.
22. RGDATA, *Talking Shop*, p.68.
23. Dublin City Archive reported that Plan Files for 73–88 South Great George's Street for this period were among the files that were destroyed accidentally in a fire at the Planning Department building in the 1970s.
24. Interview: 25 November 2009; also mentioned by several others.
25. It would make an interesting study to compare the openings of new Irish outlets to those of similar small towns in Scotland, Wales and England.
26. *Nationalist and Leinster Times*, 27 October 1967, p.7.
27. *Impartial Reporter and Farmers' Journal*, 26 October 1967, p.4.
28. *Nationalist and Leinster Times*, 27 October 1967, p.7.
29. Ibid.
30. *Carloviana: Journal of the Old Carlow Society* (December 1967), pp.18–19.
31. Carlow Chamber of Commerce, *Carlow Chamber of Commerce: Tourism and Industry 50th Anniversary 1947–1997* (Carlow: Chamber of Commerce, 1998), p.21 and p.27.
32. *Carloviana*, p.19.

33. *Irish Times*, 'The Midas Column', 17 June 1971, p.19.
34. Ibid.
35. *New Bond*, Vol. 27, No. 1 (February 1968), p.8.
36. *Impartial Reporter and Farmers' Journal*, 26 October 1967, p.4; *Fermanagh Herald*, 4 November 1967, p.5.
37. Ibid.
38. *Impartial Reporter and Farmers' Journal*, 26 October 1967, p.4.
39. *Fermanagh Herald*, 4 November 1967, p.5.
40. Ibid.
41. *Impartial Reporter and Farmers' Journal*, 26 October 1967, p.1.
42. Interview: 29 July 2009.
43. Ibid.
44. Winkler, *Five and Ten*, p.202.
45. Interview: 25 November 2009.
46. Interview: 24 June 2009.
47. Ibid.
48. Ibid.
49. Interview: 25 September 2009.
50. Interviews: 1 September 2008 and 29 July 2009.
51. Interview: 25 November 2009.
52. Interview: 24 June 2009.
53. Ibid.
54. Eunan O'Halpin, *Defending Ireland: The Irish State and its Enemies since 1922* (Oxford University Press 2000), p.507 is cited by Christopher Andrew in *The Defence of the Realm: The Authorised History of MI5* (London: Allen Lane, 2009), p.605.
55. Interview: 1 September 2009.
56. Brian Feeney, *The Troubles* (Dublin: O'Brien Press, 2004), p.49.
57. Richard Killeen, *A Timeline of Irish History* (Dublin: Gill and Macmillan, 2003), p.104.
58. Interview: 8 September 2009.
59. Ibid.
60. Ibid.
61. Ibid.
62. Interview: 30 June 2009.

Chapter 7

1. Jim O'Donnell (ed.), *Ireland: The Past Twenty Years* (Dublin: Institute of Public Administration, 1986), p.25.
2. Interview: 8 September 2008.
3. J.C.W., 'Woolworth in Britain'.
4. F.W. Woolworth & Co. Ltd, complete list of stores, November 1972.
5. Heatons was founded in Athlone in 1946.

6.   The first store to try out this method was in Leeds, Yorkshire, and thereafter the firm applied the term 'Leeds Counters' to these adaptations.

7.   Inteview: 25 September 2009.

8.   Interview: 20 August 2009.

9.   Interview: 29 January 2010.

10.   Elgy Gillespie, 'Final hours of a Woolworth's store', *Irish Times*, 8 October 1984, p.14.

11.   Full instructions for this procedure were set out in the company's store manual, which was supplied to each branch.

12.   F.W. Woolworth & Co. Ltd, General Management Committee Minute Book No. 2, meetings held on 24–7 January 1944, pp.276–7.

13.   Ibid.

14.   Ibid.

15.   Interview: 7 September 2009.

16.   O'Donnell, *Ireland*, p.35.

17.   Ibid., p.38.

18.   Seaton, *Sixpenny Romance*, p.121.

19.   Interview: 25 November 2009.

20.   Charles Prichard writing in the *Irish Times*, 19 March 1973, p.18.

21.   Ibid.

22.   *Irish Times,* 20 April 1974, p.15.

23.   Seaton, *Sixpenny Romance*, p.123.

24.   Interview: 4 February 2010.

25.   Ronnie Hoffman, 'The Management Column', *Irish Times*, 19 January 1977, p.13.

26.   J.C.W., 'Woolworth in Britain'.

27.   Seaton, *Sixpenny Romance,* p.111.

28.   Hoffman, 'Management Column', p.13.

29.   Ibid.

30.   Ibid.

31.   Interview with Paul Seaton, 14 February 2010.

32.   *Woolworth News*, No. 35 (July 1976), p.1.

33.   Hoffman, 'Management Column', p.13.

34.   Ibid.

35.   Ronnie Hoffman, 'Bread prices in North return to normal as price cutting ends', *Irish Times*, 9 September 1976, p.14.

36.   General Management Committee Minute Book No. 2, p.274, meetings held on 24–7 January 1944.

37.   Interview: 25 November 2010.

38.   David Stewart, 'Nothing could replace Galway's "Woolies"', *Galway Advertiser*, 9 August 1984, p.5.

39.   Anne Elliott, 'Small gifts to suit everyone', *Irish Times*, 7 December 1978, p.18.

40.   Ibid.

41.   Interview: 20 August 2009.

42.   Interview: 25 November 2009.

43.   Ibid. This story was told by their mother on one of the RTÉ's *Late Late Shows* and confirmed later by one of the famous brothers in conversation with a former Woolworth manager.

44.   Interview: 20 August 2009.

45.   *New Bond,* Vol. 17 No. 5 (October 1958), p.8.

46.   Interviews: 20 August and 25 November 2009.

47.   Illustrated in *New Bond,* Vol. 17, No. 3 (June 1953), p.19.

48.   'Faversham Memories', *Faversham News*, 23 March 1995, p.8.

49.   *New Bond,* Vol. 17, No. 5 (October 1958), p.16.

50.   Hubert Butler, 'The Shee Alms House in Kilkenny', *Irish Times*, 4 January 1977, p.8.

51.   Ibid.

52.   Similar legislation was being prepared to take effect in the Republic in or around the same time.

53.   Interviews: 18 February 2010 and 8 September 2009.

54.   There were nineteen store managers in the Republic. Of these, six had been initially opposed to signing the new contracts, but were persuaded to agree.

55.   'Interim Profits slip by £1.2m at Woolworth', *Irish Times*, 18 August 1977, p.12.

56.   'Woolworth Profits at £20.7m fail to keep pace with inflation', *Irish Times*, 17 November 1977, p.12.

57.   Interview: 24 June 2009.

58.   Ibid.

59.   Seaton, *Sixpenny Romance*, p.121.

60.   *Irish Times*, 10 April 1979, p.12.

61.   Ibid.

62.   Seaton, *Sixpenny Romance*, p.131.

Chapter 8

1.   Furlong, *Tourism in Ireland*, p.214.

2.   Interviews: 13 June 2007 and 25 November 2009.

3.   Interview: 9 February 2010.

4.   Furlong, *Tourism in Ireland,* p.155.

5.   Ibid.

6.   Interview: 25 September 2009.

7.   Ibid.

8.   Interview with Paul Seaton, 27 January 2010.

9.   Interview: 21 August 2009.

10.   Interview: 7 September 2009.

11.   Interview: 1 September 2008.

12.   Interviews: 21 August 2008 and 25 November 2009.

13.   *Irish Times*, 24 February 1981, p.12; RGDATA, *Talking Shop*, p.59; *Irish Times*, 7 September 1983, p.7.

14. For decades, Woolworth had always claimed Henry Street had the largest sweet counter display seen in any store in the world. Interview: 25 November 2009.
15. Ibid.
16. Ibid.
17. Interview: 12 December 2009.
18. Interview: 25 November 2009.
19. Interviews: 21 August 2008 and 25 November 2009.
20. Tim Roberts, 'Woolies looks to new outlets to restore its profitability', *Irish Times*, 1 February 1982, p.12.
21. *Irish Times*, 9 August 1980, p.14. See also Seaton, *Sixpenny Romance*, p.129.
22. *Irish Times*, 9 August 1980, p.14.
23. Seaton, *Sixpenny Romance*, p.129.
24. Timon Day, 'First half group profits collapse at Woolworth', *Irish Times*, 14 August 1980, p.12.
25. *Irish Times*, 1 August 1980, p.17.
26. *Irish Times*, 5 December 1980, p.19.
27. *Irish Times*, 23 September 1980, p.12; also referred to in 'An end to the five cent store', *Irish Times*, 26 July 1984, p.7.
28. Geoffrey Gibbs, 'Woolworth enters the price war', *Irish Times*, 19 February 1981, p.15.
29. *Irish Times*, 10 April 1981, p.14.
30. No records relating to this meeting appear to have survived. CTT Archives relating to Product Development are only held for a period of about nine years.
31. *Irish Times*, 20 November 1981, p.15.
32. Seaton, *Sixpenny Romance*, p.131.
33. *Irish Times*, 22 October 1982, p.15.
34. Ibid.
35. Seaton, *Sixpenny Romance*, p.131.
36. Sebastian Taylor, *Irish Times*, 23 March 1983, p.14.
37. *Irish Times*, 4 April 1984, p.26; additional data from the web page for Kingfisher plc company history.
38. Interviews: 21 August 2008 and 25 November 2009.
39. Interview: 25 November 2009.
40. Interview: 21 August 2008.
41. Ibid.
42. Ibid.
43. Padraig MacUalghairg, 'Woolworth shop sold for £4.75m', *Irish Times*, 5 April 1984, p.1.
44. Sebastian Taylor, 'Woolworth pays £177 for Comet', *Irish Times*, 13 April 1984.
45. *Irish Times*, 3 May 1984, p.26.
46. *Irish Times*, 26 July 1984, p.7.
47. Statement issued to the press and media on 25 July 1984 by F.W. Woolworth & Co. Ltd.
48. This was the date given in the statement issued. Closures officially took place on Monday 8 October.

49. *Irish Times*, 26 July 1984, p.7.
50. Interview: 20 August 2009.
51. John Murray, 'Woolworth to close in the Republic', *Cork Examiner*, 26 July 1984, p.1.
52. *Connacht Tribune*, 27 July 1984, p.1.
53. Interview: 20 August 2009.
54. *Connacht Sentinal*, 11 September 1984, p.1.
55. Ibid.
56. Interview: 25 November 2010.
57. *The Kerryman/Corkman*, 14 September 1984, p.7.
58. Elgy Gillespie, 'Final hours of a Woolworth's store', *Irish Times*, 8 October 1984, p.14.
59. *Wexford People*, 21 September 1984, p.9; Maria Pepper, 'We will all sit it out', *Wexford People*, 14 September 1984, p.1.
60. *Sligo Champion*, 28 September 1984, p.4.
61. *Irish Times*, 20 September 1984, p.10, and 21 September 1984, p.7.
62. *Irish Times*, 26 September 1984 p.8 and 27 September 1984, p.8.
63. Interview: 25 November 2010.
64. *Western People*, 3 October 1984, p.1; also interviews with former managers.
65. David Stewart, 'Nothing could replace Galway's "Woolies"', *Galway Advertiser*, 9 August 1984, p.5.
66. Spartacus, 'Woolworths: the end of a legend in Limerick – and an era in Ireland', *Limerick Leader*, 4 August 1984, p.15.
67. Elgy Gillespie, 'Final hours of a Woolworth's store', *Irish Times*, 8 October 1984, p.14.
68. Ibid.
69. Ibid.
70. Interview with Paul Seaton, 27 January 2010.
71. Interview with a former supplier, 10 August 2008.
72. F.W. Woolworth & Co. Ltd, List of Stores, issued August 1998, ref. 460B 3060. Closed stores, p.38.
73. Fionnuala O'Connor, 'The other face of Northern Ireland', *Irish Times*, 20 December 1982, p.7.
74. Ibid.
75. Brian Donaghy, 'Newry traders welcome Southern VAT refugees', *Irish Times*, 23 November 1983, p.13.
76. Interview: 30 June 2009.
77. Seaton, *Sixpenny Romance*, p.135.
78. www.Kingfisher.co.uk.
79. Tim Roberts, 'Further cuts in interest rates expected in UK', *Irish Times*, 7 June 1986.
80. Charles Prichard, 'Woolworths fends off Dixon's bid', *Irish Times*, 3 July 1986.
81. *Irish Times*, 21 August 1985, comments on Wellworths' first full year in the Dee Corporation.
82. *Irish Times*, 30 July 1986, p.12.
83. Tim Roberts, 'Sales rise again at Wellworth', *Irish Times*, 27 August 1987.

84.   Interview: 9 February 2010.

85.   Ibid.

86.   *Irish Times*, 14 August, 2001, p.15.

87.   Seaton, *Sixpenny Romance*, p.145.

88.   Ibid., p.149.

89.   Interview: 8 September 2009.

90.   Seaton, *Sixpenny Romance*, p.143.

91.   Francess McDonnell, writing in the *Irish Times,* 16 October 2001, p.15.

92.   Seaton, *Sixpenny Romance*, p.153.

93.   Ibid.

94.   Interview Paul Seaton, 5 February 2010.

95.   Interview: 9 February 2010.

96.   Interview: 8 September 2009.

97.   Ibid.

98.   *Irish Times*, 27 November 2008, p.22.

99.   BBC News Northern Ireland, 27 December 2008.

Index